The Frozen Keyboard:
Living with Bad Software

Boris Beizer

TAB Professional and Reference Books

Division of TAB BOOKS Inc.
Blue Ridge Summit, PA

FIRST TAB EDITION
FIRST TAB PRINTING

Copyright © 1988, 1986 by Boris Beizer

Printed in the United States of America

Library of Congress Cataloging in Publication Data

Beizer, Boris, 1934-
    [Personal computer quality]
    The frozen keyboard : with bad software / by Boris Beizer.
        p. cm.
    Originally published: Personal computer quality.
    Bibliography: p.
    Includes index.
    ISBN 0-8306-3146-1 (pbk.)
    1. Microcomputers—Programming. 2. Computer software. I. Title.
[QA76.6.B4327 1988]
005.36—dc 19   88-17-25
                                                    CIP

First published in 1986 by Van Nostrand Reinhold Company Inc.
115 Fifth Avenue
New York, New York 10003

TAB BOOKS Inc. offers software for
sale. For information and a catalog,
please contact TAB Software Department,
Blue Ridge Summit, PA 17294-0850.

Questions regarding the content of this book
should be addressed to:

    Reader Inquiry Branch
    TAB BOOKS Inc.
    Blue Ridge Summit, PA 17294-0214

To three who can claim some credit,
and must share some blame.

Mrs. Harington, PS 14, Queens
Ira Ritow
Aaron Coleman

DISCLAIMERS
AND ACKNOWLEDGMENTS

Some of the anecdotes related in this book have been synthesized from several parallel, real, situations in the interest of readability. In other cases, I have fictionalized some anecdotes which are based on real experiences in order to avoid the libel litigations which are raging through the publishing world. The names of organizations, persons, places, and software packages used in anecdotes, where such usage might be construed as derogatory, are fictional. Any similarity of such names to real names is coincidental and unintentional.

Mention of a real product or organization by name, in a favorable manner, does not constitute an endorsement. It means only that I have personally used the product or service and that I have found it to be worth the price. It does not mean, however, that it is flawless or that your experience might not differ.

The following organizations and individuals provided direct or indirect support for this book but did not in any way exercise editorial control over its contents and are in no way responsible; their contribution (solicited or otherwise) is nevertheless, appreciated: AmeriMicro Inc., American Training International Inc., Ashton-Tate Inc., Ruth Beizer, Black-Box Inc., Bitech Enterprises Inc., *Byte,* Comrex International Inc., Compstand, Epson America Inc., Fujitsu Microelectronics Inc., Hewlett-Packard, IBM Inc., *Infoworld,* Metro Software Inc., *Micro Marketworld,* Micropro International Corp., Microsoft Corporation, Peachtree Software Inc., Rising Star Industries Inc., Tom Seidman, Sydney Stern, Software Arts, *Software Digest,* Cyril and Helen Solomons, Titan Technologies Inc., and *The Wall Street Journal.*

All SHOE Cartoons reprinted by permission of Jefferson Communications, Inc., Reston, VA.

READ THIS FIRST

If the only thing you know about computers is that you've heard the word and that you've been led to believe that one might be useful to you, read the first tutorial, entitled "Getting Started—Hardware, Software, and Why" on page 203.

Terms which appear in boldface type are technical and you're not expected to know what they mean. The definition will typically be given in the first sentence in which the term is used, or one or two sentences down. Boldfaced terms are also usually defined in the glossary/index. I may repeat the boldface again on subsequent pages. Because the chapters are mostly independent of each other, the same term may be defined more than once.

The first chapter is an overview of the book: it sets the tone, states the issues, and provides a basic vocabulary. You should read the first chapter. The rest of the chapters deal with subjects which are relatively independent of one another. Therefore, instead of reading the book serially, from cover to cover as you might a novel, think of it as a set of related short stories which you can read individually as the mood strikes you or as the need exists.

The glossary/index is organized by concepts and not just by words. For example, if you look up "data-base" I won't guarantee that you'll find the term "data-base" as such on each mentioned page, but barring bugs and errors, you will find something pertinent to "data-base" on each page numbered in the index. I put a lot of stock in indexes and also a lot of work. If you have a problem with a computer or a software package, look first to the index to see if the problem is mentioned, rather than to the table of contents.

I've combined the index and the glossary as a convenience to you. It's always irked me to look in the index, see a technical term, and not be sure if that's what I wanted. I'd then have to look in several places in the text for the definition or in a glossary, if there was one. All that's a waste of time. With the combined glossary/index, the definition is right there if you need it: then you can go to the text for more information. The only reason these have been separated in the past has to do with the technicalities of producing an index—the page numbers in the index can't be finished until the book has been set in type. That was true back then, but when you've got the book on disc, are using a word processor for the text, there's no reason, other than outworn tradition, to separate them.

Most common computer buzzwords are defined in the glossary, albeit sometimes with editorial comments which may not be found in a traditional dictionary. I've used the glossary as a place to make comments about this industry and the perpetrators of software. I hope that it's obvious when I'm pulling your leg and when the definition is straight—but straight or bent, the definitions all make a point, give you a warning, or convey some information you'll find worth knowing. My attempts at humor are based on painful and expensive experiences—many of which you have also had, or will have as you increase your use of computers. It's the worst of these experiences that I've made fun of, not to minimize their importance, but in recognition that in the face of disaster, sometimes the best thing, or the only thing, to do is to laugh.

The final difference between this and other books is the set of tutorials at the back. If the technology and the market existed, I would have written this book as a computerized information package. I wanted that kind of structure because the mind does not progress in serial order like the pages of a book—it skims, skips, and jumps. It's not a disorganized way of working, but a way of taking shortcuts when details aren't really needed. We readers do that when we skim over a section of a book. As a writer, although I want the reader to read every word of deathless prose I write, I also want all the information my reader needs to be on-the-spot, as she needs it. To do that, the same material would have to be repeated over and over again, each time in a different context. This became clear to me when I found that I had written a large, technical, introductory section on installation in Chapter 2 just so that what I had to say about the installation manual made sense. Furthermore, the explanatory details in Chapter 2 interfered with the real flow of information which concerned instruction manuals and not installation—I was probably giving my reader more than he wanted to know at that point. The ideal would have been a MORE DETAIL/LESS DETAIL key. Then you could dig as deep as you wanted to and no more and I would have written no redundant material. This is not to be, so I chose a compromise. The tutorial sections at the back are midway between a passage of text and the corresponding glossary entry. I've assumed that you know what you don't know and that you know to look for details when you need them. If a term or concept isn't familiar to you, and it's not explained in that or the next sentence, then look it up in the index/glossary. If that doesn't do the trick, see if there's a tutorial on the subject. You may also find the tutorials interesting in and of themselves.

PREFACE

This book is entitled *The Frozen Keyboard: Living with Bad Software,* but 90% of it has to do with software—that's an appropriate balance because 90% of the computer quality you see and 98% of computer horror stories you hear about or live through, are in some way tied up with software quality. I became interested in software quality because of abuse by bad software. Now two decades have passed and I'm still being abused. The difference between now and then is that I have more company and more software to be abused by. I thought at first that the problem of bad software was that designers didn't know how to build good software. So I wrote some books on that subject—but the world didn't change. Then because efficiency was such an important issue in the earlier computer systems, I wrote a book on computer performance—but the world didn't change. Then I came to believe that software quality would come if designers understood and used good testing and quality assurance techniques. *Software Testing Techniques* and *Software System Testing and Quality Assurance* were intended to fix that—but still the world didn't change and bad software persists. I've concluded that my precious approach was wrong. I had addressed the wrong audience. Good software will come only because the software's users demand it. And how can they demand it if they don't know what is, and what is not quality?

This book is written for the intelligent computer user and buyer. While it applies to any computer from micro- to supercomputer, the most likely user and the greatest number of potential beneficiaries are personal computer users. The personal computer user has bought the system to extend his capabilities or to do things which are virtually impossible without computers. There is a serious application in mind—be it accounting, modeling, record keeping, running a business, managing investments, or whatever. The computer and its software is merely a tool and not an end in itself. It must compete with alternatives such as doing it by hand, using an assistant, or an outside service. This book is not for computer aficionados, hobbyists, game-players, hackers, programmers, and others whose attitude toward computers carries a heavy emotional overlay and personal involvement. If this book's reader is emotional about computers, it's likely to be anger and frustration over being victimized by bad software. Reading this book won't dissipate that anger—it'll probably make you angrier because it will tell you what you need to know to know that you've been conned. It won't alleviate the frustration but it may help you avoid it on the next hardware or software you buy. It won't help you fix bad software but it may tell you that problems of a package are unfixable and how to best live with them.

BORIS BEIZER
Abington, Pennsylvania

CONTENTS

TUTORIALS

RESOURCES

GLOSSARY/INDEX

The Frozen Keyboard:
Living with Bad Software

1
THE SOFTWARE LANDSCAPE

1. HERE WE GO AGAIN

1.1. History Repeats

The turn of the century is coming. It's nearly a hundred years since the automobile was invented. Every buggy and bicycle builder who could join motor to wheel was scrabbling for a market share. Salesmen who had learned to drive only the week before extolled the virtues of their product with the seeming expertise and confidence of automotive engineers. Deficiencies were transmuted into benefits—" . . . the reliability of a manual starting crank," " . . . made of wood instead of tinny sheet metal," " . . . and a motor so simple you can fix it yourself." There were no driving schools. The local blacksmith was the best available mechanic. Basic stuff such as brakes, steering, the number of wheels, transmission, clutch, springs, and pneumatic tires had not yet jelled. There were no quality standards. There were no safety standards. The relation between quality and cost was accidental. And hundreds of manufacturers brought out new vehicles monthly. But buyers bought and accepted inconveniences and bizarre designs because despite their faults, automobiles were better, cheaper, and faster than horses, and preferable to stepping in horse manure.

Sounds familiar? When I started this book there were more than two hundred **personal computer** manufacturers in the U.S. who, combined, offered more than six hundred models. The number of **software packages** for these computers was estimated at between 30,000 and 50,000. When *our* turn of the century comes, the two hundred will have been whittled down to a few dozen. As for the 50,000 software packages—if you're a heavy reader, you might read one book a week for fifty years or so, for a lifetime total of 2,500 books. It takes far longer to get profitable use out of a software package than it takes to read a book: a lifetime total of 50 packages might be reasonable for a nonprofessional. I don't think that there are 2,500 good software packages out there; for now, there aren't 50,000 things for which it's worth writing software; and the computer industry doesn't have enough programmers to create that much good software. Therefore, most of it must be worthless.

The purpose of this book is to help you recognize and avoid the worthless and to appreciate the useful.

1.2. Computerphobiacs Unite!

I'm an admitted computerphobiac when it comes to new software. I admire people who can sit at a keyboard, fire up the latest whiz-bang offering from Colossal Software Inc., and have it grinding out mounds of statistics, six color graphs, and management summaries faster than I can unpack the instruction manual and make a **backup copy** of the program. That first experience with a new package is as intimidating to me as a blind date. I'm confused by new terminology, strange **commands,** and obscure scribblings on the screen (assuming I can get anything on the screen at all). I have to read and reread the instruction manuals before things sink in. I *always* have trouble getting the self-teaching programs to work. And sometimes, after I've used the software for a year, I go back to the **tutorial program** and I still have trouble with it. When I get the **package** to do meaningful work for me, when I believe I've "mastered" it, I'm rewarded with lost time, lost **data, crashes,** and insulting put-downs. It's enough to give anyone a phobia.

I suppose that there are real computerphobiacs in the world, although I've never met one. These unfortunates get cold sweats at the sight of a computer **monitor.** The extreme cases break out in a rash when they handle calculators and they carry ampules of adrenalin to reverse the effects of being touched by a rampaging **printout.** I have met some men who had problems with computers because they had inappropriate sexual stereotypes working on their psyche—for example, "a keyboard is something 'girls' use." And I've met professional women who avoided public computer use lest they be cast into the same stereotyped role.

What many people call "computerphobia" is really healthy scepticism rather than a phobia. It's a reluctance to be steamrollered into "the latest and bestest" with possibly serious consequences. It's an intuitive perception that hype and glibness are being used to cover up garbage. It's a realistic concern over being screwed. That's not a phobia—it's sensible.

Computerphobia, as any other phobia, is an *unjustified* fear. I am justifiably fearful of big trucks tailgating me on the highway, jumping off bridges, the IRS, one-party political systems, and bad software.

The purpose of this book is to help you understand which fears are justifiable and which aren't. There are more than enough justifiable fears so there's no point being burdened by things of no concern.

1.3. Software Quality in Perspective

You have an intuitive understanding of the quality of manufactured goods. Better materials typically means a better product. The better product is usually more expensive to produce than the poorer product. Features also add to the cost. With a lifetime's education as wily consumer, you're likely to apply those concepts of quality to software: but the relations between quality, features, reliability, and cost for software are not like those you've learned for other products. Here are some comments on software that will help set its quality in perspective:

1. Reproduction (i.e., manufacturing) costs are a negligible part of the total cost.
2. There's no relation between the complexity you see and the internal complexity of the program. In fact, good software is internally simpler, function-for-function, than bad software. Internal complexity can be a sign of idiocy rather than of genius. Conversely, a program may be internally complicated because its designer understood some important subtleties that forced the complexity. In such cases, the "simple" approach may have a fatal flaw.
3. External simplicity, or ease of use, often requires internal complexity, which if the package is good, is completely hidden from your consciousness.
4. There may be no obvious relation between features and cost. Sometimes, useful features are a byproduct of the design and removing the feature could actually raise the development cost. Conversely, seemingly trivial features (from the user's point of view) could be almost impossible to add to a package after it is done.
5. "Big programs" can be big because they're bad. Small, tight, programs can be very good. It's not unusual to have two different programs, written to do identical jobs, with one taking four times as much **memory** and a hundred times as long to execute as the other. Function for function, good software is small, fast, and elegant (internally) while bad software is big, slow, and stupid.
6. Software quality is almost completely independent of the package's features: it's a result of the process by which the software is designed and tested and not just the design. Garbage software can result from badly executed but intellectually elegant concepts. Superb software can come

from brute-force, but well-crafted, concepts. Any software, if not properly tested, will be bad.

7. If the software isn't modified, it never wears out, can't be overworked, and doesn't improve with age.

Software quality is better compared to literary merit than to physical (hardware) products. Big books aren't necessarily good and good books aren't necessarily small. You can't tell from the reading how much work went into it. Publicity budget and hype have more to do with making the best-seller's list than quality. There may be a software Shakespeare out there, but there are also a lot of cheap romances, pornography (yes! there is porn software), and comic books.

This isn't a book on literary (software) criticism, but it may help you recognize the difference between a comic book and **the Wall Street Journal.**

1.4. You Get What You Pay For

There are several ways to get free software:

1. Be a software guru.
2. Use "free" **public domain software.**
3. Get a **pirated** copy from a friend or acquaintance.

I don't buy much software. I often get "free" copies from vendors. I put the "free" in quotes because they expect (and get) yet another independent critique from me. So that's not really free software and the price is the hard work of learning yet another package.

"Free software" in the public domain is available for the price of a blank disc from **user groups,** universities, and vendors. Public domain programs are usually inadequately tested. They rarely have legible manuals, there are no training courses, and they often don't work. Much of that software is junk. It's like confusing English Lit. term papers with literature. Most of it is sophomoric, unprofessional, and incorrect. It's mainly for people who are more interested in playing with software than in using it for some real purpose. If you're a first-time user, though, then it may pay you to buy the public domain software. It's cheap—typically fifty bucks for the lot. A "good" set will contain a word processor, mini-spreadsheet, scheduler, communications package, graphics, project management tools, and all the other packages that you might want to buy at some time in the future. Although the public domain versions are usually buggy toys compared to the real thing, playing with those toys might help you decide if you really want a spreadsheet or project management tool, say; but don't sucker yourself into thinking that these packages compare to the $300 commercial versions—you get what you pay for.

Piracy is a big problem for the software industry. If you use pirated software, then you're the same kind of creep who would make photocopies of this book. For serious users who believe in paying a fair price for value received, pirated software is not worth the trouble. You won't get **updates** or corrections. A legible instruction manual is harder to get than the software. There're no vendor support for you. The up-front costs of software (as we'll see below) are such a small part of software costs that it doesn't pay to mess with pirated copies. Piracy increases the cost to legitimate buyers because it forces a higher retail price to make up for the piracy. It stultifies the development of new software, and it puts a real crimp in vendor and retailer cooperation. Besides all that, it's illegal, immoral, and immature.*

2. WHY AND WHAT SOFTWARE

2.1. Layers and Layers and Wheels Within Wheels

Computers are run by **programs**—or as we call them, "software."** **Computer hardware** by itself can only do simple, technical things that can't be easily related to useful work such as word-processing, bookkeeping, or finance. What lies between the things it does for you and the electrons swimming about are layers upon layers of software. Some of that software is fixed in the hardware—call it very **firmware;** some of it can be modified to correct faults—call it firmware; then there's **"hard software"**, "soft software," "application software," and many finely distinguished buzzwords between. What matters is not the jargon but that each layer is another opportunity for excellence or for screwups. These software layers exist not

---

*There are several reasons why I'm testy about software piracy. Piracy is a recurrent complaint of software publishers and retailers. The publisher may sacrifice user convenience (e.g., by not allowing backup copies) in order to protect his interests against pirates. Retailers may be reluctant to let you try a package or to allow you to read the manual because they may suspect you of intending to use a pirated copy. The final reason is more personal; I've been down on pirates ever since a book of mine was pirated by a Soviet Union publisher.

**People who write or talk about "software programs" parade their ignorance of both software and English. If we have "software programs," then presumably we have other kinds of programs, such as "hardware programs." (Hardware programs of a sort do exist—they have to do with integrated circuit design. They're so technical that only a computer designer is likely to see or use one. Those who speak of "software programs," however, have never heard of, and probably would not understand, "hardware programs.")

Another favorite term of the ignoramus is "softwear"—it's counterpart would be "hardwear," which I guess is a suit of armor.

because designers want to make things mysterious but because lessons learned over the past two decades have convinced us that this layering of software is the easiest way to get something useful and reliable built; but almost everything that goes wrong with computers is caused by software failures.

We have many software layers because software designers are creatively lazy. An engineer, a physicist, and a programmer were asked to boil a pot of water which was on the floor. The engineer picked it up and put it on the stove. The physicist calculated the best path to get the pot to the stove, but left it on the floor; and the programmer imitated the engineer. Later, they were given the same problem except that the pot was on the table. The engineer again put it on the stove, the physicist calculated a new path; but the programmer put the pot on the floor, thereby doing the job by using a previously written program. The use of existing programs, often written by other programmers, is the key to software design—it's also a source of **bugs.**

The closer we get to hardware, the more primitive are the things that software can do. Consider multiplication. You learned to multiply single digits by memorizing the multiplication table, you then learned how to multiply multi-digit numbers, fractions, decimals, and all the rest. Many small computers have no multiplication hardware. They can only do addition. The programmer writes a small program (called a **subroutine***) that goes through the steps of multiplication in a way similar to that which you learned in grade school. Once the subroutine is tested, the programmer no longer goes back through the awful steps of programming multiplication, but uses the multiplication subroutine instead. The multiplication subroutine can now be used in a higher-level subroutine that calculates, say, interest payments. That in turn may be part of a finance package, and so on. Subroutines **call** other subroutines and can even call themselves. This builds a complicated tree of interdependent and interacting mini-programs. As an example, retrieving a document from **disc,** changing one letter, storing the document back on disc, and then printing the result could require the execution of hundreds of subroutines written by different programmers at different times.

2.2. Hardware and Software—A Rocky Marriage?

Hardware has always been easier to build than software because it's simpler than software. Hardware is easier to protect by patents. People understand it. It's tangible. It's physical. Software doesn't have that kind of reality but

---

*The word "routine" was used in the early days of computers to mean a small program. "Routine" is rarely used now, but "subroutine," meaning a reusable part of a routine, has remained in vogue because it's easier to say than "subprogram."

it's what makes the hardware sing. Many aspiring computer hardware companies failed because they didn't understand software. Almost every radio and TV manufacturer in the world at one time or another tried to build and sell computers.* Most of them didn't make it—often not because their hardware was bad—in some cases, the hardware was better, dollar for dollar, than anything else available—but most often because the hardware and software mentalities are at opposite ends of the mental universe and success in computers has depended on understanding software. If you think there's antagonism between vendors and victims—it's sweetness and light compared to the continuing hardware/software battles. They barely talk the same language—if they're talking, that is.

At first, software was subservient to hardware. This was reasonable because the hardware cost millions and the software was cheap by comparison. It was not unusual, in the early days, to have the computer manufacturer's sales department do the complete **application software** for the customer, sometimes prior to the actual sale. Every hardware manufacturer had its own software department. Independent software developers were rare. Software was **bundled** with hardware—that is, the software was "free" but could only be bought as a package with hardware. This changed when IBM **unbundled** hardware and software for its **mainframe** computers. IBM doesn't usually do stupid things. They unbundled software and hardware because the fractional value of the software had climbed to the point where it rivaled the hardware's value and there was lots of money to be made by unbundled software, even if the practice encouraged the proliferation of independent (and competitive) software vendors. This position was reiterated when IBM announced the IBM-PC, which was unbundled from the start, and created an environment which was inviting and conducive to independent software suppliers. IBM unbundled personal computer software because they realized that, despite their huge size and software development resources, which are probably as large as the rest of the industry combined, they did not have the human resources needed to produce the full range of software demanded by personal computer users. Unbundling was also a smart way to reduce software development risks by distributing it among dozens of tiny software builders: unbundling allowed the marketplace to determine which packages would survive.

Many hardware manufacturers have found that within a hardware house, software types are a pain in the butt; dissipate vast sums on the development of intangible products; are always late; and can't be trusted or controlled. Conversely, the software types have enjoyed the freedom from narrow-minded nuts-and-bolts bangers; the possibility of adapting their software

---

*GE, Motorola, Philco, RCA, and Telefunken, to name a few.

to many different computers; and the advantages of direct contact with users. The divorce has benefited both sides.

2.3. Who's on First?

So who writes the software if the hardware manufacturer doesn't? Look at Figure 1-1. You've bought a Belchfire personal computer equipped with the latest Belchfire software—DOSBelch and Belchall. DOSBelch is, of course, the **operating system** and Belchall is an **integrated package** that does **word-processing, graphics,** and **spreadsheets,** and ties the whole lot together with a **data-base manager.** With it you can create slick reports,

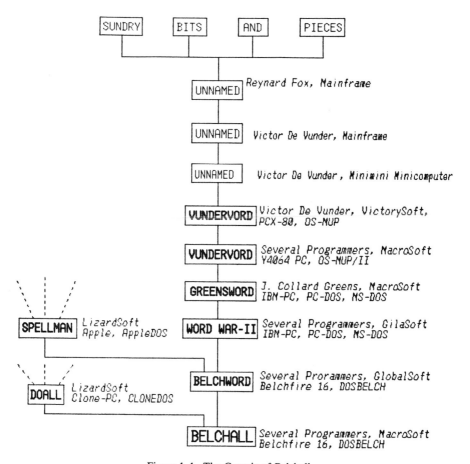

Figure 1-1. The Genesis of Belchall.

fancy graphics, tables, and all the rest. But where did it come from and who wrote it? Let's start at the top of Figure 1–1 and trace the genesis of just the word-processing part of the package.

The package started as a senior-term project by Reynard Fox at HIT (Huge Institute of Technology). He built a rudimentary word-processor by piecing parts from many other programs that were available to him: a Frankenstein's monster complete with the software equivalents of grave robbing, scars, and electrodes in the head. It was written in a strange university **language** and ran on a large **mainframe computer.** Reynard Fox left and was never heard from again. It was then picked up by Victor deVunder, a second year graduate student who was interested in some subtle word-processing problems and also wanted a package to do his master's thesis with. Victor rewrote half of Fox's stuff. It became a popular program at HIT. Victor went to work for Minimini, a **minicomputer** manufacturer, where he rewrote the package to run on their product-line hardware for internal use. It was popular there too, and he urged them to market it. They were hardware people, they had no interest in selling software, and so they gave him all the rights. Meanwhile, he had been rewriting it (yet again) for an early personal computer, the PCX80 (company now defunct), to run under the MUP operating system (no longer in use). He quit Minimini, founded Victory Software Inc. and peddled the package under the name "VunderVord". It was a hit even though it had lots of bugs: it was a hit because it was better than anything else available. Macrosoft offered him more money than he had ever seen for the package. He couldn't refuse. He took the money and ran, dissolved Victory Software, bought a dozen condominiums on Waikiki beach, and is now devoting his time to writing the winning programs for our next America's Cup challenge. Meanwhile, Macrosoft rewrote the package to run on the Y4064 PC under the MUP/II operating system. Then the IBM personal computer came out and the package was again rewritten. It acquired a new name, "Greensword," after the chief modifier of the package, J. Collard Greens. Macrosoft recognized their own limited marketing talent so they licenced the package to other software houses with a stiff royalty schedule. The best of the marketeers was GILA Software. They added features to keep it ahead of its competitors who were now beginning to crowd the field. The name changed again, to "WordWar-II." (WordWar-I was a lousy package put out by GILA and had no relation to VunderVord: WordWar-I was such a bad program that buying the rights to Greensword (A.K.A. VunderVord) and modifying its external appearance to look like WordWar-I was easier than fixing WordWar-I). WordWar-II became the best-selling word-processing package on the market. Macrosoft kept selling VunderVord, under that name, in competition to WordWar-II. Most users didn't know that they were the same program under the skin.* With the profits they made on WordWar-II, GILA Software bought control of Minimini and signed a long-term contract for the use of Victor deVunder's best condominiums as an executive retreat. Victor was last seen rounding Cape Horn in a modified bathtub equipped with a hundred square feet of sail and a two-hundred pound mini-computer for ballast. Now, Belchfire brought out its personal computer, the long awaited Belchfire 16. As any hardware manufacturer knows, you can't sell hardware without software. At that time, though, Belchfire's management didn't like the idea of selling someone else's software, so they bought the rights to WordWar-II from GILA software and repackaged it under the name "Belchword." They also bought another package from LIZARD Software (a spin-off company from GILA) called SPELLMAN, because by that time, **spell-checking** had become an essential part of word-processing. The genesis of SPELLMAN was as complex as that of WordWar-II. Belchfire didn't have the programming staff to combine the two programs so they hired GLOBALSOFT to do it for them. Later, when **integrated packages** became the rage, they bought the rights to another LIZARD Software package called DOALL, but had the LIZARD word-processor replaced with Belchword. The redesign work was, of course, done by Macrosoft. And that is how Belchall came into the world.

A quiz for the reader:

1. Who wrote Belchall?
2. Who's responsible for its bugs?
3. Who understands it?

2.4. Programming for the People?

There's lots of talk about "computer literacy," a term which is usually interpreted to mean that "literate" people have taken an elementary programming course in a popular **language** such as **Basic.** Sleazy and/or slick **home-computer** salesmen, who once peddled cheap encyclopedias door-to-door, now lay on a guilt trip implying that if your child doesn't know how to program (isn't computer literate) he won't even make it as a garbage collector in the new world. And then the local school board wants to float

---

* I didn't want to confuse things by adding to it the complexity of software that looks identical but which is different internally—compare some of the best-selling spreadsheet packages for an example. Multi-purpose, integrated, software packages can contain both kinds of components, and getting competent answers to simple technical questions can be more confusing than the old Abbot & Costello routine after which this section is named.

a million dollar bond issue to buy the latest classroom computers so that your children won't suffer the horrible heartbreak of computer illiteracy (it's worse than B.O. or dandruff). The hype is enough to make the first-time computer user feel inadequate before she's even opened the instruction manual. Getting used to a new way of working brings its share of frustration (which would be the case even if no computers were involved); but if, because you don't know how to write programs (e.g., because you're an illiterate jerk), you mistakenly feel that the fault is yours rather than the system's or instruction manuals that were originally written in Ainu and reached English via translations to Basque and Volapük, you might become a computerphobiac after all; and if not that, then at least you'll be more uncomfortable about using computers and new software than you really should be.

Programming knowledge *is* good for you and it's good for your kids; just as is physics, chemistry, biology, or knowledge of any science. Does a high school course in physics make you a physicist? Does an elementary course in Basic make you a programmer? Do you have to be an automotive engineer to drive a car? The common-sense answers to the above questions are the right answers. Programming knowledge is good for you, but because it's unlikely that you'll ever need to use Basic or any other formal programming language in your work, not knowing it is about as important as that second music course you didn't take in high-school; it's as significant and relevant as an elementary geology course is to an accountant who works for an oil company. There's a connection but let's not exaggerate its importance.

A **program** is an organized, repeatable, sequence of instructions. We all program and we are all programmed—with or without computers. We program our life when we reduce something to a routine practice. We are programmed when we learn a new skill. We were programmed to do arithmetic. And, when we learn to use new software, we program it and we are programmed. If there's programming to be done, or programming skills to be learned, they should be those that apply to the real, daily work, for which the computer is to be used.

Software has a spectrum of programmability. A word-processing package has very little to program—you can direct it to search for specified words and replace them with others. That's a rudimentary kind of program. You can specify page layouts and print **formats.** That's also a rudimentary kind of programming. If you now add the ability to create and print individualized form letters from a mailing list, then a more complicated kind of programming is needed to specify what gets placed where, so that the letter doesn't read "Dear Mr. Thompson Boulevard. . . . " Spreadsheet software provides even more programmabilitv. Data-base management packages can be as complicated as the simpler kinds of programming languages that professional programmers use. It's a spread.

1. *Most of "computer literacy" is a fad which like the "new math" will eventually pass into oblivion along with its perpetrators. It has as much meaning as "automotive literacy," "typewriter literacy," or "television literacy."*
2. *Knowing something about programming is good for you but not essential to the productive use of a computer. Put it on your list along with other self-improvement course. Don't expect to apply what you learn in an elementary Basic course to your daily computer usage. Almost every software package you can buy is far more technical than anything you can learn to do in an introductory course.*
3. *Every software package requires some kind of programming as you are programmed by every package you learn to use. How much and how technical that programming has to be depends on what you want to do and how often you have to do it. There's a spectrum of needs and a spectrum of programmability. Many users slide into programming without conscious awareness. Learn to program by small steps, and only as there's a need.*

3. THE REAL COST OF SOFTWARE

3.1. $400 Down and Forever to Pay

Software gurus aren't immune to software horrors. Fear of libel prevents me from naming the vendor; let's call them "Coddler." Coddler's business isn't computers, but office equipment. They had tried selling computers a few years back and had been so sorely wounded by the attempt that we were sure that they'd never try it again; but their interests in office equipment led them into word-processing, from which personal computers was a natural next step. So despite an earlier vow to never play the computer game again, advancing technology had forced them back into it. It's a big company and they make good hardware. Their software, for simple things, is uninspired, but acceptable; but when it comes to anything worthy of being called "software," they're blithering idiots. Their software customer service people were exquisitely polite, but incompetent.

We had Coddler word-processing systems and wanted to transfer documents to a DEC PDP-11 computer one floor down—there never was a problem on the DEC side of the **interface.** Coddler was running two-page spreads in *The Wall Street Journal* advertising the wonders of their new

network and boasting how easy it was to make their equipment talk to the world: so we didn't anticipate any problems in sending a few **files** a hundred feet. The Coddler software was **bundled** with the hardware at $1,500, but we can ascribe $1,100 to the communications hardware and $400 to the software. We bought the package, read the manual and found ourselves in wonderland.

I anticipate snickers in the background, because those of you who have tried to send data between computers know that it can be difficult. However, this story took place in a software house whose programmers design **telecommunications** software for computer manufacturers such as Coddler. We could have torn into that system's software and added the communications options. But we were experienced and we *knew* that it would be cheaper to use someone else's **debugged** software. The only difference between what we wanted to do and what they claimed they were doing daily was that we didn't intend to use a **modem;** but calls, letters, and warm statements by the salesman *before* we bought the package reassured us that it wouldn't be a problem. So what happened?

1. Basic technical information needed to make the connection was not available. This was especially irksome because Coddler had used unusual cable connections but had not documented what they had used. It took dozens of telephone calls to get them to tell us how the connectors had to be wired. Their policy seemed to be that we were not entitled to such information. We finally got several different connection schemes, all incorrect. We learned how they had really wired things by using test gear.
2. It was claimed that you could do word-processing while sending data over the communication link. It wasn't. Either the word-processing, or the communicated data were garbled, or both, or the system **crashed.**
3. It was designed to transfer a whole list of documents without further operator attention. Not only couldn't we get it to do the second document, but the operator had to hit the TRANSMIT key after every page was sent.
4. Manuals were fat, written for children, and wrong.
5. Over a hundred calls were made to two dozen different customer service departments each of which claimed knowledge of (but not responsibility for) telecommunications. I accumulated a huge list of names of persons who in one way or another attempted to solve (or who added to) the problem.
6. We eventually got the Coddler-connection to work about as well as a quadriplegic on a broken wheel chair in a storm at sea attempting to dance *Swan Lake.* That was five years ago. We disconnected the hardware, junked the software, and haven't touched it since.

I should have anticipated problems with that package. A year before, I had attempted to write a word-processing application on an earlier system of theirs. It used a special language that had ostensibly been designed for non-programmer's use. I don't know how many different computers I've programmed, but for some of the first ones, we chipped the instructions in with a stone ax. The Coddler's word-processing **application language** is the only one that ever defeated me. After weeks of frustration, I declared it "unprogrammable by man, beast, or demon." The solution to *that* problem was to **upgrade** to the newest **version,** in which all these problems were "solved". Most of the problems had been solved, we learned, by removing the troublesome features. The features they removed, as you guessed, were those that were essential to our application. I'm thankful to Coddler, though, because although their software appears to be have been produced by culturally and mentally deprived grade-school children, they, among others, inspired me to write this book.

Let's look at the real costs of our attempt to connect two computers over the CoddlerNet.

Up-front package cost	$400.
Cost of wasted labor: 100 hours @ $50/hr	$5,000.
Mainframe computer time wasted	$4,250.
Unusable hardware cost	$1,100.
Test equipment not otherwise needed	$420.
Installation of local network line	$350.
Cost of delayed work	$12,000.
Telephone calls	$475.
Pain and Suffering	$???,???.
Total	$23,995.
Up-front software cost percentage	2%

If everything had worked as advertised the cost would have been about $4,000 to get the job done, which is still ten times the software package's cost. It's possible that our problems were due to having too much experience. That's what one Coddler representative implied, when in frustration, he dropped their veneer of civility; but I doubt that. If the expertise hadn't been there, the cost would have been doubled, and in the end, crippled or not, the application would have never been accomplished. What he meant was that if we had been ignorant, we would have given up long before, and consequently *they* would not have had the problem.*

The experience isn't unique, and we all, users, dealers, consultants, and

---

*I've been told that they've cleaned their act up since then, but I'll never know. I'd never use that lemon orchard again, and certainly wouldn't recommend it to any client.

the rest, have had, will have, or have heard of similar experiences. At least we can learn a lesson from it: up-front software costs are like a ticket to an amusement park. It gets you in the door, but you still have to pay (and pay and pay and pay) for every ride—and sometimes, it's quite a ride, or perhaps a freak show. There's no way to evaluate the true cost of a piece of software unless you properly evaluate *all* the cost components and give them proper weights with respect to the short-term, the mid-term, and the long-term benefits and costs.

3.2. The Short-Term Costs

The short-term costs are those you incur from the time you decide to buy a package until you get the first productive work out of it. Use the following check list as a starting point. Attempt to keep honest track of costs based on all labor costs at the appropriate internal charge rate. Nothing is free. Try it for the next package you buy. I've not included the cost of deciding which package to buy.

1. Actual package cost.
2. Cost of processing the purchase order.
3. Reading the manual.
4. Installing the program.
5. Backup discs—time to make and cost of discs.
6. Printer paper and ribbon costs until first production.
7. Using the tutorial programs.
8. Attending a training course.
9. Screwing around with toy problems to learn the package.
10. Reading the manual while watching TV.
11. Telephone calls to the retailer for clarification.
12. Telephone calls to the software publisher's customer service department after the retailer muddies the water.
13. Cost of not being available while you're learning it.
14. Time required to enter and check the first real data.
15. Reading the instruction manual very late at night.
16. Explaining to spouse and friends how tough things are.
17. Reading the manual again.
18. Cost of explaining to boss and colleagues why the first run bombed.
19. Getting it to work.
20. Time spent congratulating yourself.
21. Boasting to colleagues, boss, spouse, and friends.

It takes me a few days to get through the above steps for simple packages and few weeks for complicated packages. If you really account for all the

costs, the typical package has a total initial cost approximately ten times greater than the selling price of the package itself. Depending on your experience, luck, and the packages you buy, you should expect a 5- to 20-fold range. I plan on a ten-to-one ratio of total cost to package price, which brings the real cost of most software up to the hardware price.

3.3. The Mid-Life Crisis

The mid-term costs extend from the package's first real use until the point where you're thinking in terms of replacing it with a more powerful version such as Belchall-II. Your use of the package has matured. You know how to exploit all the features it has and understand which additional features you would like it to have—that's when the crisis occurs, because you may be faced with changing to a new package to get those features. The package has benefits, or else you wouldn't continue to use it. But it also has hidden costs. There's the obvious costs of running it: operator time, amortized equipment cost, consumable supplies (paper, ribbon, discs, etc.), data gathering and preparation, etc. It's a good idea to occasionally reckon the operating costs and to see if the package is really worth running, and not just fun to run. You might be surprised and find yourself going back to manual methods because they're cheaper and more flexible in some cases.

Assuming that the operating costs are reasonable, and that the package seems to be cost-effective, the important remaining mid-term costs are tied to reliability. If the package is buggy and loses or corrupts data you might be using it for a long time before you realize that there's a problem. Mid-term costs should also be colored by the anticipated costs of bad or meaningless results which unfortunately look good.

You might have made a large investment in time and money to get the package working for you. Once you've done that, and got it to work, even if crippled, there are pressures that will keep you using it even if it is bad. Here are some reasons why you might continue to use a piece of garbage— and why you shouldn't.

1. Embarrassed in front of boss, colleagues, and spouse over the "mistake" you made: *don't accept blame for a piece of software you didn't write. The embarrassment belongs to the publisher, not you. Think of something more embarrassing, such as missing an important date or not zipping your fly.*
2. Assurances from the publisher that the problem will be corrected in version II, which is due out in a few weeks. *That's two of the four great lies, along with "the check is in the mail."*
3. Despite the problems, it's still far better than what's in second place. *Over the long run, first-place packages are often losers. Second place*

won't be there long, and the race is most likely to be won by a dark horse who doesn't make the other's mistakes. Wait if you can.

4. There're nothing else like it on the market. *You have to be desperate to accept that position. NEVER BE THE FIRST KID ON THE BLOCK! Wait! If it's a really useful package, there'll be at least one competitor within a year. The competitive packages will have more features, be faster, better, and cheaper, have none of the original's mistakes or limitations (but new bugs and limitations) and the original may have a far better MARK-II version.*

5. It's homely, covered with warts and fleas, but it's mine—a program that only a nearsighted mother could love *That's a personal emotional investment and probably the strongest there is.*

It boils down to waiting if you can. It pays to let others make and find the mistakes. And it pays to put software aside and not use it if it looks like mid-term costs and benefits are out of line.

3.4. The Long-Term Costs

The long term costs begin to appear when you've settled on a reasonable package (or replaced an unreasonable one) and you're using the program regularly without hassle. It's become part of your life-style and work-style. Your investment increases daily, as does your dependence. You're locked-in.

1. Your data base increases daily. Each day you add a record, a file, or a disc to what is now becoming an impressive pile.
2. The cost of transferring to a new system increases daily.
3. You and the recipients of the package's product have gotten over the novelty. What it produces is what they expect, in that form and only that form, and some other program is "not the way we do things here."
4. The fear of going to a new package, and reliving the initial and mid-term horrors increases daily.
5. **Release** 3.4 will be out in a few weeks—it's undergoing **beta testing** (another great lie).

The program's changed the way you work. It's changed your culture. If these changes are for the good, the long-term costs are worth it. It's hard to predict the short-term, the mid-term, and the long-term costs of a new package; but if you try to foresee them, even if you are wrong in the end, it may help you avoid getting locked into something worthless. And the key is to procrastinate if you can. Wait!

2

OF PROGRAMMERS AND BUGS

1. SYNOPSIS

Who builds the software. How they are trained. Their experience. How software is developed, ideally and really. Why programs have bugs. Software quality assurance. Symptoms versus bugs. The real cost of bugs. What bugs mean to you.

2. THE SOFTWARE BUILDERS

2.1. Who Are These People?

It's fun to watch grade-B computer Sci-fi movies from the '50s and '60s. Even in today's TV shows, programmers wear white coats. I've been working around computers for almost three decades but I never wore a white coat and I never saw a white-coated programmer or operator. I thought I saw one once, but he was a local butcher who had wandered in to deliver a salami. A friend of mine worked computers at a mental hospital—he wore a white coat so that the guards could tell him from the inmates. Programs are written by people. When programs fail, it's a real person who fouled-up. I like to have a clear image in my mind of who it is that's jerking me around the hall. Is this what they look like?

Tom Swift—A hyperactive kid with a squeaky voice—a permanent twitch in the right hand—he learned to program at the age of seven by working video games at the local arcade.

Douglas Goodtrue—The kid's grown up: he wears a three-piece suit now. A trim beard now hides the acne and he drives a Turbo-Frunzy-Baggetta. He started Universal Software at age eighteen (after dropping out of grade school) using venture capital provided by a local drug dealer. He grossed

$850 million last year with profits of $500 million. The stock's at 455. He intends to revolutionize the Patagonian economy by providing personal computer software to gauchos. At 28, he's a "grand old man" of the industry.

Dr. Sivana—This one is best played with a basso voice. He rumbles under his breath about "recursive produlators," "universal Turing functors," etc. In the last scene, he shouts, "Stop! Stop! You can't turn JASPER off! He's alive!" Our hero, of course, creams the computer with a handy ball-point pen and the monster retaliates by frying the nearest human—Dr. Sivana.

Those aren't real computer people. You can't correlate physiognomy with programming talent. The kid with the buzzwords could be an idiot or a kid who likes to throw buzzwords around. Some programmers wear three-piece suits and so do con artists. We're not going to understand bad software if we don't understand who writes it. We can't understand the people who write it if we block understanding by stereotypes.

Bad programmers don't follow any rules. They can be smart or stupid, energetic or lazy, organized or scatterbrained: the only thing they have in common is that they find ever-more clever ways of writing garbage. Good programmers do follow some patterns:

1. They're more intelligent than the average.
2. They're organized and disciplined with respect to their work, but there's no correlation to their appearance or behavior outside the work.
3. They have a tolerance for ambiguity—good at crossword puzzles.
4. They're properly trained, and/or educated, and/or experienced.

The point of this section is to provide insight into the process by which software is built when it's well-built, and also when it's a mess. It's peek at the inside which you may find infuriating or titillating depending on your experience. *Software is built by people* (for now).

2.2. Training and Experience

2.2.1. So Who Needs Programmers?

One of the myths that the computer industry perpetuates is that programming is easy. I think that some hardware manufacturers, especially of home computers, are the worst offenders in this respect. A close second are those sleazy schools that advertise on the back of matchbook covers and offer to "train you for a rewarding career in programming in just six weeks" (or three months, for that matter). I take a lot of potshots at programmers in this book so it's only fair to get on their side for a moment before I start. The easy-programming myth is destructive to both the user and to programming. The user is hurt because he confuses six-week wonders with pros. The six-week wonder is so ignorant that he doesn't have the foggiest notion of what he doesn't know. Amateurs will grossly underestimate the complexity of some jobs and grossly overestimate the complexity of others, they have no concept of testing or quality assurance, and in the end, will cost far more than a professional. It's up-front costs versus total costs all over again. I've heard complaints from programmers who couldn't get reasonable fees for their work because they had to compete against "programmers" who were willing to write "software" for five dollars an hour. Garbage collectors make more than that (and are more skilled!). If programming was really that easy, then you'd be better off learning how to program and to write the precise software you need to do your job, rather than wasting your time and money on ready-made software and reading this book.

If any reader who's taken an introductory programming course and written toy programs believes that programming is trivial, then let them accept this challenge. Here are two simple problems to program: (1) write a perpetual calendar routine that will work correctly to the year 2121; (2) write a routine that will check spelling errors in a document. Then, if you'll send me your results, I will, for an outrageous fee, tell you why your solutions probably won't work, and why a professional solution to the second problem will take one quarter as much memory as you think is possible to store the dictionary and will run about a hundred times faster than your solution.

2.2.2. The Software Design Profession

Software design is an engineering profession—at least that's what we software types like to claim. Actually, it's an aspiration to a profession. The present state of affairs is about the same as it was for many engineers a hundred years ago. An "engineer" was then a man who built great bridges like the Roeblings or a scientist like Steinmetz, but also a locomotive driver or a hairy guy who stank of stale beer and whose claim to the title was that he fired up a tenement's boiler. The real state of affairs of the software "profession" includes a share of scientists and real engineers, but also boiler stokers—and they all claim to be software designers and programmers.

Is it a profession? Is it yet an engineering discipline? No. It is an art, there is a body of useful knowledge, and the beginnings of science. As of now, the profession spends a lot of time debating methodology, practices, and procedures—all of which is necessary but takes time away from the real work of writing software. Accountants don't hold ten conferences a year on audit procedures. Physicians do most of their work by well-tried methods. Architects can design buildings without inventing new ways of drawing blueprints. Software design practices, and more important, standards, vary tremendously between vendors, within software houses, from project to project, within projects, and for the same person from month to month. Be kind to us, though. We're very young, have much to offer, and much to learn.

2.2.3. Training

The ideal training for a new software designer today is an undergraduate curriculum in computer sceince or software engineering at an accredited college or university. Another viable alternative is an intensive two-year course that consists of nothing but programming and related subjects at an accredited junior college or trade school. For those who are interested in some of the more esoteric parts of the profession, such as designing new programming languages and operating systems, a master's level program is essential and a Ph.D. is desirable.

Academic training suits the aspiring programmer to an entry-level job. It will take a year of additional formal and/or on-the-job training to learn how programming is done in the real world and in that software organization as distinct from the academic world. With three years of experience the apprentice programmer has become a journeyman and is ready to take on simple design responsibilities. Beyond that point, differences in early formal training tend to disappear and a heavier stress is placed on pertinent experience rather than academic training. With more experience, good programmers get better, more productive, make fewer errors, and can find and fix their errors much faster. It's not unusual to have an experienced programmer who is ten times more productive after ten years than he or she was when they entered the field.

That's the ideal, but not the real. It's a young field still, and many competent people came into it when there were no formal requirements, no curricula, and no training. There are many competent people who write software today without academic credentials and there are idiot savants with Ph.D.'s who perpetrate one software atrocity after another. More important than formal training today is talent and good experience that will allow expression for that talent.

2.3. How Software Is Developed (Ideal and Real)

2.3.1. The Ideal

The ideal development of a software package, say for use in a personal computer, begins with market research which eventually leads to a written specification of what the software is to do. We'll bypass the steps that may take place to refine the specification: at some point there's a technically feasible specification which the publisher believes will result in a marketable product. The designers begin by sketching an overall design and defining an internal **data-base.** The overall design could include a detailed definition of all the **screens** the user will see and the commands that will be used to make the software do its thing. The designers then define the **control** or **executive** part of the software. This is the part that keeps things from flying apart, that interacts with the operating system—the "brains" of the package. Up to this point, the work's been done by a few senior designers.

The next step is to write subsidiary specifications from which programs can be written. While that's being done, the designers identify the segments that can be used in many different parts of the package. These are called **common subroutines** because they're used in common by different programs. Some of these may already exist in a subroutine library and some may be variations of existing subroutines. The general design proceeds from the top down, in ever-increasing detail, until all parts of the package have been defined and specified. This process takes three to six months in a typical project, which takes about 18 months from start to finish. Note that very little actual programming has been done. Programming begins in earnest in the sixth month and peaks in the ninth.

When actual programming begins, the independent quality assurance team is called in to design a comprehensive test of the entire package. As routines are completed by the programmer, they are tested, first by the programmer, and then perhaps again by an independent test team. They're also subjected to detailed technical reviews and audits which may be conducted by other programmers, the programmer's technical supervisor, and quality assurance. At month nine, enough of the software has been written to begin system test and integration. This is done by first assembling a backbone of essential subprograms to which other features and functions will be added later. The integration process continues with ever-more complex tests performed as more and more of the program is assembled. By the twelfth to fifteenth month, the design team believes that it has done complete testing and is not aware of any bugs. The package is then turned over to independent test and quality assurance for another go-over. The final stage of testing is to send the package out to independent, so-called **beta testers** for more tests.

During all that testing, the software is subjected to situations which the typical user would never dream of. Keys are hit at random and in patterns, things are stopped before they're started, the testers attempt to copy and destroy data that doesn't exist, give duplicate names to things, try to get as much going simultaneously as possible, use the largest **files,** longest **fields,** and the worst cases which the system can handle. In other words, there's an effort to "break" the software. In all, testing, consumes at least half of the total labor required to get the package working. If we take into account the cost of external independent testing, then the test and quality assurance cost rises to about 75% to 80% of the development costs.

2.3.2. The Real

Reality is cutting corners. Two corners are cut: the initial design and quality assurance. Programming starts before there's a clear design concept and software is released prior to proper test and review. Instead of expending 50% to 80% of the budget on testing and quality assurance, untested software is sent to the field. The result is that customer service, rather than programming, has to handle user complaints. Eventually, more money is spent fixing the program after it's been released than would have been spent testing it correctly prior to release.

2.3.3. Why the Differences

There's pressure to get the package out before the competitor. There are all those pressures that marketing brings to bear on any engineered product, with all the same consequences. However, the biggest reason for the differences is that there's a vain hope that somehow, this one time, it will be possible to get software working without encountering any bugs. If that myth were real, then not only would time be saved, but so would half of the development cost. Everybody wants to believe this myth: programmers, managers, marketeers, and users—everybody except experienced cynics, especially those concerned with quality assurance. I call it "the Mr. Spock syndrome": we desperately want to believe that we are little Mr. Spocks; that we don't suffer from the human imprecisions and frailties that lead to bugs. So instead of concentrating on methods that prevent bugs (good design practices and tools) and methods that find bugs (good testing and quality assurance), we waste effort on wishful thinking. Bad management is another reason. There are many software development managers who make programmers feel guilty over bugs. In some shops, bug guilt is so great that programmers are immobilized and won't do anything that's even slightly creative. Another important reason for bad software is that we've got managers who have no personal experience in writing software. They lack the perspective to hire knowledgeable subordinates, they can't appreciate quality software when they see it, nor smell the stench of bad software. They are easy prey to myths and shortcuts, with the expected results that such ignorance brings. In other words, we've got just as much bad management as any other field, but because we're younger and less experienced, the bad results are more frequent and more drastic—and who pays? You do.

3. WHY SOFTWARE HAS BUGS

3.1. The Fundamental Problem

Programming is a bitch. Some virtuoso practitioners of this art claims that it is the hardest work every dome by man. I dont agree because working a Siberian salt-mine and rowing a galley was harder occupations. And as for tough mental disciplines, I don't think that programming compares to Polynesian navigation or to preliterate bards. What makes programming a bitchis that it requires humans to achieve something which they're not good at—perfection. A typical piece of programming (a large subroutine say, consists of about 500 statements. Statements average a half-line of text. Any tygopraphical or conceptual errors in any line will be bug, whose symtoms can range from obvious to so subtle that it is never found. Furthermore, the symtoms do not usually manifest themselves directly in the area of the work done by the faulty statement. To see how toubh this can be, examine this paragraph carefully and see how many many tygopraphical, spelling, and grammatical errors are in it (all deliberate).

The programmer doesn't write in a reasonable natural language such as English, but in an artificial language in which every written character is significant. A careful programmer will have one to three errors per hundred statements prior to testing. I've called this error rate the "public error rate." The private error rate is much higher. The programmer, of course, corrects most of these errors as the work progresses. The program is then tested, which reveals more errors, which are then corrected. This continues as components of the software are integrated into ever-larger pieces. A typical software package consist of 10,000 to 20,000 statements, while an **operating system** consists of 30,000 to 100,000 statements. Most bugs that remain after testing and after the program is released are bugs that can't be caught by the programmer because they arise from the interaction of programs. Furthermore, it is neither practical, nor theoretically possible, to test all such interactions. Another bitchy thing about it is that in good software, as bugs are corrected, the remaining bugs are subtler, ever-more arbitrary in their occurence, and ever-more unpredictable as to symptoms. The most

expensive bug I know of was in a control program for the *Mariner* Venus space probe. A comma (",") was left out of one statement, with the result that the probe and about $18,000,000 went astray.*

Human beings are good at intuition, generalization, and synthesis. We're big picture thinkers. That's diametrically opposite to the ultra-precision which programming demands. Yet, if a program is to be good, the programmer must be able to conceive that big picture lest she program something useless in meticulously correct detail. That's the final bitchiness: in addition to asking programmers to do something which humans aren't good at, we insist that they retain human outlooks.

This isn't intended to be a plea for "be kind to programmers' week" or "have you taken a programmer to lunch lately," or "I BRAKE FOR PROGRAMMERS" bumper stickers: there are technical tricks (as in any skilled trade) to help make the seemingly impossible possible. But it's a hard-won skill, much of which is contrary to human nature as we understand it. Spock *is* my ideal programmer—but notice how every once in a while even he goofs, and even he displays some residual human and/or atavistic Vulcan weakness. When that happens, we have bugs.

3.2. Programmer's Immunity

My wife's had no computer training. She had a big writing chore to do and a word-processor was the tool of choice. The package was good, but like most, it had bugs. We used the same hardware and software (she for her notes and I for my books) over a period of several months. The program would occasionally **crash** for her, but not for me. I couldn't understand it. My typing is faster than hers. I'm more abusive of equipment than she. And I used the equipment about ten hours for each of hers. By any measure, I should have had the problems far more often. Yet, something she did triggered bugs which I couldn't trigger by trying. How do we explain this mystery? What do we learn from it?

The answer came only after I spent hours watching her use of the system and comparing it to mine. She didn't know which operations were difficult for the software and consequently her pattern of usage and keystrokes did not avoid potentially troublesome areas. I *did* understand and I unconsciously avoided the trouble spots. I wasn't testing that software, so I had no stake in making it fail—I just wanted to get my work done with the least trouble. Programmers are notoriously poor at finding their own bugs—

---

*It's been reported as a lost period, a semicolon, and other punctuation marks. The putative cost varies from a few million to a hundred million dollars. It doesn't matter what the real story was, except that it was a microscopic error with a galactic cost.

especially subtle bugs—partially because of this immunity. Finding bugs in your own work is a form of self-immolation. We can extend this concept to explain why it is that some thoroughly tested software gets into the field and only then displays a host of bugs never before seen: the programmers achieve immunity to the bugs by subconsciously avoiding the trouble spots while testing.

3.3 Testing

Because we know that bugs are an inevitable consequence of the programmer's humanity, good software designers accept the fact that there will be many bugs in the programmer's initial work, and use design procedures that (1) prevent the bugs, and (2) find them when they do occur. The most important thing that can be done to prevent bugs is to design software so that it can be easily tested. Once software is written, there's no magic that will eliminate its bugs except copious testing. Test design is similar to software design and requires much the same talents. Approximately half of the effort required to get a program to the point where it can be used, is (or should be) expended in test design and testing. For consumer software, such as for personal computers, the test design and test effort should be increased so that it is 75% to 85% of the development cost. For software used to run nuclear reactors, the test and quality assurance costs should be about 90% to 95% of the total.

Software testing is not the act of hitting a piece of software with lots of **garbage,** or with random data, although that's what many software developers believe. They also confuse testing effectiveness with the amount of testing done. You could run a million dumb tests and not learn what can be learned from a few smart tests. Smart testing is technical, requires an intimate understanding of software in general and the package being tested, specifically. It requires training beyond software design training.

The above is what should be—what are the realities?

1. As of 1987, after over three decades of software development, you could count the number of books on software testing and quality assurance on your fingers and toes.*
2. Most programmers don't know how to test their own or anyone else's software. They're ignorant of what testing techniques exist, and of how well those techniques do or don't work.

---

*On one hand, if you count in **binary.** I immodestly claim two of that hand-and-footful of books.

3. As of 1987, few universities offered courses in testing or software quality assurance.
4. Many programmers and software development managers were aware of testing methods but they didn't use them, or weren't allowed to use them had they wanted to.

3.4. Software Quality Assurance?

It's clear that if there are so many opportunities for foul-ups in the development of software, even by conscientious, competent programmers, then quality assurance is essential. Software quality assurance methods exist. They include: independent testing, reviews, audits, paperwork controls, tools, statistical data gathering and processing, and many other things. The methods exist, but they're applied sporadically, if at all, and are in much the same state as testing is.

One of the reasons that there's almost no software quality assurance is that there's never been a real pressure for it until personal computers came along. Mainframe software development is usually done by an in-house data processing department that plays to a captive audience: there's no accountability, and consequently, no QA. Eventually, things work because the bugs are found and fixed, but it can take years. The personal computer business is different. There are dozens of competing packages for any one application—buggy best sellers won't remain best sellers long if the bugs don't get fixed. The only reason some programs managed to survive in their earlier versions was that there was no competition and the buyers didn't know. As competition increases and as buyers lose patience with bad software, the pressure for software QA will increase, and with that pressure, software will get better, and possibly acceptable. However, I've recently attempted to get information from many different hardware and software vendors, on the methods and policy they used for software testing and quality assurance. You'd think that if they had a plan and a policy, they'd have some slick PR stuff ready to send and that they'd boast about how good their QA is. Not one of those I've asked has ever answered my questions. I can't believe that *all* my requests and *all* my letters went astray. What's more likely is that they don't have a policy, they don't have a plan, and there's no consistency with respect to quality assurance.

4. BUGS AND WHAT THEY COST—AND COST, AND COST

4.1. Symptoms Versus Bugs

There's conflict between software users and developers: the user's concern is *what* the program does or doesn't do, while the programmer's concern is *why*. Users see symptoms, but programmers look for causes. Consider the difference between software and manufactured products. In most products, the symptoms are closely related to the cause. The simpler the product, the closer that relation is. If your kitchen sink leaks, you look under it, and not in the attic: but as products become more complicated, the distance between symptom and cause increases. If your car misbehaves you might be able to say that the problem was in the engine, but unlike earlier cars, for modern cars with their complicated emission controls, you can no longer, without expert knowledge, localize the problem further. With more complicated systems, such as humans, the relation between symptom and cause is even less obvious. We've learned to accept this consequence of complexity. Software is someplace between a modern car's engine and a biological system.

There's no correlation between the severity of a bug in technical terms and the severity of its symptoms: awful bugs from a user's point of view may be trivial to programmers and vice-versa. By the time a package gets into the field, though, most of the remaining bugs are little annoyances to both programmer and user. From the user's point of view, the program does queer things here and there with no apparent pattern. From the programmer's point of view, he doesn't know if there's one, three, or ten different bugs about which users are complaining: and the lack of pattern makes it difficult for the programmer to find the source and fix the bug.

4.2. Entomology For the User

4.2.1. General

There are recognized technical bug categories. In organizations that employ viable software quality assurance methods, bugs are placed into these categories, from which statistics can be developed which can in turn lead to new quality assurance and design methods that will help to prevent and correct such bugs. Does this mean anything to the user? What would you do if a programmer told you that the reason you lost a week's work is that there was a *type error,* or a *indirect-index error?* Such categories are meaningless to users. What the user wants is a way to categorize the *symptoms.*

4.2.2. Symptomatic Bug Categories

The symptomatic bug categories are: data corruption, data loss, processing errors, control loss, and cockpit error induction.

1. *Data Corruption*—The program produces a correct result, but creates errors in an area far from that in which you're working. For example, lost appointments in a personal scheduler. If you enter an appointment for January 4, and it appears to be correct, but unknown to you, the entry for December 14 is clobbered, that's data corruption. If you were playing with

the January 4 entry and *it* was clobbered, that's improper processing (see below).

Data corruption is the worst thing a program can do to you because it's usually subtle and unrelated to the work at hand. It may be days or weeks before you discover the problem. If the problem is systematic, it's not as bad as if it's random. You can usually avoid systematic corruption by avoiding the cause. It's also easier to reproduce, and consequently, it's likelier to be repaired once it's been reported. Random data corruption is the worst because you can't evolve a working style to avoid the problem and because customer service may not believe you when you report it.

2. *Data Loss*—Blame yourself for extensive data loss. Many bugs result in data loss. Make it a habit to create copious, frequent backups for everything. I do at least one backup a day for everything I do. In some cases, I'll backup every hour or two, depending on the package, the complexity of doing the backup, and so on. Even a daily backup is annoying but I've yet to use a package with which I could confidently work for days at a time without backups. It's not fair—good software shouldn't require such frequent backups—but it is realistic.

The most common data loss is the loss of a file or an entire disc. Data loss bugs can be vicious. Some bad packages lose data as a result of attempting to do a backup. One solution for that problem is to put a **write-protect tab** on the original when doing the backup.* Another solution, for critical work, is to have two or three backups.

3. *Processing Errors*—When the program fouls things up in an area close to where we're working, we call it a processing error. Processing errors are usually obvious and the error can often be corrected by retrying the command. Their biggest impact is that they erode confidence in the package. For example, you're a good speller and you use a buggy spell-checking program. You notice that it doesn't catch every error. What do you do then? You lose confidence in the package and you spend more time proofreading than you should. With numerical packages, such as spreadsheets, it may be impossible to spot processing errors unless you insert special check calculations, all of which take more effort. In a data-base management system, erosion of confidence leads you to manually check files to reassure yourself that no important records's been misprocessed.

4. *Control Loss*—Control loss occurs when the program no longer allows you to control it. The primary example of control loss is a crash. Other forms of control loss include any kind of very long operation which cannot be aborted. Control loss (and crashes) often have associated data corrup-

---

*But some software won't allow you to do that.

tion or loss. We call such instances of control loss **raving crashes.** Benign crashes usually lose only the work done during that session. Because that which you were working on is usually lost after a crash, crashes not only lose that work, but also cause additional work because a system that habitually crashes will force you into more backups than you would otherwise make.

5. *Cockpit Errors*—A program may have bugs which leads you to make a **cockpit error.** A nasty example is a program that tells you that you've lost your data (for no apparent reason). You believe it, grumble, and repeat the work. The data wasn't really lost, but your restart and the other actions you took as a result of the program's lie causes the data loss. Such bugs are a pain. After a while, you learn where they are and which can be ignored, and you don't fall into that trap again—but every time it happens, whether you get caught or not, it leaves a psychological scar.

4.3. Bug Severity in Personal Terms

The symptoms of Section 4.2 impact the way you work and the world. All bugs have consequential damages; and all vendors disclaim responsibility. If you've ever read the fine print on software warranties, they even disclaim responsibility for having the program work at all. A typical agreement reads: "no . . . warranties with regard to performance or accuracy of data of any kind . . . merchantability and fitness for a particular purpose . . . " Someday, software vendors won't be allowed to blithely deny their responsibility for bad software as now they do.

Bad software's impact differs from user to user. In some cases, data corruption is an annoyance, in others, the same bug means bankruptcy. Only you can judge which applies to you, and therefore, only you can judge how much tolerance you can have for bad software. It's a useful exercise to establish risk categories before committing yourself to a package, or to the use of a computer, for that matter. Here's a list of categories to use as a starting point:

1. *Mild*—the bug's symptoms are aesthetically offensive: for example, misaligned columns in a report.
2. *Moderate*—Misleading or redundant outputs. Bugs that induce cockpit errors.
3. *Annoying*—More frequent occurrences of the type in 1 and 2 above. Problems are perceived but there are ways around them. The bug may cause others to complain, such as truncating a name, or sending dunning letters for unpaid bills of $00.00. Call a bug annoying if you have cause to curse it daily.

4. *Disturbing*—The program refuses to do reasonable and legitimate things which it was designed to do. For example, refusing to print page 34 of a 57 page document.
5. *Serious*—Obvious data loss which can be avoided by backups.
6. *Very Serious*—Unknown (at first) data loss or corruption.
7. *Extreme*—All of the above if they're frequent.
8. *Intolerable*—Subtle, creeping corruption of a large data-base—especially dangerous for numerical data. For example, gradual erosion of the validity of inventory data. The point at which the damage exceeds the cost of the software, the ancillary costs, and all the rest. The point at which litigation starts.
9. *Catastrophic*—Sufficiently dangerous to destroy the entity that uses the system. Typically, by this time, it is you who's being sued or is on trial.
10. *And Worse*—If you think it can't get worse, consider software that corrupts other software, that corrupts other people's data, or software that kills. And software *can* kill.*

4.4. The Advantages of Old Software

Software can't change by itself. It changes only if the software's builder does so. If you have a package that you bought a year ago, it'll be no better or no worse today than when you bought it. It can seem worse because as times passes your applications get more complicated, your data base gets larger, and you use more features and options in more combinations than you had before. These changes in your usage increase the likelihood that you'll trip on a bug that has been there all along.

Conversely, don't assume that the copy you buy today is the same as the one you bought last year, even if the **version** and **release** numbers are identical. The version and release numbers apply to the package as a whole and not to the individual programs within the package. It would be rare to have a bug so pervasive that every program in a package had to be changed to fix it. Consequently, most bugs affect only one or two out of a possible twenty programs in the package, and the vendor does not renumber either the package version number or the release number, but only the release numbers of the affected programs. It's no different from any other consumer product. You know that there are changes from week to week on automobile assembly lines: it's only after those changes have accumulated that a new model is declared. Some vendors, for some packages, do provide update services that will allow you to get the latest variation, but most don't.

So even though the software can't change itself, it is continually being changed. If the software is good, and effectively marketed, there will be a

---

*A bug in software that controlled an x-ray system has killed several times.

stake in increasing profit by reducing customer complaints. The package's success means that it will be upgraded, not only for new features (which the vendor will be sure to publicize), but also to correct old flaws.* The longer a package has been around, the likelier it is for *subsequent releases* to be bug-free. It pays, therefore, to buy old software and to always get the latest version.

---

*I've yet to see an ad which said "Buy BELCHALL III—we've fixed everything you hated and which didn't work in BELCHALL II."

3

READ THE MANUAL—IF YOU CAN

1. SYNOPSIS

Why people complain about instruction manuals. Why manuals are so bad. What's in a good information package. The tutorial package. Tutorial programs. Help screens. The reference package. Hidden manuals.

2. LAMENTATIONS

2.1. Lamentations of a User

Here's a two-hundred page manual for a word processing package. The publisher wanted it to be "user friendly," which he thought meant giving it an instruction manual written for children instead of adults. The first few pages are a sell-job that tells me how wonderful computers are and why I shouldn't be afraid of them, how great word processing is, and why *this* package is the greatest of the great. Several frustrating hours preceded success with the first exercise because the installation instructions were unintelligible as well as wrong. A call to the retailer, another call to the software publisher's customer service department and I'd finally got the thing started. The manual's first instructions were:

> "We will start by typing 'The quick brown fox jumped over the lazy dogs.' Don't worry if you make a mistake, with BELCHWORD all your stupid fumble-fingered typing mistakes can be easily fixed. Begin by:
>
> Type the letter 'T'.
> Now type the letter 'h'.
> . . . .
> Now type the last letter, 's', followed by a period. End this sentence by touching the RETURN key."

I suffered through five pages of this pap and decided to skip ahead to the meat. On page 20, I was lost by:

"Produlators are inconclusive when used in conjunction with semaphores. If you want inverse margination, you must read chapters 12 through 14 before continuing, otherwise you may damage your disc drives."

A bad manual had been "fixed" by tacking-on a patronizing beginning, but with no thought to consistency and the workings of the adult mind. Such manuals are useful only if you don't need them. What's more, their unevenness makes you feel like a fool—few computer users have the confidence to assert that the instruction manual is garbage—most will assume that the trouble is with themselves.

You *will* get into trouble if you don't read the instruction manual before you start—but you don't read the manual because if you're not insulted by patronizing prattle at the beginning, then it's because you realize, after a few pages, that it's unreadable.

2.2. Lamentations of a Retailer

Buyers who complain about good software packages (retailers tell me) have trouble because they haven't read the instruction manual. They act as if they expect to learn the package by means of private tutoring sessions conducted over the telephone. This refusal to read instruction manuals, to go through excellent tutorial material, to not accept that some things (such as data-base management, communications, and spreadsheet packages) can be complicated, is a headache for the software retailer. It doesn't take a degree in finance to realize how little time the retailer can afford to spend training the buyer before his profits are up the flue: it's about one hour per package, and that includes the time spent selling it, installing it, and answering questions after it's sold.

Second only to the buyer, the retailer has the highest stake in excellent instruction material. Second only to the buyer, it's the retailer who's frustrated and angry over poor instructions. Retailers will push a package which has good instructions over a more powerful one that may cost less because they know that they'll have less service costs with the simpler package. The retailer may not even tell you about package Y, which he has judged to be too difficult to learn.

2.3. The Software Developer's Lament

I've watched the transformation of one of my favorite vendors from an informative, cooperative organization to a defensive, suspicious, and occasionally hostile group. When personal computers were new, they treated us like they did buyers of their mini- and mainframe systems. It was easy to get to the technical people for information that wasn't in their manuals. As they sold more personal computers, there were more users who had less experience and needed more help. The service they had been giving became unprofitable, so they interposed a layer of less technically qualified persons to answer inquiries and complaints. And what was worse, that information, instead of being free, was now available only if you had purchased a "customer service" subscription. Nothing's free anymore—or what you get for nothing is worth just that.

From their point of view, they're embarrassed by the success which has bred all those ignorant new computer users. They're even less tolerant of buyers who flood them with technical questions and problems whose real origins are avoidable cockpit errors. They're annoyed by smartass techies who gobble hours of valuable service representative time with gripes over valid design decisions. And then there's the hordes of idiot users who haven't even tried to read the excellent tutorial material and the poor souls who just won't accept the fact that computers may not be all that easy to use and who probably will never achieve competence.

Some vendors have a siege mentality when it comes to customer service. They wouldn't be under siege if their software worked and if their manuals were helpful.

2.4. The Critic's Lament

I'm tempted to start the critic's lament by saying "A pox on all your houses", thereby antagonizing you, my reader, the software development community, and the retailers and vendors with whom I deal each day. The problem is that everybody seems to be operating under mythical expectations instead of reality. The retailers hype, the buyers buy and fall on their faces, then the retailer claims ignorance while the vendor raises the drawbridge, drops the portcullis, and stocks the moat with alligators. Nowhere is the game played worse than in manuals and information—because more often than not, there's *nothing wrong with the product a that a good information package wouldn't fix.*

Both buyers and sellers have rights and responsibilities. Both must forget the myths and TV-hype that accompanied the introduction of personal computers and made it all seem so easy.

The Buyer's Rights—Expect a professionally written information package that can be understood by a person of average intelligence and education as appropriate to the package. It's reasonable to assume that accounting packages will be used by trained accountants and bookkeepers and that word-processing packages by almost anyone. The manual must be informative. It should have the components discussed in Sections 3 and 4 below. *And it must be correct.*

The Buyer's Responsiblities—Don't expect to master the package without working at it, no more than you should expect to master a technical book that way—no matter what the salesman told you. You shouldn't expect an education in computers, or word-processing, or data-base management. You can't expect to exploit all the package's features on the first day, or even after a week.

The Retailer's Responsibilities—Be fair about warning new users about the complexity of some packages. Steer them to a simpler (and possibly less profitable package) if that's more suited to their needs and current level of understanding. Offer and urge new users to attend training sessions and to buy after-market books (the best of which you should stock). State exactly how much support will be provided up front and what additional support may cost.

The Publisher's Responsibilities—Apply the same standards that book publishers use for writing style and expertise. Hire professional writers to create manuals, not hacks and not failed programmers. Test the manuals independently with an effort that's comparable to the independent testing of the software. Use intelligent novices and expert critics. Adopt good after-market manuals if you can't write them yourself.

2.5. The Information Package

You buy two things when you buy a software package: (1) the software and (2) the means by which you learn how to use it. I call those means the **"information package."** The information package is pointless without the software and the software is unuseable without the information package.

Using a package goes through several phases and each phase requires different information. The phases are: buying, installing, learning, using, and exploiting. These lead to the following components of the information package: the pitch, installation, tutorial, reference, and application. The pitch, installation, and applications are discussed in the tutorial sections at the back of this book. The core of the information you need is contained in the vendor's tutorial and reference packages, which are discussed in this chapter.

3. THE TUTORIAL PACKAGE

3.1. Why Tutorials

Learning is a process which changes you. It follows that you need a different kind of manual when you're starting than after you've had experience. This leads to a paradox: what's good for a novice can be exasperating to an expert; what's essential and efficient after you've learned the package is confusing when you start. The users' knowledge is a spread. Some users have no previous experience with this or any other package, while some are expert enough to create it. Both extremes and everyone between must be satisfied. If the manual is pitched for the novice, experts are annoyed—if aimed at the expert, the package fails commercially. If aimed at the middle, they all hate it. It's a problem for manual writers; here's three ways they solve it:

1. A tutorial manual and a separate reference manual.
2. Combine the tutorial data and the reference material without confusing the novice or boring the expert.
3. Address only one group—e.g., novice, middle, or master.

The third approach, although common, doesn't work. The novice is confused, the expert is frustrated, and there's really nobody in the middle. I like the second approach, but it takes superlative writing skill and more effort than most publishers are willing to put into a manual. The first approach is the one most commonly used today. There are two manuals—an elementary tutorial manual and a more detailed, but terser, reference manual. When the package is inherently complicated, there may be three manuals: a basic tutorial, an advanced tutorial, and a reference manual. Whether this material is bound as one manual, two manuals, or three sections of one manual, is unimportant. What counts is that there be an obvious division between tutorial and reference material.

3.2. Tutorial Manuals

Why, if there's a tutorial program (see Section 3.3. below), is a written tutorial manual still needed? It's needed because you can't study the tutorial program in bed or on the train.

A proper tutorial manual (or program) consists of a series of lessons and exercises that an intelligent person can execute to learn the basics. Being elementary doesn't mean that the manual is patronizing or insulting, or even boring to the expert. The main difference between an expert's use of a tutorial and a novice's will be the speed at which she goes through it. The novice may take days while the expert takes hours. The tutorial may be on paper, or be a program, or both. It has the following characteristics:

1. Statement of the lesson's objectives—e.g., to learn how to set up pagination. The objective's statement is made only in terms of previously described operations and terminology.
2. Summary of what was learned in terms of operations and terminology introduced in that lesson.
3. At least one example for every operation and variation discussed, including:
   a. Pictures of all screens before and after the operation (this is automatic for tutorial programs).
   b. Unambiguous specification of all commands entered and keys struck—keystroke by keystroke.
   c. Description of what happens, as seen by the user.
4. A collection of questions and their answers, gleaned from experience, in the form they're usually asked.
5. Cross-reference to the reference manual—for example: "For more information on pagination, see R101 and R105."
6. It doesn't have to be slick. There could be a set of programmed lessons and an actual manual which is printed for you by running a program. It's not a bad approach, and it is sometimes used with low cost software. The difficulty with such "manuals" is that graphics are sparse and it can be hard to discuss some things without using pictures.

Whether the tutorial material is on paper or on disc, it should follow a lesson plan. The following plan is appropriate to almost any package; an egg roll processor, say:

Lesson Zero—Prerequisites and Installation. This refers to the prerequisites and installation of a tutorial program for the package rather than the installation of the package itself. Some packages have a simplified installation procedure in a "getting started" section which can be used with either the tutorial programs or with the printed lesson plan. The ideal is to build the lessons around a minimal configuration that requires little or no installation.

Lesson One—Starting the Egg Roller. I always have trouble getting started the first time. I get into trouble because I follow the instructions literally, just as a novice would, and start-up instructions are often wrong. What's more frustrating than not being able to start the package? Instruction manual writers tend to assume things that the reader doesn't know. A common failing is not telling the reader how to load the program disc. It's falsely assumed that the reader has read and understood the operating system manual. Lesson one should be a rote, key-by-key startup procedure that assumes no prior knowledge—from turning the system on, up to the point where the package's first screen appears. If it's not patronizing no one will be insulted by it. This is a short lesson that's at most one page long.

Lesson Two—Stopping the Egg Roller. You can always stop a program by turning the hardware off or by popping the disc out: and doing it that way can destroy the program disc, the data disc, or both. About half of the tutorial manuals I've read don't tell you how to stop. That's like teaching a driver without telling him where the brakes are. This is another short lesson of a page or so.

Lesson Three—Getting Help. A short lesson on how to get help while running. For example, the use of **help screens** and help keys (see below). Reassurances that using HELP will not destroy work (if true).

Lesson Four—Creating and Naming Egg Rolls. Whatever else the package does, it will be used to create **data objects.** Creating data objects includes naming them, and may also require you to specify other parameters. Creation commands in data-base management packages can be complicated, while in word processing they're often so simple and automatic that you hardly know you've done it. At this point in learning the software you want to know enough about naming and creating egg rolls to get on with the lessons, and no more.

Lesson Five—Saving Egg Rolls. Some instruction manual writers must have cast-iron kidneys. They assume that once you start, you'll go through to the end (where how to store objects is revealed). You must store things before you can stop. It makes sense therefore, just as you must know how to stop after you've learned to start, to learn how to save after you've learned to create.

Lesson Six—Fetching Egg Rolls. You've stopped the lesson in the middle, saved your work, stopped the program, restarted it, and now you want to pick up where you left off. You have to fetch an egg roll—so that's the next lesson.

Lesson Seven—Backing Up Egg Rolls. This is less important for tutorial sessions, where the loss of an object is annoying, but rarely serious. However, once you're using the program in earnest, it's essential that you back up all work—copiously and frequently. Some (poor) packages force backups to be done only by using the operating system. Often, backing-up is just a matter of storing another copy with a different name. Whatever the procedure is, you must be told.

Lesson Eight—Deleting Egg Rolls. It's amazing how fast a disc fills up with junk. Good packages allow you to delete useless objects without leaving the package. Most force you to confirm the deletion of an object.

Lesson Nine—Egg Roll Status. You can't be expected to remember how many objects you've created, their names, their attributes, and their current status. It's brutal to require you to leave the package to get that information, so (decent) programs have a directory or status command that you can use to get such information.

Lesson Ten and On—Playing with Egg Rolls. The above fundamentals apply to every package. Beyond those lessons, things get specialized, but there are still many areas of commonality that can be exploited to achieve a uniform structure for lessons even though the details will differ from package to package. For example: copying, printing, editing, merging, sending data to other packages, getting data from other packages. These general lessons should precede the more specialized lessons that are peculiar to the package. Once the basics are done with, there's a lot of flexibility to the order in which things can be presented. It's best if the manual (at that point) is subdivided into functional areas (e.g., printing, report layout, editing, etc.) so that you can read the lessons with a priority appropriate to your special needs. There are few things as frustrating as being forced to plow through a bunch of features that you'll never use in order to understand that which you need. Within each such functional section, the basics for that section should be presented, and the section itself should follow the structure of the entire tutorial material.

If publishers collectively followed a common, rational, plan for their instructions manuals, they'd find that user support requirements would decrease substantially for all of them. One of the advantages of buying software from the same publisher can be that there is a uniform tutorial plan, so that going from package to package is a familiar, rather than a strange, experience.

What do you do if the instruction manual isn't rationally organized? Do it yourself. Look for the above lessons and rearrange the pages (or copies of them) if you have to. Alternatively, find the lessons and tag the pages accordingly. Then follow the tutorial manual in the rational order (as above), rather than in the order in which it was written. Good manuals will require little or no rearrangement while bad manuals will make a total rewrite seem easier.

3.3. Tutorial Programs

I've had more problems with tutorial programs than with the packages they're intended to teach me about. Otherwise good packages are accompanied by hostile, patronizing, and incredibly buggy tutorial programs. I've crashed four out of five tutorial programs—in normal attempted use. It's as if the tutorials' designers don't realize that the tutorial program's purpose is to educate a novice (for that package), who is likely to make mistakes. Because tutorials aren't "the real thing," I suppose that designers think they don't deserve the same care. Actually, tutorials deserve more thought and more care. Far more important than seeing a demonstration, ask the dealer to allow you to run through the tutorial program (if there is one).

A tutorial program isn't a demonstration, even though there may be a demonstration mode. The user is usually passive in a demonstration, while active when running a tutorial program. That's the important distinction. There can be no errors in a demo because you do little or nothing (but the equivalent of turning the page). The tutorial allows you to enter data, make mistakes, and all the rest. It's a simulation of the real thing. So there's actually a spread in tutorial packages ranging from a pure demonstration to a highly interactive, structured, learning experience. The closer the tutorial is to a simulation, the more useful it will be. Simulations can be complicated. Simulators for such things as the space shuttle are more complicated than the things they simulate. The ultimate tutorial program, that allowed you to safely explore every nuance of a package, would be more complicated than the package itself and more expensive to design. There's been no demand (yet) for such training tools by personal computer buyers. There's no evidence that they're willing to pay $400 for a package and $600 for its training software—even though it might be a good deal. Therefore, most tutorials are limited. They correspond to the introductory tutorial manual. They're intended to teach you fundamentals and nothing else. Good tutorial programs have the following characteristics:

1. A lesson plan similar to that discussed in Section 3.2. above for tutorial manuals.
2. More like a simulation than a demonstration.
3. As interactive and free as possible—within the constraints of following a lesson plan.
4. Forgiving to the nth degree. Catches all errors and gently points them out without a put-down.
5. Keeps the lessons on track despite your errors.

6. Reviews of what was learned in each lesson. Some method of self-evaluation; possibly, automatic examinations (although I haven't seen that yet).

7. Can be safely stopped after every lesson, started at any lesson, and can rerun any lesson in any order.

8. Uses previously prepared data objects which you can manipulate and modify rather than forcing you through the laborious, error-prone steps used to create the object. You should be asked to enter only that which is needed to illustrate the lesson; everything else should be on disc. No matter what right or wrong thing you do, when the lesson is restarted, the original object is still there and hasn't been changed or lost.

9. Split screens or some other method such as color to distinguish between the tutorial's operation and the package's simulated operation. For example, it's one thing to quit the package and another to quit the tutorial. If you simulate quitting the package, it doesn't mean that you want to quit the tutorial.

10. Identification of your inputs, the package's responses, and the tutorial's responses—for example, by using color, boldface, italics, or inverse video.

11. On-screen references for further details—e.g., "For more information on editing egg rolls, see Chapter 12 of the reference manual."

12. Field-by-field, explanations of whatever appears on the screen and how to interpret it.

13. Explains, where appropriate, how the tutorial's behavior and the actual program's behavior may differ.

14. Explanations of what would actually happen if it's not possible or practical to do something in the tutorial. For example: "At this point, the package would print three copies of the egg roll."

15. Some indication of how long it could take to finish a time-consuming operation. For example: "Sorting an egg roll can take several minutes—let's assume that it's been done—here's the result."

16. Adult conversation—no babytalk, no patronizing.

17. A tutorial program's tutorial manual that states: tutorial program prerequisites and installation, how to start, how to stop, how to repeat a lesson or step, how to bypass lessons, and how to get to specific lessons.

18. Self-protecting, fully debugged, and robust.

Just because there's no tutorial program or because the tutorial is poor doesn't mean that you should reject the package. After-market tutorials that satisfy most of the above requirements are available for many popular packages from American Training International Inc., among others. After-market tutorial producers may also provide tutorial programs under the package's publisher's label. In such cases, there will probably be no independent tutorial. And in some instances, you may have a choice of several tutorials, some of which may be the same. The typical tutorial package's price is about $40 or $50. It's a sensible investment for expert computer user or novice. Add the cost of an after-market tutorial (if necessary) to the package's initial cost.

3.4. Operational Tutorials (Help Screens)

Not all of the important tutorial material is in the manuals or in a tutorial program. Most users forget what things mean and what they do, especially if the program has a lot of useful but complicated commands. You can always (or should be able to) look things up in the reference manual, but often that's inconvenient. Good packages solve this problem by using **help screens.** At any instant, only a few operations make sense. The help screen is a screen that gives you a quick summary of the available choices and/or commands, what they mean, what they do, and how to activate them. Every decent package has help screens or the equivalent. Every decent package has a uniform, safe, method of activating the help screen. Some examples in order of decreasing desirability:

1a. An explicit HELP key.
1b. A special function key (say F1) designated for "HELP."
1c. An ordinary key used in conjunction with a control key, or ALT shift key, such as ⟨control⟩H, ⟨control⟩?, or ⟨ALT⟩H.

Help can be complicated and one help screen may lead you to another. For example, the first level might simply list the available options or general subject headings. Then, you can select which area you want in more detail. Good help systems have several additional characteristics:

2. Exactly the same method (e.g., keystrokes) used to invoke help throughout the package.
3. Increasing depth and details under your control.
4. Ability to move between help levels at will.
5. Ability to cut off long lectures—e.g., STOP HELP.
6. References to chapters, sections, or pages in the reference manual and/ or in the tutorial manual.
7. Ability to print the help screen.

Finally, it should be obvious that HELP should not interfere with what you were doing. A help command that stops the ongoing operation, that loses data, that forces you to restart, is not just hostile—it's vicious. Who needs that kind of "help"?

4. THE REFERENCE PACKAGE

4.1. How Much Is Enough?

What's the right size for a reference manual, or for that matter, for any part of the information package? Complicated packages need bigger manuals than simple packages. Judge the complexity of the package by the number of distinct commands you can give. A package with a hundred commands is twice as complicated as one with fifty commands and you should expect an information package (and price) that's about twice as big. Make comparisons and judge excellence after correcting for the package's complexity. It's not the number of pages that counts; it's the number of pages per command. Similarly for index terms and glossary entries.

Manual writers seem to think that they have a dilemma: if they include all the facts, then even the best-written reference manual will be intimidating to most users; if they leave out any facts in order to avoid overwhelming the reader, then customer service will be overwhelmed by questions. There is no dilemma. The problem is that both users and writers don't know why the reference manual was written and how it's supposed to be used. Think about it. Is an encyclopedia intimidating? How about a dictionary? Or the telephone directory. If you thought you had to read any of those works from cover-to-cover in order to use them to advantage . . . silly, isn't it. A reference work is a reference work and not a tutorial. It's intended to be a source of information—all the information that all the users need.

A good reference manual is organized by subjects. It can, within a subject, progress from simple to complex if the material lends itself to that treatment, but alphabetical listings of commands or functions can work just as well. The information should be indexed in different ways so that however you think of it, you're likely to find a path to the data you need. I'm amazed at the self-contradiction of elegant data-base management packages that let you access data by dozens of different keys, but give you only one key (the index—if that) to the contents of their own reference manuals.

Good reference manuals have 1.5 or more pages per command or major command variation (for **menu-driven software,** it's about the same per menu option or sub-option.)

4.2. Reference Card

Whether the program is controlled by typing commands, by **function keys,** by touching the right spot on the screen, by selecting options from a menu, by some combination of the above, or by none of the above, each such action is a **command** to the package. Simple packages may have as few as 30 different commands. Most single-function packages (e.g., word processing, data-base management, spreadsheet) have about 150 commands, while integrated packages have 250 or more commands. The more a package does, the more commands it has. The more it does, the less likely you are to remember all the commands. In practice, 90% of your work is done with ten commands. You learn those quickly enough. You also learn, but forget, the other commands if you don't use them often.

A command reference card (sheet, chart, index, summary list) is an essential part of every information package. I have an urge to trash any piece of software that doesn't have one. The list is organized either by functional areas or by key letter (first letter) or both, and it has the following information:

1. The command itself or a picture of the menu option.
2. The format of any data to be entered, and/or the command's format (i.e., the command's **syntax**), as appropriate.
3. A *very* short statement of what it does—e.g., "STOre = stores a record."
4. A key to the appropriate reference manual pages.
5. A key to the appropriate tutorial manual section.

Reference cards come in all sizes and shapes: neat plasticized cards with a built-in stand, folded sheets, credit card size, single color, multicolor, rough, slick, etc. The good ones are sturdy and protected from coffee spills because these cards get a lot of use and abuse. Whatever their size and shape, a lot of thinking went into the useful ones. They strike a balance between clarity and utility on the one hand, and not trying to cram the entire reference manual onto one page, on the other. Good or bad, though, any card is better than none.

4.3. Glossary

Glossaries can be long or short but that has nothing to do with their usefulness. An information package without a glossary is probably poorer than one with—but before you count the number of terms in the glossary, see how many of them are useful. The purpose of a glossary is to provide definitions for technical terms and jargon which the reader is unlikely to find elsewhere. That doesn't just mean new words: it also means new usages. For example, what does the word "format" mean? It has different meanings as a verb and as a noun, and means completely different things in word-processing, spreadsheet, and data-base packages. You could look "format" up in a dictionary, or even in a computer dictionary, but that might not help you understand what "format" means for this specific package.

Then there's jargon. Jargon can be specific to the computer field, or to the package. Terms such as "infix," "left binding power," "flattened," and "recursive" need explanation (assuming that they had to be used in the first place). An introductory manual, for a computer say, might define general computer terms such as "disc" and "backup" because it's assumed that the user may not know their meaning. When you see such definitions in an advanced manual, for a technical package, it's just puffery and a waste of space. I've seen exactly the same basic glossary used in a half-dozen different packages from one publisher. It looks as if there was an instruction manual standard which required the inclusion of a glossary—so the writers copped out and used that stock glossary, but key technical terms and package-specific jargon were not defined.

Glossaries don't work by themselves. They work in combination with text and indexes. A good glossary and information package has the following characteristics:

1. Every special term, jargon, or usage is marked when first used—say by using boldface (my favorite method).
2. Every boldface term has a definition in the glossary.
3. There are at least two index entries for the term—the place in the text where it was first defined and at least one other place where it's used— why introduce a term if it's not used?
4. The glossary includes not only terms and jargon which appear in the written manual, but also those which appear on screens and in **error messages.**
5. Any foward references (which should be avoided) are also given a glossary entry.

4.4. Error Messages

This subject gets me angry. A good package will detect when you've painted yourself into a corner. If you attempt to store something on the disc, and have run out of room, its reasonable that the package will tell you that that's what's happened and that it will give you an opportunity to get out of the corner. Not all such messages result from your actions. Sometimes, the program detects illogical conditions that indicate that something has gone wrong. For example, an error in reading the disc (did you inadvertantly touch the surface?). Sometimes illogical conditions result from software bugs, or a temporary hardware malfunction. Whatever the cause, you want to know about it and how to recover, if possible. I'm angered by software vendors who don't explain these messages. You do something innocent, the screen blanks out, and then you see: "ILLEGAL UUO AT USER LOCATION 1DA079—ABORTING." One of the things that infuriated me about Coddler's software was the way it handled error messages. The package would lay one of those message on at almost every opportunity. Naturally, there was no error message index, or any other reference to what these messages meant. I called the customer service department and was told that such information was *not for public consumption!* The program talks to me, but I'm not allowed to know what it said? That's what I call a "FUSS."*

Designers don't have to be defensive about asking you for help. Because that's what one of those messages really mean. The program doesn't know what to do—HELP please! There must be a dictionary of all error messages which the package can send you: a good one has:

1. The message number.
2. Repetition of the text as it appears on the screen
3. Explanation of all terms, parts, fields, or numbers that may appear in the message.
4. The probable cause or causes.
5. The action, if any, you can or should take to correct the situation. There may be several actions possible, or alternative actions, and all alternatives could be ugly—but at least your options are explained.

There may be some messages whose presence indicates that something that's so illogical has occurred that you had better look for a service person. Such messages may be accompanied by arcane numbers which are not explained. If that's the case, write the numbers and things down, or do a **screen dump** if you can, and then quit, and run the **hardware checkout programs** (if your system has them) before you call customer service. Only one such message should be allowed. It should read:

046 FATAL PROBLEM: CASE # nnn; ABORTING

or something like that. If it happens during a thunderstorm, after you've spilled coffee on the keyboard, or spit on the disc, then there's no reason to be alarmed. Run the checkout program, restart the system, and try again with a different data disc and another copy of the program disc and/or operating system. Call service if the problem persists. But if that kind of

---

*Fouled-Up Software System if you want to be euphemistic.

message appears more than once a month without provocation, then it's probably a programmer's cop out.

4.5. Index(es)

An information package without an index is hardly worth the trouble. That's such a miserable piece of documentation that you might as well not bother—not unless you're willing to create your own index. If we use the number of different commands or basic commands and major options as a basis, the indexes for the combined tutorial and reference manuals range from three to twenty page numbers per command: two or less is meager, five is adequate, and fifteen or more is good. A good package could have several different indexes, for example:

1. Normal subject/concept index.
2. Command index.
3. Keystroke sequence index.
4. Help messages index.
5. Error message index.
6. "How to" index.

I don't think you'd want all of these as explicit, separate, indexes. It would depend on how good the other sections were. They can also be combined. Commands can be indexed under the heading "command" within a normal index. Definitions should follow the same convention used in the text. If definitions are in boldface, say, then so should the page number.

4.6. Limitations

This is another area where software and manual writers get defensive: the package's limitations. I like to know such things as what's the longest document, the biggest field, the smallest number, and so on. Whatever the package does, whatever computer it runs on, it has limitations. Some of these are forced by the hardware, some by the operating system, and some result from designer decisions. It really doesn't matter why there's a limit; what matters is that there is. It's interesting though, that the publishers who hide their limits also hide the messages related to the limits. What are they ashamed of? That they can't process to infinity with finite resources? Who do they think they're fooling? Every user will sooner or later bump up against the limits. Any good reviewer will check the limits experimentally if there's a suspicion that the limits are unreasonable. And if the vendor's reasons for being coy about limits is that they believe that publishing such limits might hurt their competitiveness, then any smart competitor will test and find those limits and will be sure to publish them in a comparison.

Look for an explicit limitations section. If you can't find it, check the message directory. The next step is to contact customer service and ask for a list. My willingness to try the package is proportional to the ease with which I can get this data. Also, and perhaps this is caused by unfair bias on my part, programs with hidden limits tend to have obvious bugs. Don't waste your time if there's an alternative.

4.7. The Reference Section

The reference section is the largest part of the reference manual. It's typically organized alphabetically by command words for command-driven software and functionally for menu-driven software. I like an organization in which every command (or menu option) is given its own page or pages. For command-driven software, each command should have the following information:

1. Command name or keyword (e.g., STORE).
2. **Command syntax** and acceptable variations.
3. Short (one line) definition of purpose.
4. Definition and discussion of the form and function of every field which can appear in the command.
5. One or more examples of the command's use.
6. Screen appearances before and after, if appropriate.
7. Narrative discussion of the intent and use of the command.
8. Specification of any aftereffects of the command—(e.g., source file destroyed).
9. Warnings, limitations, or potential problems.
10. Reference to related commands.
11. References to applicable error messages.
12. Technical details related to the execution of the command. For example, mathematical formulas for variance or net present value, algorithm used for sine, etc.

The information for menu-driven software is similar except that there's a greater reliance on the use of screens and less on formal syntax. Each use of a menu is actually a procedure, so that the reference section must define your options at every stage of the procedure. As with command-driven programs, limitations, aftereffects, cross references, usage, and intent, are also essential. The organization of a menu-driven reference section will typically follow the **menu tree** and progresses menu by menu and by sub-menu within menu, rather than alphabetically.

4.8. Supplementary Appendices

A good information package attempts to be self-contained and attempts to anticipate your questions. It's a matter of self-defense. The publisher proves credibility by providing a toll-free number which you can use to get more information. The typical call takes fifteen minutes, or costs the publisher about ten dollars after overhead's been included. A widely distributed, but bad package, will generate thousands of calls. Adding a hundred pages of supplementary material to the information package is a cheap way of preventing those calls. From your point of view, each call is at least as expensive, and you want to avoid the calls as much as the publisher does. What might you find in good supplementary appendices?

1. Special cases and situations. There are always situations that behave strangely or in an unexpected way.

2. Tricks. There may be special tricks that can be used to do things that you might not think are possible. A collection of these accumulates (after a while) from user responses and requests and its sensible to publish them.

3. Technical assumptions and procedures. Some packages may do sophisticated things even though from the user's point of view, they're not obvious. Whenever mathematics is involved, there's a mathematician out there, who for good reasons wants to know precisely how a specific calculation was done. The same applies to finance and accounting. Publishers who try to be cute and hide this information underestimate the questioner—people who know to ask such questions often also know how to find the answer experimentally. It's easier to publish this data.

4. Communicating with other packages. This is an area of increasing importance. The publisher may not know why you want to transfer data to or from another package—but it's really not her business. Typically, this section consists of specifying the procedure used to get the data into an ASCII format. This may involve removing special control information which could be misinterpreted by the other package. At the least, it's an appendix that describes in detail, what the package's files look like (at least those files that can be used to communicate with other packages). A good use for this section is the information that you might need to convert data that had been generated by a competitor's package.

5. Complex or "dangerous" features. Sometimes, a feature or command is so complicated and powerful that a separate appendix is warranted. Sometimes, innocent commands can have disastrous aftereffects if improperly used. In either case, the publisher may put this in a separate reference section.

6. Comparison with previous versions. If this package is the latest of several versions, and if there have been major improvements, or changes in operation, it's a good idea to spell such changes out. If I've been using the MARK-II version, and get MARK-III, I look to this section for a summary of the differences and what I have to learn anew.

7. Comparison with competitors. This one is a two-edged sword and used only if the publisher believes that his package has a significant advantage—either functionally or in terms of ease of use. It provides the buyer with a justification for having bought this package rather than the competition's. It can also contain useful technical material related to converting data. It's primary use, however, when properly done, is to provide a quick introduction for the experienced user of another package. For example, if you've been using SOFTSPREAD and have now bought the more powerful SUPERSPREAD from a competitor, it's nice that the new package gives you a quick course on its use, which is written in terms of your assumed prior experience with SOFTSPREAD.

4.9. The Hidden Manuals

Some of the most important information isn't printed: it's stored on the disc and shipped along with the software. It's done to reduce cost or to provide additional security against piracy. These documents might include:

1. Important notices and warnings.
2. Supplementary information and references which will eventually get into the printed manuals.
3. Detailed definition of the version, release, and sub-release numbers for every component program, including the day, hour, and minute of the release and the programmer's name or initials.
4. New features and commands not yet placed into the manual.
5. A file of bugs, their symptoms, and how to get around them.
6. Contacts for technical information at the publisher, or user's groups.
7. Dedication and acknowledgments.
8. The chief programmer's name and address.

It's not always obvious which files these are. The way to find them is to routinely print the package's directory (e.g., use the operating system's DIR command) and look for files which are *not* program files (i.e., files with **extensions** such ".COM," ".SYS," or ".EXE"). The files you want will have extensions such as ".DAT," ".DOC," ".MAN," ".INF" and/or names such as "DATA," "SUPPLE," "INFO," etc. If in doubt, display all files except those which you know are programs. Sometimes the information *is* produced by a program which you must invoke by the appropriate operating system command. For example, the information you want is produced by a program called "MANUAL.COM." Activating that program produces a nicely formatted document of supplementary information. I've rarely seen any part of the printed manual even hint at what supplementary information is on the disc; which is why I've made it a practice to routinely examine all disc files.

In some cases, and this will probably become increasingly popular in the future, there is no printed information package as such: the entire thing is on the disc. It makes sense. The publisher provides you with an up-to-date reference package at little or no cost. You can print it yourself. The publisher saves postage, printing costs, and all the rest, which is presumably passed on to the buyer. I'm sure, that as laser discs become a common peripheral and the preferred medium for selling software, we will see the elimination of printed manuals and their replacement by on-disc manuals.

4

CRASH, CRASH, TINKLE, TINKLE

1. SYNPOSIS

What is a crash? How can you tell if the system has crashed? Real crashes and pseudo-crashes. Clean and crazy crashes. After the crash is over. Why software crashes. How to avoid crashes. How to cause crashes and why you should.

2. SHRIEKERS, LOOPERS, FREEZERS, AND BABBLERS

2.1. What is a Crash and Who's Responsible?

A **crash** is any condition of a computer and/or program in which you can no longer control what's happening. A crash is to software what a failure is to hardware. The only saving grace of crashes is that the failed software is easily returned to the conditions that prevailed at some time prior to the crash: **recovery** is usually possible.

Whatever nonsense you hear from retailers, software publishers, or system vendors that might lead you to believe that you're responsible for a crash—forget it. It's consummate bullshit. Most crashes are caused by software design errors. A few crashes are caused by the workings of a capricious* universe and are neither your fault nor the software designer's; but even then, the software designer's responsible for a clean aftermath to an unavoidable crash.

CREDO—SOFTWARE DESIGNERS ARE RESPONSIBLE FOR CRASHES.

---

*The system I used to prepare this manuscript is robust. Even as an abusive user, I can't fault it in the crash department. But, why was it that I had so many crashes while writing this chapter? It knows! Don't tell *me* it doesn't know!

Software designers *are* supposed to worry about crashes and to build crash-avoidance into their software. A competent software quality assurance department devotes many hours of testing to forced crashes. One big difference between good software and bad, is that bad software has no internal protection against crashes and therefore crashes a lot, while good software is robust. Taking the blame for crashes is like feeling guilty about an airline crash or an auto crash caused by a mechanical failure (assuming that the auto was properly maintained).

2.2. Crash Symptoms

2.2.1. How to Tell If It's Crashed

You know there's been a crash by the symptoms. If you've never experienced a crash, then you're either very lucky or you haven't used computers very much. Alternatively, you don't know how to recognize the crashes you've had, or you're a liar, oblivious, or an oblivious liar. You can tell there's been a crash because of: what you see on the screen, the keyboard's behavior, the disc's behavior, what printers do, and what you hear on the **audio monitor** (see the tutorial).

2.2.2. On The Screen

The first sign that something's amiss often appears on the screen. It's not just what appears and stays there, but also what flashes on, what gets cruddied up, and what doesn't happen.

Crazy Screen. The screen erupts in strange patterns of random characters, graphics characters, blanks, erasures, or other garbage such as the example of Figure 4-1.

Frozen Screen. The screen is frozen—nothing changes when something should: a blank screen is another variation. A frozen or blank screen typically occurs along with a frozen keyboard.

Corruption. You've got a normal screen, except that some of the menus are slightly corrupted. See Figure 4-2 for blatant examples. There's a tendency to ignore minor corruptions, of just one character say, a line out of place, or something in bold face that shouldn't be. These may seem like little things, but the corruptions mean that the program has lost control—crash territory.

Suicide Note. The package leaves you a suicide note such as:

042: ABORT. RETURNING TO OPERATING SYSTEM.

9^#V¹□M ♣♠^#V¹9s#rz=↑⅃¹ ¹
                              9^#V9s#r¹9^#V⫴□U ♯¹
                                                      9s#

r¹
   9^#V¹ □ T‖□_ ℝℝ¹⇔¹
                  9s#r¹
              9^#V⫴ℝℝ ¹♣⁴□0µ□_µ⁴07µ□   π∷□Jµ¹-♣⁴□'Lꟼ*W≤⁶¹-♣
⁴□,.ꟼꟼℝ ¹♣⁴□0µ□_µ⁴07µ□ ⫴µ □Jµ¹-♣⁴□'Lꟼ*W≤⁶¹-♣⁴□,.ꟼꟼℝ □⁴?□ ¹M⁴□⊪ ꟼ□≤>¹♯¹9s#rℝ ¹
          ^♯⁹‖□⁴?¹L⁴□⊪ ꟼ¹   9^
#V¹ □λ T¥¹⁶¹''⁶¹]≤⁶¹]≤⁴□   9^#V⫴□⁴Cꟼ¹M⁴□⊪ ꟼ□≤>¹♯¹9s#rℝ □‡ ⊄ G⊥y y ℝꟼ
♯¹9s#r¹θ⁴□θꟼ''X♠¹┃t●¹P⁴□θꟼ''#≥¦┃t●¹9^#V⫴□θꟼ'' ♠¦┃f □ ¹}2↓♦*X♠''Z♠□ᵣf*#≥''Z♠♠⁴□⁴wꟼ⁴□¹''
=≤□≤>¹   ≥⁴□ nꟼ□⬛µ¹≥''≥¹ ≥⁴□Σꟼꟼ¹⁶⁶¹ ≥⁶¹-♣⁴□?♂ꟼꟼꟼ¹⁶¹f●⁶¹⫮♣⁴□?♂ꟼꟼꟼ¹⌐♣⁴□0µ-□Jµ-
SCHDTIME.DATSCHD.DATSCHD.NDX□V ¹L⁴□⊪ ꟼ□3 *γ♣¦┃t∞¹⫴⁴□♯µꟼ¹⁶¹↓⁶¹≥⁴□1Eꟼꟼꟼ-Exiting S
CHD A:VALDOCS.CHN□V □-□⊪⁴□-ꟼ-□V □-└¹ 9^#²↑¹⁴□βꟼ□A-A:$$$.SUB□V ¹┘¹''♦¹⫴JJ-□V ¹-*.
⫴□'□ℝA□> □U♯-□> *µθDM*σθ♯□♯σ8-□> □so8-□> *µθ♯*+++♯*σθDM*△θ♯¦∫θθ □¹9N♯F♯^#V¹'$□ᵣ⫮
⌐*-⊪⊪ □¹♦¥-⊪⊪ □¹⫴J¹¦⧸¥→*¢Σ''⌐Σ-¹9^#V*⌐Σ♯¦¹⌐9} ¦ ⎕*⌐Σ♯¦¦→¹♦-Choose your option:<
E>nter or change an→¹≥''≥¹♯¹9s#r¦¦┃↑¹9⁶¹←Σ⁴□ Zꟼꟼ¹¦¦T¹''↑●¹\♦⁶¹9⁶¹9^#V⌐□⊪ ꟼꟼꟼ♯¹9s#r
9^#V⫴□U ♯¹9s#r¹9^#V¹ □ fℝ¹⇔♯¹9s#r¹9^#V⫴ℝℝ¹♣⁴□0µ□_µ⁴07µ□   π∷□Jµ¹-♣⁴□'Lꟼ*W
≤⁶¹-♣⁴□,.ꟼꟼℝ¹♣⁴□0µ□_µ⁴07µ□⫴µ□Jµ¹-♣⁴□'Lꟼ*W≤⁶¹-♣⁴□,.ꟼꟼℝ¹9^#V♯-□‡ ⊄ ℝ
                                                                       ℝ_→□V ⊪*≥
♯¹9s#r□
      ¹-≥''≥:♪≥o8}2‖≥¹}2π≥¹-≥⁶¹⁴□
ꟼꟼᴊ5   ¹n
            ⬛

                                                              ⟨ 11:18 ⟩

Figure 4–1. Crazy screen.

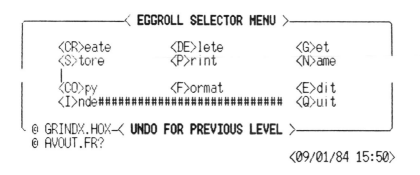

Figure 4–2. Examples of Corrupted Screens.

The next thing may or may not be the operating system prompt. Suicide notes are programmed. They should be used only when the internal self-checking parts of the software have determined that it's better to quit than to continue. Suicide notes, if they're infrequent, are better than other forms of crashes; the programmer's retained what little control there is and the aftermath of such a crash is likelier not to have data loss. Conversely, some very bad software uses suicide notes as cop-outs for easily recoverable user errors.

Alice in Wonderland. You're working along nicely, there's a hiccup, a flash on the screen, and the next thing that appears is the operating system prompt, or worse, after a short pause you find yourself in a completely different part of the forest—possibly another package, a menu that you couldn't get to from where you were, or anything else that indicates that you've suddenly been teleported. GET OUT! Just because you've landed in something that seems to work doesn't mean that it does. Limit your losses by quitting as cleanly as you can. If you can still save your work from the part of the forest you're in, and *if you've got a backup for that work,* you might as well try saving things; but don't have high hopes.

2.2.3. The Keyboard Symptoms.

Freeze. This is the most common crash symptom. The keyboard appears to be frozen—that is, it doesn't respond to any keystroke, including the **panic keys** (UNDO, STOP, ABORT) if you have them. A frozen keyboard is often accompanied by a frozen screen. If nothing responds and nothing changes, then you have no choice but to curse and lose the work. A frozen crash on the audio monitor either sounds like dead silence (rare) or most likely, a steady, high-pitched, almost pure, whistle. If you suspect a frozen crash, turn on the audio monitor and check for that whistle.

Crazy Keyboard. Another, relatively rare, form of crash is one is which keys don't do what they're supposed to. For example, sudden shifts to locked capital letters or to the graphics sets. But not all the keys need be affected and the fewer the keys affected, the more likely you are to miss it. Try to quit clean, especially if it can be done with the function keys or panic keys. The ESC key and CONTROL key in combination with other keys are possibilities for getting out if the normal process doesn't work. This behavior typically means that the operating system has been corrupted and consequently, you should do a **cold restart.**

2.2.4. Haywire

The system starts doing crazy things with the disc and printer, and possibly the screen. The combination of the package's design, your way of working, and the tasks you do, eventually fall into a pattern. Every piece of hardware is part of that pattern. That includes the printer, the in-use lights on the disc, the chirping of the disc drive, modem lights, and so on. Whenever such signs fall out of the pattern, or continue indefinitely, there may be a crash.

Discs. Learn when the lights go on and off and when to expect the "chirp" the disc makes when it fetches or stores data. Uncontrolled chirping, lights on with no disc in, the motor turning when it shouldn't—any of these, if they continue for a long time, probably mean a crash.

Haywire Printers and Peripherals. This is the kind of crash you most often seen in the movies, but in reality it's very rare. Uncontrolled printing, garbage printing, complaints from the system on the other end of the telephone line, wild plotting—if you can't stop it, is a crash.

Stinkers. Go to the local electronics hobby store and buy a few cheap integrated circuits, transistors, and a small piece of printed-circuit board. Alternatively, buy a very cheap transistor radio. Take the stuff home, and heat the lot on the stove or with a blowtorch. You will soon be treated to the world's lousiest, but most expensive perfume, "Essence of Silicon." Learn this smell—it's an expensive smell. Although it's rare for software to cause hardware failures, it can happen, and the result is often a stinker, or worse, a shrieking stinker.

Shriekers. This is probably the worse kind of crash there is. The computer makes a clearly audible sound (without an audio monitor). It *is* possible for software to do that kind of thing to some hardware, although it's rare. *Any* audible sound, other than the usual fan hum, disc noise, etc. indicates a serious hardware or software problem. If you hear any sound like that, turn the power off immediately.

2.3. Pseudo-Crashes and Their Avoidance

2.3.1. Real and Pseudo-Crashes

It's one thing to crash and another to think you've crashed when you haven't. Almost all crash symptoms can occur without a crash if the software is bad enough. That sort of thing leads you to believe that there's been a crash. You then take what corrective action you can, such as a restart, with the result that you lose the work just as surely as if there had been a crash. How do we tell real crashes from pseudo-crashes?

2.3.2. Impatience

Impatience is the main cause of pseudo-crashes. The telephone company did a study to find out how quickly people get impatient while waiting for a dial tone: they were annoyed after a one second delay, angry at five, and furious beyond that. We have a short fuse when it comes to machines. We expect instant responses and give no quarter for how long the operation might take.

Some things take time—even for computers. Examples include: sorting records, searching large files, copying discs, reorganizing data, conversion of large files to a new format, and merging files. If you deal with analytical and mathematical software, it's easy to ask for work which can take hours on a personal computer. It's not unusual for a program to clear the screen and lock the keyboard during long operations: which might lead you to believe that there's been a crash.

The duration of long operations is typically not proportional to the number of items processed, but worse (see Chapter 8, Section 3.5 for details). For example, sorting 1,000 items doesn't take ten times longer than sorting 100 items, but twenty times longer. Some operations can go as the square of the number of items, (i.e., 10,000 times for the above example) and some, as the cube (a million times) or worse. The result may be that an operation which takes a few seconds for a few items takes hours for many. Pseudo-crashes by impatience would be rare if processing time were always proportional to the number items processed, but that's not the way the world is. Consequently, the designer has a responsibility to prevent pseudo-crashes.

2.3.3. Pseudo-Crash Prevention Features

The following features, if present in a software package, will help you prevent pseudo-crashes.

Warnings. A warning for any operation that might take more than a few seconds. If it's under a minute, a notice that say's "WAIT PLEASE" or "WORKING" is adequate. For longer durations, the program should calculate the expected duration in accordance to the appropriate law for that process and state:

OPERATION MAY TAKE MORE THAN . . . MINUTES.

Progress Reports. I like progress reports for long jobs. I like to be told when the job is half done. If the program can give you a warning of how long a job may take, then it's usually not difficult to also provide a progress report instead of just "WORKING." Sometimes, the progress report can be a lot easier to provide than a prediction of the job's duration and in most instances, it's adequate.

Halt/Interrupt Keys and Commands. Good software lets you change your mind. There's always a STOP, HALT, or PAUSE key available during long operations. Hit that key and you're given a progress report and an opportunity to either continue or to quit safely. Bad software forces you to go on, no matter how long it takes, and your only alternative is to shut the system off (and lose the work). Alternatively, bad software does stop when you tell it to, but it loses the work for you anyhow, and then dumps you into the operating system.

2.4. Crashes From the Inside

This section is slightly technical. It describes some generic situations which result in crashes, but not how the software got that way. Reading it may give you some insight into software and crashes, but it's not essential to understanding the rest of this book or to using a computer.

Executing Data. Both programs and data are stored in the computer's memory, albeit in different parts of it. You can't tell just from looking at a memory location if it's holding instructions for the computer or a letter to your aunt in Milwaukee. I simulated the crazy screen example of Figure 4–1 by deliberately treating computer instructions as if they were text. Individual instructions are normally executed one at a time, and one after another. Whenever the program has a decision to make, it may jump to another part of memory for its instructions. If that jump is bad, for whatever reasons, the program jumps into your letter and starts to interpret the text as if it were instructions. That's what we mean when we say that the program is **executing data.** The program will do something, but it's unlikely that it will do anything reasonable. It has crashed. Most crashes are directly or indirectly caused by, or result in, data execution.

Clobbering Code. Code-clobbering is the flip-side of data execution. The program stores a copy of your tax return into its own middle—electronic hara-kiri. But it won't die until it attempts to use that part of the program—hours later. Again, the program is executing data or a combination of corrupt code, good code, and data. The results are the same as for direct data execution (except for the time delay).

Loops. Much of what a program does involves repetitive operation. For example, it checks a word's spelling, fetches the next word, checks it, etc. This kind of repetition is called a **loop.** All loops should eventually stop (when the work is done). Programs that crash in a loop do so because either the loop is incorrectly designed so that it never terminates, or the program executes data, which results in a loop. Because loops are repetitive, they can produce pure tones when heard on the audio monitor.

Halt. Every computer has a halt instruction—the program stops and does nothing else. There are legitimate technical reasons to have halt instructions in a program.* There are also many bugs which lead to incorrect halts. If the program executes data, then one of the things it might run across is a bit pattern that looks like a halt instruction. However, the odds of garbage causing a loop is higher than that of causing a halt instruction, which is why loop-death is more frequent than halt-death. Because nothing happens after a halt, the audio monitor is silent.

Out of Resources. You need resources to process things—the most common are main memory and disc space. These are (by software) subdivided into convenient chunks called **blocks.** When you add a paragraph to your letter, say, the program fetches another block. When you erase the letter the blocks are returned for future use. Unfortunately, programmers and programs lose track of resources, or may not handle things correctly when you have run out of resources. The result can be that the resource is fetched out of an area that's used for programs, leading to code-clobber.

Deadly Embrace—Lockups. A **deadly embrace** is like meeting a person in a narrow hall—you shift left to pass and he shifts to his right. You go right and he shifts to his left. You can't pass each other if this keeps up. A computer is often doing several things at the same time: setting the next second on the clock, printing, reading the disc, doing something. The operating system keeps track of things, but bugs can occur when there's an unexpected conflict between these simultaneous processes. A **lockup** is one of those situations where several processes are trying to get to the next step, but preventing each other. A **deadly embrace** is an illogical situation in which two processes depend on each to continue but

---

*For the techies—the halt may be there to wait for an interrupt, such as a disc or printer I/O completion. The program will continue, but at the higher priority level where interrupt processing is done. That's why flipping peripheral device switches, popping the discs in and out, and opening and closing the disc drive doors may sometimes get you out of a crash.

both are waiting for the other one to finish first. Because that's a more complicated loop, the audio monitor pattern is repetitive, but rarely a pure tone.

3. THE EFFECT OF CRASHES

3.1. Clean and Dirty Crashes

All crashes result in lost work and lost data. All data are stored in memory—the computer's internal or **main memory,** and the mass storage memory such as a floppy or hard disc. A **clean crash** loses only the data in main memory (and, of course, the time you spent doing the work). With a clean crash, you can reboot the system, restart the program, and take off from where you last stored intermediate results. The nicest software with the cleanest crashes does things in such a way that many intermediate results are automatically stored for you, without your intervention, so that even some of the time may be recoverable. It's important to know how clean or how dirty a program's crashes are because that will affect how much work you have to do to recover and how much effort you should put into backups.

3.2. Dirty Crashes

3.2.1. Setting a Scale

We really shouldn't distinguish between "clean" and "dirty" crashes, because *all* crashes are dirty—so it's really measuring how dirty and smelly crashes can be. We can't discuss consequential damages because that's highly individualistic. The same bug and symptom has a completely different impact for me than for you. There *is* a universal scale, however. We can judge the smell by how difficult it is to restore the system, and all of your data, to the conditions which prevailed prior to the crash—that is, how difficult it is to **recover.** I've assumed that in all cases you have made copious backups (or attempted to, or believed that you have done so). Because if you haven't been doing backups, then you're far too trusting to be using a computer. The cleanest possible crash, of course, is one in which you simply hit the reset button* and continue (with justifiable confidence) as if nothing had happened. The worst possible crash is one which destroys not only your data, but your floppy, the entire content of your hard disc, your backups,

---

*Your computer doesn't have a reset button? Silly system! Turn the power off and on again.

and all copy-protected software, and ends the affair by a complete computer melt-down.

3.2.2. Some Crash Aftermaths

Here's a not too rigorous set of milestones on the scale of crashes from clean to dirty:

Data Destruction and Corruption. Obvious data destruction is a relatively clean consequence of a crash. The more data destroyed, the worse it is. If it can be confined to a single record, that's better than a complete file. Data destruction is usually correctable by going to the backup and redoing the work. Corruption is always worse than destruction because it is usually distant from the area (record, file, etc.) in which you were working at the time of the crash. You learn just how bad data destruction and/or corruption is for a program (or system) by comparing the file(s) which are on the on-line disc with the backup; also by noting how much of the work you had been doing was actually lost. It's a good thing to know for the packages you use frequently. There are no rules—only experience.

Directory Destruction. I hate this kind of crash. You don't lose the data, but you do lose access to it, which amounts to the same thing. Typically, the **directory** gets fouled. If it happens to a floppy, that's not so terrible. But suppose it's the directory to a 20 megabyte hard disc? You have the backup floppies, but it could take hours or days of hard work to reload all that stuff. Always check the directory of anything you were using after a crash. Most operating systems do provide facilities for directory reconstruction, but they're technical, tricky, and error prone. Use them as a last resort.

Program Destruction. This is one of the reasons I despise **copy-protected** software. I've no objections to software that requires you to use the master disc to make a working copy. It's cumbersome, but it's a reasonable compromise. Copy-protected software that can't be copied by using ordinary operating system utilities is a pain. It has a built-in arrogance that assumes that no bug will ever cause program destruction. If the crash destroys, or worse, corrupts the copy of the program on disc, you may have consequential problems very far down the road—you must *always* assume that the copy of the program in memory was destroyed. Wherever possible, I use a **write-protect tab** on the program disc, because it can help prevent some program destruction. However, it's not always possible to do that. For example, I use several different printers with a word processing package. Switching the printers involves, among other things, changing some data on the program disc. It would be a pain to have to remove the tab every time I changed printers. Some programs use the program disc to store working files and data: write-protecting that disc would prevent the program from working.

Operating System Parameter Destruction. This is a little more insidious. You have installed your operating system. The characteristics of your configuration are stored in the operating system program. The crash can corrupt that data. The result is that other programs now behave strangely (if you're lucky enough to notice it) but not the program that caused the damage (see the ghost of Frankenstein's monster's dog, below). When the operating system's behavior is one of the crash's aftermaths, then you may have long-term, subtle problems that may appear to be a hardware problem. If this happens on a hard disc, then you could be strung along for a very long time before you realized what had happened.

False Reset. Some computers have a small, battery powered internal memory that keeps the time-of-day clock going and is also used to store some other parameters of the way the system is set up. Hitting the reset button, or turning the power on and off, *does not really reset everything* for systems with this feature. If this convenience is properly implemented, then there's no real problem. However, a poor or buggy implementation can result in this data being corrupted, so that the normal reset procedure doesn't clear the problem. If your computer has such a feature learn what's stored in such memory, and what's going on while the power if off, so that if you see symptoms such as a crazy time of day, you know that you should do a complete system reset as part of your recovery procedure.

3.2.3. The Ghost of Frankenstein's Monster's Dog

You've suffered what seems to be a clean crash. Alternatively, the crash was dirty, but you think you've recovered by using your backup data. Does this mean that you have recovered? It depends. You should not, until you have confidence in the software, assume that the damage done by the crash was only to the program you were running and, if to data, only to the data you were using. The bug that caused the crash is a Frankenstein's monster. The villagers light the torches, hunt the monster down, burn the castle, and then go home for a good night's sleep; but there's still the monster's ghost to worry about. Any data file that was on the discs, and any program on those discs can be mauled by a crash. A crash is a loss of control. The symptoms have no rhyme and little reason. Therefore, anything could be destroyed or corrupted. Prudence dictates that you regard anything that could have been reached by the raving program as potentially damaged. A very conservative approach would be to completely back up the software, as well as the data. A simpler approach is to backup only the data. You can do this by doing a disc copy to create a backup disc rather than just copying the file that had been changed. The second thing you can do is to make sure that backups are always done to a completely separate disc. Backups done to the same disc are almost useless.

What about the dog? Or is it the dog's ghost? Backup data and backup copies of programs reduce the probability that the aftermath of a crash sticks around. It reduces the probability to an acceptably low level but it does not eliminate the possibility as an absolute thing. There's no mystery—software cannot teleport bugs from one disc to another across hyperspace—but failing software can corrupt any data or software that it can reach. And while that software, say, doesn't itself misbehave, it could cause a bug to propagate like a deadly **virus** to the next, disc, and so on. You're usually safe and the above sequence is far-fetched. However, one of the nastiest problems I ever had was when the virus was carried by the backup disc. The only way to assure that nothing has perpetuated would be to start all over again, with the master copies of all software, recreate all the files, reinstall the system, and all the rest—and do that without a crash or hitch, and then, you can be confident that there's no monster's dog's ghost around.

You can help avoid the ghosts by recreating the system after you've used it for a while. Reinstall the software, the operating system, and the rest. You're less likely to make a mistake the second time around, and therefore less likely to leave a ghost.

3.3. Precautions After Crashes

What you do after a crash depends a lot on the package and how much (or how little) confidence you have in it. The least you must do is restart the program. The most might be to completely reinstall the operating system, recopy the program from the master disc, and continue the work with a fresh backup copy of the data. It takes time to gain confidence. Therefore, your post-crash recovery procedure should be more elaborate at first. You would use *all* of the following tactics only for a very bad package that circumstances forced you to use. If you had to do all of that, then you'd probably be better off not using the computer at all, or trying a new package. The actions can be subdivided into two domains: what you do with the software and what you do with the data. The tactics are given in increasing order of complexity for both domains.

Software Tactics.

1. *Reboot and Reload.* Always reload the operating system and all software after a crash. That is, do a **cold start.** Shortcut this procedure only if you have a lot of confidence.
2. *Power Off and On.* If the cold start doesn't work.
3. *Software Check.* Some software and/or operating systems have check facilities (i.e., programs that check the software) that you can use to tell if the software's been corrupted. Use them.
4. *Back Up Software Copy.* Try using the backup copy of the software if the working copy doesn't work; but make a new working copy from the master first.
5. *Installation Check.* Check the package's installation parameters (e.g., the printer type, screen size, color selection, etc.) to verify that they've remained as you set them *even though what you did or what happened doesn't seem to have any logical connection with those parameters.* Compare the values with the list of values you printed out (and kept) when you first installed the package. Go to the master and redo the entire installation if you see *any change at all,* even if it's slight and you don't really care about the difference—say a light green screen background was changed to light blue. The point is, that if those parameters have changed, then something, something worse, may also have changed.
6. *Operating System Check.* Run the check program on the operating system itself.
7. *Operating System Installation.* Check the operating system's installation parameter values as for the package installation check in 5 above.
8. *New Operating System Copy.* Try a backup copy of the operating system.
9. *Reinstall.* Go back through the entire installation procedure, starting with the operating system and then the package, from scratch. Use entirely new discs, etc. I wouldn't do this twice for any package.

Data Tactics

1. *Retry.* Make sure you have a usable backup of all the data and then try it again. Try to recreate exactly what you were doing when it crashed.
2. *Data Disc Check.* Run the disc-check program (if you have one) on the data disc to make sure that it's okay. Use the backup if it isn't.
3. *Back Up Data.* Make an exact duplicate of the backup data disc using the DISKCOPY operating system command and then try it again with the new backup disc.
4. *Test Cases.* Develop a repertoire of small but complicated test cases

whose results you can instantly verify. You could adapt one of the examples provided in a tutorial for this purpose. If there's a problem, then it's likely that you'll have to try a software tactic to recover.

5. *Break It Up.* Try dividing large files into smaller ones and then doing it again.

6. *Alternate Route.* There are often two or more different ways of doing the same thing—especially copying files. Sometimes you can recover a lost or butchered file when you've lost the backup by reading and copying it under a totally different package, such as the operating system.

7. *Undelete.* You delete stale copies of files as you go along. Often, the package does it for you, so that when you update the file, you really write a new copy of it, and the old copy is merely marked as deleted, but is actually not deleted. The undelete function (also called "recover backup file") resurrects such copies.

8. *Recovery Programs.* Some operating systems provide data or directory "recovery" programs. It's a last resort, and worth trying, but they never seem able to recover from the bugs that caused the crash.

3.4. Precautions Before Crashes

3.4.1. Putting It In Perspective

The time to worry about crashes and backups is before the crash. How much effort you put into recovery precautions, meaning backups, depends on what you're doing and how important it is. If you're using the computer as a word processor, say, primarily to create individualized form letters, then all you need do is back up the form letter and the mailing list. If the program were to crash in the middle of a run, all you'd have lost would be the one or two letters that were being done at the time. Conversely, again with word processing as an example, I write long documents (such as books), whose loss represents a huge time loss which is potentially greater than the hardware value—I take elaborate backup precautions. If you were using a spreadsheet package for financial calculations with possibly large consequential damages, then you would also take elaborate backup precautions. Establish your backup policy based on the assumption that whatever data you have will be totally destroyed by a crash. Then consider the following:

1. What is the true cost of bringing the latest backup data to the point at which the crash occurred? Compare that to the cost of doing backups.

2. What is the consequential cost in lost time, lost opportunity, schedule slips, and all the rest, of going through the recovery from the previous backup?

3. What is the emotional cost in frustration, embarrassment, and anger (yours or others) of losing the data and of recovering from the previous backup?
4. How much of a gambler are you? How willing are you to expose yourself to crash risk in order to achieve the higher productivity that not doing backups allows?
5. What is the additional cost of materials (discs, paper, etc.) for the backup?

There are probably another dozen questions along this line that you can ask yourself. You don't have to do a formal analysis for personal use. Just thinking about it will lead you to a viable, flexible, personal policy. Conversely, if it was your task to establish a departmental or corporate backup policy for a secretarial or word-processing pool, or for a group of contract writers, say, then a formal analysis would be warranted. Reduce everything to the same cost measure. Gather statistics on the frequency of crashes in your application. Multiply the recovery cost by the crash probability to obtain the effective crash cost. Evaluate the cost factors for the proposed backup policy. The backup policy cost must be lower than the effective crash cost in any useful policy:

[crash probability] × [recovery cost] = [effective crash cost]

good policy = backup cost is less than effective crash cost

3.4.2. Program Backup Options

Program backups are straightforward. You use the master copy of the software that came with package to make two copies—I make three. The master is stored in a safe place after you've put a write-protect tab on it. Use the operating system DISKCOPY command. Further work, such as installation, is done with a copy. You install the copy and then copy *it* to create an installed working copy, which is what you use daily. Date all copies. Use only the highest quality discs which have a built-in hub reinforcement ring.*
If you're installing the program on a hard disc, then do that in addition to the copies you make on a floppy. The publisher's copy protection policy can make the above more difficult (or impossible).

Some publishers limit the number of copies you can make. Some publishers even provide you with a single backup copy, and you cannot, except by using highly technical means, make an adequate number of additional backups. If your disc fails, why, just continue working with the master (they say), or stop the world for a week or two while the U.S. mail delivers the bad copy to the publisher and the publisher sends you a fresh copy. What

---

*New high-density floppies don't have reinforcement rings and apparently don't need them.

is worse, such publishers may also use the junkiest floppy discs on the market, rather than the best. Floppy discs wear out. People sneeze on them. Flick ashes on them. Such protection policies are unrealistic. A package which is in daily use for several hours, may have to be replaced two or three times a year. Consider the vendor's copy policy, the physical environment in which the package is used, how clean and careful the users are (long fingernails can do extraordinary damage), and include that in your buy decision if there's a restrictive copy policy.

You shift to the backup program copy when you suspect that a crash has been caused by corrupted software. Take the backup copy, and copy it to create a new working copy. Date the new working copy. My next step is ritualistic. I then take a long pair of scissors and cut the old disc in half. I do that for me and for the publisher. For me, it eliminates the possibility that I may inadvertantly use that bad disc again. For the publisher, I am protecting his interests by assuring that the possibly faulty copy will not be picked out of my garbage can and used in violation of copyright.

3.4.3. Data Backup Options

The technology provides you with more options for backing up data than you might imagine. Here are some options, their weaknesses and strengths:

1. *Same Disc, Package Control.* Use a command in the package to create the backup, which is then written on the same disc. This is the weakest form of backup because the crash-causing bug can (and will often) destroy the entire data disc. Backups made on a hard disc are also vulnerable, although a little less vulnerable than backups to the same floppy disc. If your hard disc is partitioned into volumes or directories, back up to a different directory.

2. *Different Disc, Package Control.* A little stronger, because if the backup is successful, then it's unlikely that both the working data disc and the backup are destroyed by the bug. A minimal backup policy is to have some backup on a separate disc. For example, the working copy on a hard disc, with backup on a floppy.

3. *Operating System Disc Copy Command.* The operating system is used to copy the entire disc. This is usually an exact copy and may therefore carry problems over (such as a mixed-up directory) to the copy. Copying from a hard disc to a floppy does not usually have that problem.

4. *Operating System File Copy Command.* This is a bit better than the disc copy command because a new directory entry will be created for the copy. It is also more cumbersome when you have several files to copy in order to create a backup.

5. *Streaming Tape Unit*. This is tape unit which records all transactions made to a hard disc. Recovery is possible, but time-consuming, technical, and difficult. We will, in the future, surely see reasonable recovery software that does do a proper recovery from a streaming tape unit (if possible).

6. *Paper Backups*. This is my penultimate backup method. For most of my work, it's the thinking time I'm trying to save and as a last resort, I'm willing to type things in all over again. I have a paranoid obsession about data loss and I pay for it by using vast quantities of paper. A fast draft-quality printer is a prerequisite for this approach. I normally dump a copy of whatever I've written or processed whenever I store it, which means every five to 10 pages of text. I use the same method for spreadsheets, data-base packages, graphics, and all the rest. If your computer does not allow concurrent printing and processing, or if you don't have a **spooler,** then you're severely limited in the extent to which this very effective approach can work for you.

7. *Spooler Backup*. My printers are equipped with a 64k or larger spooler unit (also called a data-buffer). This has several advantages. For systems (hardware or software) that do not provide printing concurrent with processing, the spooler acts like a printer that's ten times faster than normal and consequently you can get back to productive work quickly. Most spoolers allow you to make a second copy, if you're paranoid enough to want them. Another advantage is that you can send the copy to the spooler without actually printing it. This quickly stores yet another backup inside the spooler, without having to waste the paper or suffer the noise. I use spooler backup late at night when the printer's stammer might awaken my wife.

8. *The Wastebasket*. This is the ultimate backup, especially if you get into the habit of using paper backups. I do only one disc backup a day, but I do three or four paper backups a day. The old paper is *neatly* placed in the wastebasket, in proper order. The wastebasket is *neatly* dumped into the garbage can at the end of the day. That garbage can is put out for trash collection only once a week. That's a lot of backup levels. I've suffered only one complete data loss in the last five years and it was because I attempted to shortcut my backup ritual.

3.4.4. Backup Experiences

Although this section was included in a chapter devoted to crashes, crashes are not the main reason for doing backups. *For every time I've had to use a backup because of a crash, I've had three occasions to go to the backup because of my own goof.* The most common goof is erasing or overwriting the wrong file. Novices make more mistakes and will therefore have more reason to need backups. Here are some (of my own) experiential observations on backup methods and the frequency with which they've been used.

1. *Copy on Another Disc.* Ten to twelve times a year. Eight times for goofs and four for software problems.
2. *Spooler.* Once in the past year—caused by a goof.
3. *Paper Backup.* Four times—once for software glitch, three for goofs—destroyed all copies of the file.
4. *Wastebacket.* Six times—all goofs.
5. *Garbage Can.* Twice, goofs both times.

And we won't count the one unsuccessful attempt at garbage can recovery—the garbage truck was too far down the street for me to catch it. I'd love to have statistics on what other people do, but it's impossible to get. It could be that I'm unusually unlucky or inept—or possibly it's honesty.

3.4.5. The Backup Ritual

The only way to achieve a successful backup policy that's appropriate to your needs is to make a ritual out of it. For each kind of thing you do, define points in your working procedure and make a backup (of some kind) at that point—no matter what. It is to be a formal, relatively inflexible ritual. It eventually becomes so ingrained in your work habits that you are no longer conscious of the fact that you're doing it. And that's when it will serve you best. Here are some components to use in designing your own ritual:

1. Do a full backup disc copy at the end of each day.
2. Store files and intermediate results whenever the telephone rings, or at any other interruption.
3. Back up before you change the software you're using.
4. Store at the end of every (section, page, paragraph).
5. Store before eating and before coffee.
6. Paper backup after every store.
7. Disc duplicate (by renaming the changed file) always.
8. Wastebasket after every print.
9. Garbage can after the daily disc backup.
10. Store after every ten items entered, backup after every hundred, printout after every backup.
11. Do house-keeping, and especially cleanup of stale files, only once a week, and as another ritual of its own.

4. WHY SOFTWARE CRASHES

4.1. Hardware Failures

Hardware failures are usually solid and a lot more goes down the tubes than programs and data when that happens. Fortunately, real hardware failures are rare and getting rarer all the time.

4.2. Hardware Malfunctions

Hardware malfunctions are temporary: they're electronic hiccups. Good hardware designs go a long way toward eliminating hardware malfunctions, but they can't be perfect—not at any price you might be willing to pay. As an example, a computer which is not much different from a typical personal computer, if designed to operate in a spacecraft, costs 100 times as much— and that's real, justifiable costs that go into such things as elaborate testing, gold-plated contacts and connectors, silver wiring, shock-protected hardware, and so on. The effects of hardware malfunctions are generally unpredictable, but many of them result in crashes. Here are some sources of hardware malfunctions and what you can or can't do about them:

1. Power Transients. All computers have some built-in protection against power fluctuations. Power transients can be either drops (brownouts) or high frequency noise. Either can cause malfunctions. See the tutorial on power for precautionary measures.

2. Jostles and Glitches. The disc drives are sensitive to jostling. If you go around bumping your computer (or the stand), expect problems and crashes. Cables are another source of problems, and can induce glitches not only at the connector, but merely by bending the cable. See the tutorial on connectors and cables for more information. As a primary rule, don't bump and don't bend.

3. Vibration. Computers get turned off, not on, by vibration. Don't expect it to work if your fillings shake loose whenever a truck rolls by. If you can feel vibration, it's excessive. Your solutions are: find a different place to work; eliminate the source of vibration; buy a military- or industrial-rated computer; float your office in a pool of mercury. Old buildings, offices in trailers or on top of a disco, are problematic.

4. Interference. Fluorescent lights, large electric motors nearby (especially those with brushes), power tools, CB radios, a nearby TV or radio station, or any other source of electromagnetic radiation can be a source of debilitating interference. Don't expect to use a personal computer on a typical factory floor without special shielding. In this respect, the biggest mistake you can make is horizontal thinking. You look for interference sources in a horizontal plane—in your office, say—but ignore what's happening on the floor above and the floor below. Interference can (depending on source and strength) propagate about 30 feet—that means you have to think in terms of what's happening two floors above and two floors below. The biggest source of interference could be your own printer. Do a quick and dirty interference survey by using your transistor radio **audio monitor.** Hold the radio five feet away from the computer and tune it to a weak station. You should be able to pick up the computer within two or three feet. See what else you can pick up (say the induction welding plant on the next floor). Any source that's as loud as the computer is a potential troublemaker. Interference isn't a common problem, but it shouldn't be ruled out.

5. *Static Electricity.* Static electricity is blamed for computer problems far more often than it is the problem. If it were as big a problem as some claim, we'd have to drag anchor chains from our waists and wear steel caps with built-in lightning rods. It can be a problem. If your environment (meaning air, carpets, humidity, etc.) is such that you get sparks and shocks, then you may have a static electricity problem. Use an **antistatic mat** on the floor. Discharge yourself on a doorknob before using the computer, and keep the cat out.

6. *Disc Errors.* Data are written to discs using elaborate codes that allow the computer to detect reading and writing errors. By the time the system tells you that it can't read a disc, it's probably tried several times and failed each time. You're unaware of the many disc reading malfunctions that occur. Avoid these problems by: using high-quality discs; using a disc cleaning kit periodically;* being sure the disc drive is level; treating the floppies gently (don't fold, force, spindle, mutilate, spit, sneeze, spill ash, or sweat on them).

> Be gentle to your disc my dear,
>   Especially when you change it;
> It's beneficial to career,
>   And marks you as my favorite.

7. *Alpha Particles.* This form of radiation is claimed to be a common source of problems—but then so are cosmic rays, X-rays, and all other forms of radiation. There's not much you can do about them short of working a thousand meters underground in a lead mine. If stray radiation is a significant source of computer glitches in your environment, get out of there fast because it'll be lethal to you long before the computer gets damaged.

8. *Heat and Humidity.* If you're sweating, it's not only uncomfortable, but it's too hot and/or too humid for most computers to work reliably. Electronic circuitry doesn't like heat. Think not only of the external heat, but also the heat created by the computer itself. Make sure that the fan works. Keep the air inlet and outlet clear. Check and clean the air filter

---

*Check manufacturer's recommendations; overcleaning can hurt some disc drives.

twice a year. Feel all parts of your computer when you first get it to learn what the normal temperature is. Feel the computer periodically to make sure that there's no excessive heat buildup.

9. *Bad Luck.* There are a lot of electronic pulses racing around inside any computer and inside every chip. Once in a while those pulses gang up the wrong way and cause an internal glitch. Tough luck. Good hardware, though, is self-protective.

4.3. Software

Most crashes are caused by software, not hardware. Unfortunately, unlike hardware, there's not much you can do to about fixing the cause of software crashes (but see Section 5 below). You can and should bitch to the publisher, especially if you're sure that it's a software problem. All crash-causing software problems are ultimately traced to what a programmer did or failed to do. Bugs are not inexcusable. What counts is how many there are, how debilitating they are, and how often their symptoms occur. No software can be guaranteed to be bug-free and no software is impossible to crash—that's not only a pragmatic observation, but it's also fundamental and theoretical. It's a matter of degree: but that isn't a license to produce untested garbage. Let's assume that when you use a package you use it intensively. Here's some criteria for judging quality:

0–60	hours between crashes		—don't buy it
61–125	" " "		—marginal
126–250	" " "		—just bearable
251–500	" " "		—fair
501–1000	" " "		—good
1001–2000	" " "		—excellent
2001 plus	" " "		—great

If you have many operators using the same package, get the above numbers by dividing the total number of hours of usage by the total number of crashes experienced by the group. Also, we should increase the above scale by one notch for every three years. Therefore, in 1990, we'll mark 125 hours as garbage and expect three years of crash-free operation for greatness.

5. HOW TO AVOID CRASHES (OR CAUSE THEM)

5.1. Do's and Don'ts for Crash Avoidance

Those of us who work in software quality assurance spend a lot of time devising fiendish situations that make programs crash. The greatest compliment I've ever gotten was from an angry programmer who accused me of being "diabolical." The following list of do's and don't are based on the experience we've gained with software testing, and a knowledge of the specific kinds of technical bugs which programmers are apt to write. If you want to know why these methods work, then you'll have to learn more about software and software testing then you probably need or want to know. There are, though, two great principles that guide crash-causing bugs and the crash avoidance methods are based on them:

FIRST PRINCIPLE—Things are always worst at the extremes.
SECOND PRINCIPLE—Simultaneity is a bitch.

First Principle Methods

1. *Avoid big anythings if you can.* Don't use big files, big records, big fields, big anything.
2. *Avoid nulls.* Don't use files with no records, empty records, the number zero, empty fields.
3. *Leave room.* Always allow enough room on the disc for two copies of the largest file you're working with. Break up files if you must (and can). Try not to have more than half the disc full.
4. *Avoid binary powers.* Numbers, especially large numbers, which are powers of two such as 2, 4, 8, . . ., 256, 512, etc. are sometimes a problem. Also, numbers one smaller, such as 255. Of binary powers 256 is the most sensitive, followed by 65,536.
5. *Keep away from limits.* Keep clear of any published limit on anything. If I'm told that a data base can only have 32 fields per record, I wouldn't use more than 30. The limit warning applies to almost anything.
6. *Break it up.* Divide the files into smaller pieces and break up the work into smaller tasks.

Second Principle Methods

7. *He who hesitates wins.* Let the program finish what it was doing before you give it the next command. Allow things to settle before you go on to the next thing. Use the audio monitor to learn when the program's really ready for another command. Pause before hitting a command key, and after.
8. *One at a time.* Even though the software can print and process simultaneously, do so only after you've gained confidence. Avoid all other simultaneous operation possibilities. Don't print or copy the file you're working with. Don't delete the file you're copying. Don't calculate while you're receiving or transmitting.
9. *Don't scramble the keys.* Type deliberately and avoid simultaneous keystrokes.

10. *KISS.* This stand's for "Keep It Simple, Stupid!". Avoid compound commands with many options if there's an equivalent sequence of simpler commands that can do the same thing.
11. *Don't use windows (much).* Nice feature—many bugs.

Unprincipled Methods

12. *Avoid legalisms.* The manual doesn't say you can't use a negative record number. If you do, don't be surprised if there's a crash. Complex compound conditions that you dream up will work only if the programmer shared your dreams.
13. *Avoid the nonsensical and illogical.* Only very good programmers protect their software against maniacal users with off-the-wall senses of humor.
14. *Avoid insertions and deletions.* Inserting something into the middle of a file or record, or deleting something, is often a problem.
15. *Don't change structure.* Even if the package allows you to, avoid changing basic data structures such as file structure, record definitions, keys, page formats, record print formats, etc.
16. *Be narrow.* Interpret the manual in the narrowest way you can, and trespass those limits with caution.
17. *Don't expect robustness.* See chapter 7 on robustness. Avoid doing things that only a robust program can handle.
18. *Find the tender spots.* Every package has tender spots—places, operations, and features where the software is likelier to crash. Find them, remember them, and avoid them.

Any software that's so tender that the only way you can coddle it into working without crashing is by applying all of the above methods is useless. If the software is supposed to print and process simultaneously but crashes instead, it's a grievous flaw. If it's supposed to allow several windows, but crashes on some combinations, then it doesn't really have windowing. You *should* be able to go to extremes and the programmer *should have* anticipated the worst you can dream of. And if the programmer didn't, then the software QA department (that mythical beast), should have. Judge software quality (in part) by the extent to which you have to coddle the software to avoid crashes.

5.2. How to Cause Crashes

It might seem that the last thing you'd want to know is how to force crashes. If you're tasked to buy many copies, or if you're trying to judge a package before you buy it, then knowing how to force crashes is useful. It's also a good idea to put a new package through its paces to see how robust (or tender) it is. Causing crashes is easy—reverse the above list. Do everything that's to be avoided, and avoid everything that's safe: try big everything (simultaneously), try nulls, don't leave room, hit the binaries, violate the limits, don't hesitate, pound the keys, get it all going, be legalistic, nonsensical, and illogical, be broad in your expectations, and don't tiptoe through the menus—stomp and trample 'em.

5.3. Smelling an Impending Crash

I've sailed with old salts who can smell bad weather coming. You might scoff at their seeming superstition, but I advise you to do so only after you've reefed the main, battened the hatches, donned foul weather gear, and clipped your safety harness on. After the storm you've time to be scientific and then you'll find that they smelled ozone, the effect of lowered barometric pressure on surface flora, and many other technical things. Human intuition is marvelous. It's a background processor that integrates a thousand subtle signs to come to a valid conclusion without ever bothering your conscious mind. It's archetype reporting by exception—and it works for crash smelling. Trust it! Sailors say that the time to reef sail is when the thought first occurs to you. The time to back up is when you get that uneasy feeling that the software's about to crash. Trust your feelings!

I know you won't let me get away with just an appeal to intuition (even though that's the best guide), so here are some signs that may indicate an impending crash—usually in sufficient time to clean up, back up, and get out.

1. *Responsiveness.* An about-to-crash system may be sluggish. It has a "sticky" keyboard. The pace slackens and the computer seems to be working harder.
2. *Disc panic.* A lot of unusual scrilling and squirching from the disc—abnormal hyperactivity.
3. *Balky.* Running the program seems to be more like mule skinning than finance.
4. *Lying.* It tells you things that you know aren't true.
5. *Flashes.* Flashes of crazy stuff on the screen which you barely see, at unusual times and for no reason. A warning message appears and is instantly erased. A prompt or menu from another part of the program, or from another program altogether. They flash on and then off, and then (soon) it's crash, crash, tinkle, tinkle.
6. *A new order.* Menu lines appear in a different order, a dialogue jumps all over the screen, the normal sequence of things has changed.

7. *Wonderland.* New prompts and new screens you've never seen before. A welcome message from the first programmer to work on the package, or from a company you never heard of. A sudden jump to another part of the forest. An out of context prompt. Anything that makes you ask "How the hell . . . ?"

8. *A new beat.* If you're using an audio monitor, it sings to a new (and often irregular) beat.

9. *I didn't do that!* Get out, fast!

10. *Cryptic complaints*—such as "ILLEGAL UUO AT USER LOCATION 06A@44" and then seeming to go on normally. Messages such as "HELP! HELP! I'm trapped in a Chinese fortune cookie factory".

11. *Repetitions.* Repeating a request more than once, when you know you haven't made an error.

If, on the basis of the above symptoms, or anything else (such as a gut-feel) you believe that there's a crash coming, here's what you can do (in order of increased risk and desperation):

1. Hit the STOP key if there is one. This is the key that stops the current action but keeps you in the program.

2. Hit the UNDO key. This is the key that stops the current operation and undoes whatever's been done by it.

3. Hit the QUIT key. This is the key that gets you out of the program. The data you were working on may be lost, but you'll probably not clobber anything else.

4. Pop the program disc—usually safe, but don't count on it. Working data will probably be lost.

5. Pop the data disc. Risky, but occasionally helpful.

6. Block the operation—for example, if you smell a crash during printing, turn the printer off, or reset it. Similarly for any other involved connected device with its own reset.

7. Interrupt the action—for example, request a new window, initiate retrieval while printing, force simultaneity. It could be a whole lot worse, but it could also be better.

6. RELAX!

Rereading this chapter gave me a vision of readers cringing from their computers—up in a tree and out on a limb, gnawing their fingernails. It wasn't my intention to fill your sleep with nightmares nor to give you ulcers by describing all the things that can go wrong. You *will* experience crashes, but it would take years of abuse by many different, bad, pieces of software, most of which will never reach the marketplace (or stay there if they do) to experience all or even a small part of what's been described in this chapter. Nor should you think that your software will have all that bad behavior. Think of this chapter as you would a medical text: only a hypochondriac would expect (and experience) all the symptoms in the book. Relax! Don't become a software hypochondriac—but know what *could* happen, and be prepared with the right response if ill luck should befall you.

5

OF MICE AND MENUS

1. SYNOPSIS

Input, process, output—the quality triad. The user's changing needs. Menu-driven software. Mnemonic versus iconic. Pointing methods. Hybrid methods. Menu control.

2. TALKING TO COMPUTERS

2.1. Input, Process, and Output—The Quality Triad

2.1.1. An Uneasy Dream.

I have a recurring dream—or is it a nightmare? Instead of spending hours each day at a keyboard, staring at green worms on the screen, I'm pacing around my office, talking to my computer. When I make mistakes, it chides me in a pleasant voice and suggests a correction. Meanwhile, in the background, it's reworking my spelling and style, formatting the manuscript to satisfy the editorial software, doing my tax returns—a dream. The nightmare starts when it refuses to do something routine. It tells me that it's a *beta-4* and that such work could be done by a mere *epsilon*. Then there's the wrangle over how to split the royalties—though what it intends to do with the cash it's already accumulated is beyond me. And now it wants a coauthorship, it won't control my coffee brewer anymore, and it doesn't do windows!

2.1.2. Love and the Computer

We and our computers are symbiotes. The more you use it, for all its faults, the stronger that tie becomes. It's an uneven relationship (for now). It does all that work, for which we give it a few cent's worth of electricity, but no

86

love. Is that kinky? Love lavished on a machine? But what about America's love affair with cars?

For most of us, interpersonal relations are the most intense of all. Just following that might be the affection between man and domesticated animals such as dogs, cats, and horses; but human-computer affections are not far behind, and for many, far ahead of pets. And for some unfortunate hackers, computers are an adequate substitute for human intercourse.

All intense relations are expressed in communication. What's more, the communication's form shapes the relation. Love and hate are close: a few ill-chosen words can change the former to the latter—a few ill-chosen commands can turn your love of a package to hatred. The means you have to communicate with the computer, and the means by which it communicates with you, will profoundly affect how you relate to it. It is a profound effect because it is, despite our veneer of objectivity and rationality, an essentially emotional, rather than intellectual, experience. If it isn't an emotional experience, why curse the crashes, why complain that ''it's mocking me,'' why the anthropomorphisms?

2.1.3. Input, Process, and Output

A computer accepts our inputs, processes them, and conveys the results of that processing by some kind of output. Quality is expressed in all three areas, but this chapter and the next are devoted to input, while Chapters 7 and 8 focus on processing quality and performance. Input can be further divided into **command input** and **data input**. This chapter is concerned with command input, while data input is a large part of Chapter 7.

All computer operations start with commands—you must tell the computer what you want it to do. Unlike human languages, where we as individuals exercise vast controls over our means of communications, with computers we are constrained by some unknown programmer's imagination (or lack thereof). There was a time when the computer's small memory and low power forced programmers to use primitive, cumbersome, methods of exercising control. It was a choice between that and sacrificing important functions. However, the personal computer's power is now so great that almost anything can be implemented—implemented with ease—if only the designers think of it. If the programmer's vision is limited, then you will be frustrated by an inarticulate and inflexible language. I call it a ''language'' because that's what it is. That's what you must learn to work computers. How that language is structured and presented to you affects the ease with which you can learn it and with which you can exploit it to express your own needs and personality. Good software is characterized by many options and variations, by a consistent logic (read grammar) to the **com-**

mand language, and by how easily you can predict the form of a rarely used command.

2.1.4. Our Changing Needs

We are at least three persons in our dealings with computers and software: a novice buyer, a student, and a master. Nowhere is the different approach to these persons more telling than in the means provided for commanding the computer. Each of these persons has vastly different perceptions, needs, responses, and frustrations. How software is designed to meet each person's needs is what this chapter is all about.

1. *The Novice.* More than anything, the novice wants a quick understanding of what the package does and how to get it to do it. This package is only one of many competing packages and the choice will often be not the best, but the package which was easiest to understand in the store. We are all novices with a new package. It is when we are novices that we are the most vulnerable. It is when we are novices that we are most easily swayed by toys and novelties which are easy to understand but which will soon become incredible annoyances.
2. *The Student.* That which was appealing to the novice is at first also helpful to the student in us; but as learning progresses, it is logical and operational consistency that helps us to learn. Inconsistent command methods require us to learn a hundred ad hoc rules. We can't apply what we learned here to there.
3. *The Master.* Satisfying the master is the most difficult task of all. The master is impatient with cumbersome methods that tediously repeat the lessons learned months before. The more proficient we become the less patience we have. We know the entire command sequence we want to use, no matter how complicated it might be. Our fingers and our minds are one and they're forever running ahead of the computer. Our work is automatic and there's no longer a self-conscious awareness of how we communicate with the computer. What we want now is speed and shortcuts and damn the tutorials.

The short-sighted designer believes that there's a conflict between those three persons' needs—that satisfying one must be at the expense of the others. So we have vendors who base their design concepts on pandering to the novice. They provide the novice with what he says (from his limited point of view) he *wants,* rather than with what he *needs.* The other extreme caters to the master with no concern over the awful process by which the novice becomes a master: that's just as self-limiting. The wise designer knows that there are three persons, and many others in between. She exploits the computer's power to satisfy all their needs without sacrificing anything.

2.2. Command Methods

2.2.1. An Overview

Figure 5-1 is an overview of methods that can be used to command computers. The methods are first divided into two broad categories: **menu-driven** and **command-driven.** In **menu-driven** software you command by selecting things from a menu of options presented to you on the screen. In **command-driven** software (Chapter 6), you control by typing commands

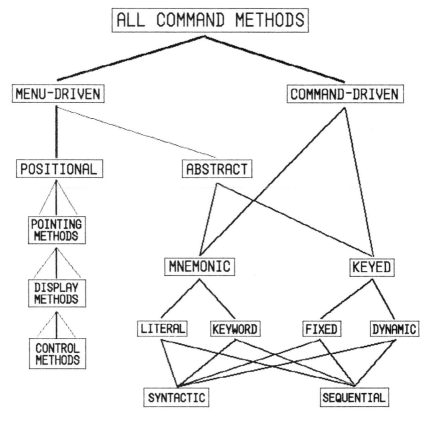

Figure 5-1. Command taxonomy.

or special keys. That's the broad division, and most of this chapter is concerned with explaining what the other boxes in this figure mean. Note that there is a box, "ABSTRACT," which overlaps both categories. This taxonomy is not rigid. There are actually more lines between the boxes than one could sensibly draw, and more boxes than would make sense.

2.2.2. Pure Menu-Driven Software

The left side of Figure 5-1 is a straight line down. In pure menu-driven software, option selection is positional. That is, you must move something, such as a cursor, to a place in the menu and thereby make a selection. There are different ways of pointing to things on the screen, of which the cursor is the most common; but you can also point with your finger, a mouse, or a lightpen, or touch the screen at the right spot. How are the choices displayed? That can be anything from codes, to terse words, sentences, pictures (icons), or some combination of these. Finally, there can be many menus, and there are different methods by which you can select them, or go from one to the other.

2.2.3. Command-Driven Software

Command-driven software has a more complicated taxonomy. The first major subdivision is whether the command is done by a (typically) single keystroke or by typing a mnemonic or command abbreviation. The kind of mnemonic used, be it a specific character sequence such as "^S" or a sensible word such as "STORE", is the next level down. On the right, which is driven by specific keys, we ask whether the keys have constant purposes or do their purposes change much like the purpose of a screen position changes from menu to menu. The final subdivision, which applies to all command-driven systems, is whether the keys are struck in a sequence to get something done (as analogous to going from menu to menu) or whether we must type in a single, complicated command, with many parts.

2.2.4. Hybrid Vigor—Is there a Conflict?

The middle part of the figure, under the box labeled "ABSTRACT", shows that there is overlap between command-driven and menu-driven software. Menu-driven software can actually use all the methods that apply to command-driven software, creating a hybrid method which is often more convenient than any pure method. What's more, many good packages provide both command-driven and menu-driven options for the same functions, and do it so smoothly that you don't notice the difference. The closer you are to the novice side of the spectrum, the more you'll like menu-driven software. Conversely, as you gain experience, you'll want a command-driven package. There's no reason (except for poor software design) why you can't have both. There's no conflict—except in the minds of designers who can't see how to do it.

Actually, few designers are so foolish as to built either an absolutely pure menu-driven or command-driven package. The extremes are either unworkable or unlearnable or both. Programs are hybrids. The flip-side of these observations is that you should be wary of any single method touted as the end-all and be-all of methods for controlling your package ("iconic pop-down functionally ergonomic command menus"). It's probably not the end-all, it certainly isn't the do-all and be-all. Like any pure method it's going to have problems. Who is it aimed at? The unwary novice or the master? And after all, remember that it's only one part of the package— command input. There's still data input, processing, output, and several other things that go into good software.

3. WHAT DO MENUS LOOK LIKE?

3.1. Simple Lists and Choices

You've probably seen and used menus before, but you may not have really looked at them—their simplicity is deceptive. Here is the simplest possible menu. It requires a yes/no answer.

```
          Do you want me to bake another egg roll?

            Type "1" for YES and "0" for NO
```

This is a miserable piece of software because:
1. The association of "1" with "yes" and "0" with "no" is unnatural. It's a "code" you have to learn, and each such code is another barrier to ease of use. From the programmer's point of view, it's natural because he uses that association all the time (for technical reasons). This programmer has forced you to move toward him, rather than building what you need.
2. It's technically archaic and unnecessary. There was a time when it was difficult to use a more humane approach to yes/no questions, but that's

long past. This approach is typical of either very old software that's been reworked or very old-thinking designers who haven't been reworked. It's also lazy.
3. What will happen if you type something other than 0 or 1? Really bad software crashes. Miserable software picks one or the other, without consistency or reason. Merely bad software assumes something for you, but does it consistently. Good software repeats the question.

A good piece of software would have asked it like this:

Do you want to bake another egg roll? (Yes/No)

This version differs in several noteworthy ways:

1. The "YES/NO" is natural. There's no new code to learn.
2. The programmer's indicated that you can type the whole word "YES" or any part of it, in either upper or lower case, as long as it begins with "Y" or "N" as appropriate to your choice. Any of the following will work for "YES": "Y", "y", "yes", "YES", "YE", "yE", "yessiree-bob".
3. It's shorter. It takes less time to display, less time to read, and less memory is wasted on superfluous garbage.
4. She's removed that patronizing, anthropomorphic "me." This programmer doesn't try to insinuate her personality into the software, nor does she make a pitiful attempt to put you at ease by making the computer, a machine, seem to be a person. An important psychological miscue has been removed.

Here's a typical, simplistic, multiple-choice, menu that we find in many packages:

```
            1.  CREATE EGG ROLL
            2.  STORE EGG ROLL
            3.  FETCH EGG ROLL
            ....................
            8.  DESTROY EGG ROLL

     Type in your choice number and then RETURN.
```

This menu was probably written by the same programmer who did the first yes/no menu. It's bad for the same reasons:

1. It uses a code—the numerals "1" through "8" have no special association with the meaning of the choices. What is worse, the same numerals will probably have different meanings in every menu.
2. It's almost as archaic and unnecessary as the use of "0" and "1" for "yes" and "no". It's again typical of very old software (or unreconstructed programmers).
3. Often, as with the yes/no menu, such junk is vulnerable to wrong numbers and letters instead of numbers.

It should be clear that I intend there to be some other choices between 3 and 8. However, a new, simple, and otherwise good, word processing package from "Big Blue" was not only marred by using this archaic selection method but compounded the fault by a menu which included choices from 1 to 5 and 9, but no 6, 7, or 8. Even the best of us have an off day.

Here's a more reasonable approach:

```
                <C>reate  egg roll
                <S>tore   egg roll
                <F>etch   egg roll
                ................
                <D>estroy egg roll

         Type your choice and then RETURN.
```

This time, the programmer's used a natural, self-teaching, convention. The choice is selected by typing the first letter (or more) of the **keyword.** Even if I'd never seen the package before, I'd guess that any of the following could be used to destroy egg rolls: "D", "d", "des", "dEsTrOy", "DEATH!", "DARTH-VADER". Also, and this may not be obvious at first, this menu took 26 characters less of memory—good software is often like that, not only better, but more efficient.

In all the above methods, good or bad, you were given options, of which you selected one. Each choice was presented as a short sentence. How you made the choice is not important at the moment: it will be discussed later. Lists of options have the following advantages:

1. Although short one-liners are best, the text for each choice can be as long as need be for clarity.

2. They're natural, easy to learn, and hard to forget.
3. There's a limited range of possible errors (if all invalid selections cause the "choice" to be rejected, that is).

Menus based on option lists have the following disadvantages:

1. They can take up a lot of valuable screen room, especially if the package always has a menu on the screen.
2. If they appear only on call (known as a **pop-up menu**), there's the continual disorientation and malaise induced by having your work obscured by the menu.
3. They tend to be slow and annoying once you're proficient with the package.
4. They use a lot of memory, which can be a problem for large packages running on computers with small memories.

3.2. Command Areas and Menu Lines

You start the package and this appears at the bottom of your screen:

CREATE   STORE   FETCH   DESTROY

You select the choice by any of several methods, such as the first letter, pointing to it, or by pressing a **function key**. A typical computer has the function keys on the top row and it's natural to associate the key below (on the keyboard) with the word above (on the screen). If, as on the IBM-PC, the function keys are on the left side of the keyboard, a more natural arrangement for the above menu might be:

It's a better arrangement because it associates the key's position on the keyboard with the function's position on the screen. Is this choice selection method really a menu? Yes and no. It is a menu because a menu appeared on the screen. It's not a menu, because if you know that the function keys have been assigned to those choices, then whether or not the choices appear on the screen as a menu doesn't really matter. So the boundary between command-driven and menu-driven software isn't all that sharp.

A command area can appear almost any place on the screen which makes sense. The most common choices are the first and last screen lines. Command lines are simple menus with several advantages:

1. They don't take up much screen room.
2. The command line can always be on the screen.
3. They're obvious and easy to use.

   As with anything, there are disadvantages. The biggest one is that it can be difficult to contract a complicated action to a single word.

Command-line menus can be very compact and can have many choices. For example, the typical spreadsheet package has a command line in which each letter designates a different command. Command lines are often combined with **status lines** which give you important information about the software's operation or the data you're working with. For example, in word processing: what page you're on, the time of day, cursor position, and so on. Command line menus are a compromise—a fair one at that. The menu's limited to a one or two word description (or icon), which is a whole lot better than an abstract code, but there isn't the penalty of taking up a lot of screen room with menus, or the annoyance of seeing the work continually obscured by the menu.

3.3. Icons

Iconic menus are command-line menus in which the action to be taken is expressed not by a word, but by a small picture, or **icon.** I've shown no icons in this book because the graphics are expensive, it would have raised production costs, and therefore, the book's price. Icons appeal to the child in us. Here are some icons used in a popular personal computer:

A *clock*—time of day

A *trash can*—delete something

A *drawing hand*—paint something

A *sheet of paper*—write something

A *computer*—the operating system

Icons have a childish charm. They're fun (at first). But frugivorous hype to the contrary, there's no evidence that they're easier to learn and use than words if you already know how to read and write. If I were designing a package for preschool children or foreigners, say, to teach them English, then there's no contest over the the superiority of icons.

Iconic forms aren't new. Most written languages started that way. Pictorial writing was developed to a high art by the Maya, Egyptians, Chinese, and Japanese, to name a few. But such languages evolve toward the replacement of the icon's original, limited meaning, by a purely conventional meaning which has almost no relation to the object which it originally signified. For example, in Egyptian hieroglyphs, the icons eventually adopted the value of a syllable in addition to their pictorial meaning. It takes an expert calligrapher to recognize that the Chinese symbol for "trouble" is two women under the same roof. Every literate culture we know of starts with some form of pictorial writing which eventually evolves into an abstract (although not necessarily alphabetical) written form. Look at our alphabet and trace its ancestry—can you see the "house" in "B," the "camel" in "C," or the "door" in "D?"

What's wrong with icons is their meager expressive power. That's what the Egyptians learned four thousand years ago. They're fine for nouns, marginal for verbs, difficult for adjectives, and hopeless for adverbs. Yet, the typical command we give to a computer has the following form:

VERB the [ADJECTIVE]^n NOUN

I've yet to think of an icon for "create" that wasn't either obscene or blasphemous or both: it's as hard as trying to find a rhyme for "wolf." Concepts such as "and," "or," "not," "include," "exclude," "backup," "recover," "reformat," "extract," "insert," "continue," and "translate," are hard to express pictorially. It can be done, of course (witness ancient hieroglyphs), but like teaching a pig to dance ballet, who wants to? Iconic languages can grow only by the addition of new icons or by grouping icons so that the grouping takes on a new meaning which is implied by its components. Take the first approach and you're soon drawing subtle distinction which only a trained expert can perceive. Take the other approach and you get classical Chinese with its 16,000 symbols. The power of icons is so limited that even iconic software uses them only for the top-level (and most observable) menus, but quickly revert to words at the next level down, or for most adjectives, adverbs, and conjunctions.

The second objection to icons is more subtle. Mayans and Egyptians wouldn't have this problem, but most of western culture associates pictorial communication with childhood. Show me a picture of a garbage can with a fly buzzing over it* and I can't take that software seriously. And if I'm forced to use it, I'll sting from being so patronized each time I do. It's a put-down. It implies that I'm too stupid to understand the word "delete"

---

*The frugivores eventually removed the fly.

or "destroy;" that I'm so childish that I'm more comfortable with a picture of a clock than with the word "TIME." And if I asked for the time, would it say to me: "the little hand is on the four . . . "?

A picture may be worth a thousand words, but not one transitive verb.

Now that we've put icons back into their cute little trash can where they belong, have they no place at all in good software? They do when what they depict is inherently graphic, or when it's done for emphasis. For example, it's much easier to show the following patterns than it is to describe them:

These icons are welcome in a graphics package, where they might be used to select how a bar graph was to be shaded. The next example uses graphics for emphasis and control.

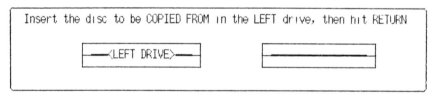

This usage of icons and graphics is like a road sign. It gives us quick information when a wrong decision might be harmful. Like graphic road signs it's use is limited to warnings. The above example is not insulting because copying discs is a dangerous business: it's a sure way to destroy the work *and* the backup. The left symbol's open door reminds you into which one you put the source disc. The closed door on the right also warns you. It saves me the trouble of looking at my right and left hands before I start the copy, which is what I do on other systems. I'd have no objections to using graphics like the above to select between several dangerous options—as long as it wasn't overdone and that there was some sense to what constituted danger.

4. MENU SELECTION AND POINTING METHODS

4.1. A Clarification

Menus present you with choices. How do you choose? Go back to Figure 5-1. It shows two main selection methods: **positional** and **abstract.** In positional methods you point to your choice by some means or another, while in abstract methods the choice is made by the keys you hit. As usual, neither method is clearly superior.

4.2. Positional Methods

4.2.1. General Characteristics

Positional selection methods work by pointing to the choice which appears on the menu. They differ in what is doing the pointing and how to get the pointer where you want it to be. The most common pointer is a **cursor.** I say ''a cursor'' rather than ''the cursor'' because most packages define their own cursor. An underline is a typical cursor for word processing. Graphics packages may use cross hairs or a small circle with cross hairs in it. Other packages use inverted video. Almost anything is possible.

Not all positional methods move the cursor. For example: the tab key might be used to move between choices so that each choice is highlighted as it is selected, but the normal cursor doesn't move. A package that does this actually uses two different pointing methods—one for normal use and the other for menu selection. It's confusing. Sometimes, bad software produces multiple cursors—it leaves little turd-like cursors lying around all over the screen. It's a typical crash precursor.

There are many fancy gadgets used to move the cursor around. But fancy or simple, cheap or expensive, that's all they are: a method for pointing to something on the screen. Nothing more and nothing less. Of no more value and no less value.* This section concerns pointing methods, their advantages, disadvantages, and how they can be well-done or ill-conceived.

4.2.2. Cursor Control Keys

The keys used to move the cursor can also be used to point to choices. If the keyboard has cursor control keys, the software should use them. If it doesn't have such keys, the typical practice is to redefine the numerical keypad keys as cursor control keys (if you have them). A worse choice is to use the function keys, because that'll cause inconveniences later on. Finally, the designer may define normal keys used with the ⟨CONTROL⟩ key or ⟨ALT⟩ key for cursor control. ''^E'', ''^S'', ''^F'', and ''^C'' are typical choices. Frankly, though, keyboards that don't have permanent cursor control keys are a pain. Multiple-use keys (such as using the number pad keys) are confusing, error-prone, and hard to learn.

Inconsistent design of pointing methods is a grievous fault. For example,

---

*It's from this point of view that I relegate mice to the cute but insignificant little rodents that they are.

several word-processing packages use cursor keys within text, but force you to use tab keys or other keys to move the cursor to a choice within a menu. Another variation moved the cursor with either set of keys but only the tab control keys could do the selection—using the cursor control keys moved the cursor, but that which the cursor was on wasn't actually selected. Confusing. It's better to use the same dumb method throughout than to use several different, individually convenient, but conflicting methods to point to things. It's bad enough that we have to put up with that from package to package, but to suffer such abuse within a single (supposedly integrated) package is absurd.

The best cursor control in menus I've seen is in the Rising-Star/Epson Valdocs integrated package. Cursor motion is done by normal cursor control keys in menus, but the motion is constrained to operate only between the choices that appear on the menu. If the menu has two columns, the LEFT/RIGHT keys alternate between them. The UP/DOWN keys automatically take into account the item spacing, and so on. It's fast, because a few keystrokes can get you from any part of the menu to any other, thereby alleviating one weakness of cursor pointing methods.

Once you've pointed to something you must indicate that you've made a choice. Reasonable packages expect you to hit a key—say ⟨RETURN⟩. Here again, consistency is mandatory. One of the worst packages I ever used executed the command as soon as the cursor landed on a choice. You had to be careful and for some menus you had to really sneak around to avoid an unwanted selection.

4.2.3. Mice, Pads, Balls, Joysticks, and Other Gadgets

All of these are methods for pointing or moving the cursor. You push the **mouse** on a flat surface and the cursor moves in the direction you pushed it. When the mouse reaches the desired location, you indicate your choice by whomping it on the head (or pushing a key on its top).

While mice are relatively new, other cursor movers have been around for decades. A **touch pad** is a soft, rubberized pad on the keyboard. Where you touch it determines the direction in which the cursor moves. How hard or far from the center you touch it determines how fast it moves. When you get it to where you want it to be, you mark your choice with a RETURN key, say. It doesn't add to the desk clutter, but beyond that, it's about as controllable or (uncontrollable) as a mouse. **Touch tablets** are paper-sized touch pads. Where you put your finger is where the cursor goes. They're conceptually similar to **touch screens** (see below) with the additional disadvantage of increased desk clutter. **Joysticks** are used to move the cursor to a point determined by how hard-over in that direction you've moved the stick.**Track balls** are essentially the same kind of thing except that the joystick's been compressed into a ball. All of these gadgets can be programmed either to move to an absolute screen location or to provide movement at a controlled speed in the selected direction from where the cursor is originally.

There are three problems with these gadgets: two minor and one major. The first minor problem is the added cost. The second minor problem is the room it takes on the keyboard or on your desk and the extra clutter of another piece of string (the mouse's tail or the joystick's wire). The major problem is that it forces you to change your thinking (and your finger's thinking) from keyboard to gadget and back to keyboard. If you're using keyboard-dominated packages, such as word processing, spreadsheet, or data-base, then the continual shift back and forth, especially for menu choice selection, is annoying. Conversely, if you're doing a lot of graphics, then the direct, nonrectilinear control you can get with these gadgets is a joy—cursor keys seem positively primitive by comparison in such applications. What are you using your computer for?

4.2.4. Light Pens and Pointer

A **light pen** is a penlike device that senses light. Although it happens too quickly for you to see it, what you see on the screen is rewritten many times each second. An electron beam constantly sweeps across every square millimeter of the the screen. The light pen "sees" that beam going across, because to the light pen, the screen is constantly erased and refreshed.* Say that the screen is rewritten thirty times each second in a fixed pattern that starts on the upper left and progresses, line-by-line, to the lower right (similar to a TV screen). By noting the exact time at which the beam was sensed by the light pen, we know exactly where the pen was on the screen. Software takes it from there. A **touch screen** works on a different principle. Some have microscopic wires imbedded in the screen's surface and sense the change in electrical properties induced by your finger. The Hewlett-Packard touch screen is simpler. There are semiconductor lasers on one side and the top, and corresponding sensors on the opposite edges. When you put your finger on or near the screen's surface, you interrupt horizontal and vertical laser beams whose intersection marks your finger's position. You can't see the beam because it's in the infrared part of the spectrum. Software figures out where your finger is.

Light pens provide high resolution, which makes them especially effective

---

*Actually, it catches the beam on the way back—when it's going from right to left to start a new line.

for graphics work: it's probably the best method around for that purpose and it's been used for decades. Touch screens don't have the resolution for graphics work and are in that respect, inferior to joysticks, mice, and other gadgets. Touch screens and light pens do have the advantage of allowing the programmer to define a seeming infinity of **virtual buttons.** The whole screen can be filled with buttons, and what's more, each one can be labeled as the designer wishes.

On the debit side of light pens, there's that extra wire to tangle up with the telephone cord. Both methods, as menu selectors, suffer from the same problem as the other gadgets—keyboard to screen and back to keyboard, which is an increased demand on hand-eye coordination. Both have been accused of causing a syndrome called **"lead arm."** Some people, apparently get tired from moving their hand up to the screen and back down to the keyboard all the time—hence "lead arm".

4.3. Abstract Selection Methods

4.3.1. Keyed Versus Mnemonic

In **abstract menu selection** methods, your choice is indicated by typing something abstract, such as a number or letter, which is related to the menu choice. The use of numerals is a prime (and bad) example of abstract selection. The use of the first letter of a keyword is a good example. We subdivide abstract selections into two main groups: **keyed** and **mnemonic** (see Figure 5–1).

4.3.2. Keyed Methods

In **keyed methods,** the key struck has no inherent relation to the menu choice—it's arbitrary. For example, using numbers, letters, or function keys (F1, F2, etc.) to correspond to the first, second, third, etc. choice. All keyed methods involve learning a code and are therefore difficult to learn and remember. Unlike command-driven software, in which the key's meanings are designed in accordance to a master plan which applies to the entire package, in menu-driven software, the value of an abstract key, such as "1," "2," etc., is arbitrarily related to the position of the choice on the menu screen and therefore the value changes from menu to menu. That is, the numeral "1" means something different on every menu—which fact is another small impediment to learning the package.

Keyed methods based on function keys, where the function keys' positions on the keyboard obviously and consistently correspond to the menu's legends on the screen or on the command line, are acceptable. The ideal would be function keys which have built-in, program controlled displays—change the function of the key and change the legend on key's cap. The menu is displayed on the keys themselves. It's technically possible, it's wonderful, but also wonderfully expensive, for now.

4.3.3. Mnemonic Methods

In **mnemonic methods,** you indicate your choice by typing a single key or several keys which are mnemonically related to the choice. Here are several approaches:

First Letter Selection. This is the most commonly used method. The first letter of the choice is set off by some means such as: ⟨C⟩reate, **C**reate, Create, Create, etc. It's understood that you can type the letter "C" in either upper or lower case, as you wish.

1. It may be difficult to find enough different words, each of which starts with a different first letter. With most menus, which have less than eight choices, this isn't usually a problem. But it can be, and can lead to artificial choice designations and inconsistent terminology. Good planning and more, smaller menus, will avoid the problem. If it's done well, you don't even notice.
2. It's inconsistent with flexibility and allowing the user to type any sequence following the first letter. For example, if the choices are "CREATE" and "RESTORE", the user who types "CRE" as an abbreviation for "CREATE" finds himself on the "RESTORE" option because the program thought he changed his mind. This can be fixed by forcing a pause of a second or so between choice changes, and by other means.

Multiple Letter Selection. Multiple letter selection just extends the above idea to two or more leading letters of the choice designation. It's rarely used. It tends to be confusing and it doesn't get out of the problems of single letter selections all that often.

Keyword Selection. In keyword selection, each choice in the menu is described by a single keyword, or by a sentence which begins with the keyword—"CREATE," "STORE," "EXPAND," for example. Selection is based on a variable number of letters, depending on the choice mix and the letters the keywords start with. For the above three cases, the single letters "C", "S", and "E" would suffice. Some systems may insist on the entire keyword, which can be frustrating and slow. However, it's not a bad idea to do that for things like "DELETE-FILE."

4.4. The Best of All Worlds

The ideal method of menu selection combines all of the advantages and incurs none of the disadvantages. Positional and abstract selection are provided and both menu- and command-driven features are accommodated.

1. Menu choices are rationally laid out with meaningful words for each choice.
2. Normal cursor control keys can be used to get from choice to choice. The four cursor keys work, they automatically skip over empty lines, and the LEFT/RIGHT keys go from column to column. Any selection DOWN or RIGHT from the last choice jumps to the first choice. Any selection UP or LEFT from the first choice wraps to the last choice.
3. Each choice starts with a distinct keyword, all of which have a different first letter. Typing that letter automatically moves the cursor to the corresponding choice. The first several letters following that are ignored.
4. Normal execution requires the ENTER key to confirm the choice, but if the key letter is struck with the control key held down, (e.g., ^C) then execution is immediate.
5. When there is a progression of successive menus, holding the control key down while typing a sequence of (remembered) key letters, has the effect of "piling up" the choices for those successive menus.

4.5. Default Selection

Every menu presents a set of choices. At any instant, there is a likeliest choice. Software which makes a default choice selection for you, already in place when the menu appears, is nice. If you can control the default, it's nicer still. In positional selection methods, the default choice is marked by having the cursor on that choice when the menu appears. In menus that require a typed-in response, the default appears in the proper place when the menu appears. In either case, if you agree with the default values, you simply confirm them (with the RETURN key, say), or you type over any that you want to change. Here are several different ways of handling the default values, from bad to excellent.

1. A fixed, but stupid selection, inconsistently applied.
2. No default selection at all. The cursor is gone or no choice is written in.
3. The choices are arranged in a logical order with the first choice the likeliest. The cursor is always positioned on the first choice. Fields that require data have the likeliest values put in, but the default value is fixed.

4. You can change the default values by entering them and then storing the lot by using the STORE key.
5. The software remembers your previous choices and uses them as the default values until changed.
6. The default changes from context to context, for the same menu in accordance to rational rules. For example, if you've done more than two file deletes in a row, the next default will be to DELETE FILE.

Many other variations are possible. Good default methods allow you to zap through one menu or a sequence of menus just by hitting the RETURN key (or whatever key is used for choice confirmation). If the menu's display is suppressed when you do this, it's almost as fast as (or faster than) a command-driven system. Most good packages use one or more of the above (good) techniques for default selection, but I've yet to see a package that does it consistently. They all behave as if the default approach was designed by each individual programmer without coordination with the others in the project.

5. MENU COMMAND AND CONTROL

5.1. Selection Entry and Confirmation

5.1.1. General

Once your pointer is set on the choice, by whatever method, the next step is to indicate to the program that you've actually made a choice—that is, confirm your choice. The approach depends on whether a pointing method or abstract selection method is used.

5.1.2. Pointing Methods

Because pointers may be difficult to control, any pointing method which makes an immediate choice, without giving you a chance to confirm it, is almost useless. The most common key used for confirmation is the RETURN or ENTER key (usually the same key). Mice, joysticks, and light pens usually have their own buttons for the purpose. The most important thing about the method used though, is that it be consistent with the rest of the package. I've seen as many as three different keys used in the same integrated package to indicate that a choice selection has been made, with no apparent reason for which is used where. Sometimes it's the RETURN/ENTER key, sometimes the ESCAPE key, the UNDO key, or a function key. Programmers who use inconsistent methods think that they're off the hook because they've told you in the menu that *this time* menu choice confirmation is done with the STOP key. Technically, it's dumb and inexcusable. It actually takes more software and more money to use inconsistent methods, but less thinking, coordination, and planning. Don't put up with that kind of garbage—complain.

5.1.3. Abstract Methods

Abstract selection methods can work with or without explicit confirmation because they are really a kind of command-driven software. If the reaction is immediate, that is, if you hit the "A" key and the A-action is immediately initiated, then what purpose did the menu serve? It's an automatic help screen for what is really a command-driven package. Menu-driven software is slower—that's one of its virtues. The deliberately slower pace with the more explicit command actions gives you a chance to think about things before you act. If the key's reaction is immediate, then much of the value of menu-driven software has been destroyed. There should be, as with pointing methods, an explicit keystroke to confirm the choice. And as with pointing methods, complete consistency as to which key is used for the purpose, or if any key is used at all, is essential. Alternatively, as was shown above, it's still possible to provide high-speed, immediate execution, for the master by using the SHIFT, CONTROL, or ALT key in conjunction with the normal key.

5.1.4. Reconciling the Differences

As with so many things in software, the conflicts often result from the designer's limited imagination. The rational compromise is to give the user a choice over whether the program should react immediately to a choice selection or whether it should wait for a confirmation from the RETURN/ENTER key. This can be an installation option, or it can be done automatically. This flexibility adapts to the novice and student and permits a careful, slow, deliberate, but error-free pace. Conversely, the master can run ahead at breakneck speed, if that's what she wants to do.

5.2. Running Ahead and Buffering

Most command-driven software provide **command buffering.** That is, commands are stored as you enter them, and the whole string of commands is executed as soon as possible. This also applies to menu-driven software when each command may fetch up another menu in a series. For example, say that you want to print a file. The succession of operations are:

⟨PRINT⟩—Single keystroke selection of the print menu by using the PRINT key.

⟨filetype choice⟩—Select one of several file types to print by a single letter choice from a menu. Let's use "A" for ASCII.

⟨filename⟩—enter the file name in response to a menu query. Let's call it "Myfile".

1—select one copy.

D—select double-spaced printing.

L—select letter quality.

Let's say that each of these questions appeared on a different menu. As a novice, you make the choice, menu-by-menu and allow each menu to appear and stabilize before selecting the next choice or answering the next question. There are many possible variations in how you communicate the fact that you are putting down an entire sequence of commands. One reasonable approach is:

⟨PRINT⟩⟨RET⟩A⟨RET⟩Myfile⟨RET⟩1⟨RET⟩D⟨RET⟩L⟨RET⟩

This is consistent with normal menu operation but the program suppresses the menu display because it recognizes that there's a whole string of commands—this speeds things up. You get the speed (and the risk) of command-driven software, but if you're unsure, or slow that day, just pause at any point (or hold the key down) and the menu appears.

5.3. Menu Display Control

When you're a novice, you want to see all of every menu every time. When you're a master, you know them all, and you've no patience with it. But as a student, or even as a master, you can get confused or forget the menus for rarely used operations. So you want to see the menu then; a narrow-minded, arrogant, and unimaginative software designer will throw her hands up and demand that you "make up your dumb mind," but a good designer will take this as a challenge. It takes precious time to display a menu. Furthermore, whenever a menu's displayed, be it in a command line, a dedicated menu area, or a **window,** it's distracting because your work is (temporarily) obscured. Menu control is the ability to control just how much of each menu is displayed and when. There are several good approaches to this, which can be used either singly or in combinations:

1. *Suppression by Categories.* A set of categories is established. You can call yourself a "novice," "intermediate," or "expert." Each category suppresses a different set of menus and also changes the menus' appearances. The "higher" the level, the terser the menus are, and the fewer the menus that are automatically displayed: but if you hold the key down, the menu appears.
2. *Automatic.* The next menu's display is suppressed if you type another command and/or command confirmation before the display is completed or before a preset time interval of say, one second.
3. *Multiple and Alternate Form.* Each menu has at least two versions. A full version, which is the default (until changed), which takes the most screen room and which has the clearest explanations, and a short version that consists only of keywords or other mnemonics. The short version appears in a command line or dedicated command area. You can control which version is to be displayed for each menu by some simple consistent means, and then make that version the default version. Holding the key that selected the menu down, or the HELP key, brings up the full version.

5.4. Conversion to Command Mode

It's clear from the above that there really isn't a sharp division between command-driven and menu-driven software. And given good controls, it is possible for you to convert your working style from menu-driven into one that's close to command-driven *exactly to the extent that you wish.* There are, however, some characteristics of properly designed command-driven systems that don't fit in well with menu-drive, so that you're not really converting a menu-driven package to command-driven, but to something between, which can be almost as good for many users. If the package is to allow conversion to true command-drive, then it must be designed as a command-driven package from scratch, and then adapted to menu-driving to suit the needs of novices and students, because it's almost impossible to do it correctly the other way around. If the designers don't think things through, and (as is so often the case), merely tack on a command-drive option onto an essentially menu-driven package, then you'll find that while you can get many of the benefits of command-drive, you can't get them all. You can get so far and no further, and the whole scheme falls apart because you just can't remember all the options and sequences. The package doesn't have the inherent logic of a command-driven package. Eventually, you start thinking in terms of another package, because as a master, you've lost patience with the unconvertible menu-drive.

6. UP AND DOWN THE MENU TREE

6.1. Menu Nesting

Figure 5-2 shows a simplified **menu tree** for a typical disc management function. It's not important what the entire thing is, nor what all the boxes mean. What counts is that there are many boxes and that they're interconnected in many ways. The first level, the top of the tree,* "DISC MANAGEMENT," is selected by a function key. The first menu has four choices: "INITIALIZE DISC," "COPY DISC," "COPY FILE," and "DISC MANAGEMENT." "COPY FILE" provides a further choice: one file at a time or many files simultaneously. In either case, the "COPY" menu includes both copying and deletions. Whatever you select at that point, will require that you identify which drive(s) is(are) used. The "MANAGEMENT" box also splits and merges again. I've shown nine more menus at the bottom of the figure. They aren't connected to the other boxes by lines because they connect to almost all the other boxes in a bewildering mess of lines that would make this drawing look like the work of a spider on LSD.

The menus are **nested:** selecting a choice on one menu leads you to another. Let's add to the complexity. At various points in your traversal of this tree, you can get listings of file directories, say. You can then use the PRINT function key to print either those directories (with many different print options and variations), or to print the actual menus as they appear on the screen. You might want to do that to get a record of exactly what you had been doing, or to record default options on paper. Similarly, you might elect to STORE some menu default values at some point, or to FETCH some values which you had previously STORED.

No one can really draw you a diagram of how all the menus relate to one another. This is especially true for integrated software packages. Such diagrams tend to be approximations in which some paths and byways have been left out for clarity's sake. In fact, no one may know all the possible paths, but that isn't really important. We can assume (or hope) that the programmers have constructed a sensible logic that defines how the menus relate to one another, and that all the essential controls have been put in

---

*Computer types draw trees upside down.

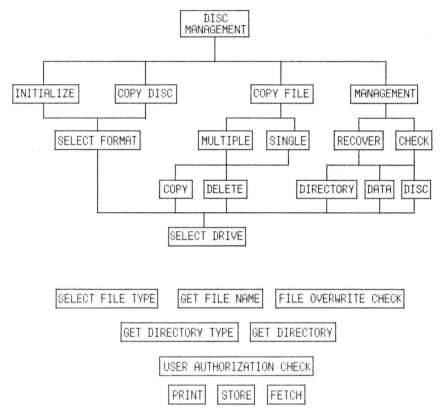

Figure 5–2. A typical (simplified) menu tree.

place. What counts is not the structure of the tree, but the tools you've been given for tree climbing.

6.2. Up, Down, and Across the Tree

Going down the tree is straightforward—it's implied by the succession of choices you made in previous menus. You have no direct control over that. The programmer has built that into the program's logic. If it's correct, every menu you need will appear on every path. However, don't assume that the menus always appear at the same level or in the same order. For example, if the PRINT menu is selected to print another menu, then it can appear at any menu. You normally follow a menu path from the top of that set of menus to the end of some branch, at which point your final selection causes all that you have selected to be executed. There are then two choices for the designer:

1. Return to the first menu on that branch (DISC MANAGEMENT in this case).
2. Return to the lowest point that makes sense. For example, if you have been deleting files, go back up only to the point where you can select another file to delete.

Here are some characteristics of good and bad software in this respect:

1. Awful software leaves you stranded, with no control (on some branches), so that the only way you can get going again is to quit.
2. Bad software may bring you back to a point in the tree which is meaningless, but give you no way to get to a meaningful point, thereby forcing you to do something you don't want to do.
3. Cheap software takes you out of the tree altogether and allows you to select a new starting menu—all the commands you entered and all the choices you made in the previous tree are lost.
4. Better software does the same, but keeps what you've done, so that when you enter the menu again, your previously entered values and choices appear as defaults.
5. Good software gives you complete control over menu climbing. It stores your previous selections, and puts you at a place on the menu which makes good sense (for most people, most of the time), but if you don't like it, you can still move to where you want to be.

Here are some tree climbing controls which good software gives you. They are given in order of decreasing importance. These are all single-keystroke commands:*

1. QUIT. Leaves this menu tree altogether. Can be executed at any point prior to the final selection (the one that actually starts the action).
2. BACKUP. This key takes you back exactly one menu *along the path you took to get to where you are.* This can always be used, at any point in any tree.
3. TOP. Like QUIT, but to the top of the current tree.

---

*Don't expect exactly these key names. And some controls could be combined. For example, BACKUP may be done by an "UNDO" key, and "FORWARD" may be implicit in every menu.

4. FORWARD. Displays the next menus in order, but executes nothing. It allows you to see what can be done.
5. HELP. A help screen that explains the current menu's options. It does not count as a menu from the point of view of control.
6. UNDO. Undoes (if possible) whatever permanent thing may have been selected by the previous menu. It tells you if undoing is not possible.

Good software warns you when you're about to enter a dangerous part of the tree. While one-way menu streets are undesirable, they are sometimes unavoidable. In such cases, good software warns you before you start down the street. Lateral controls (for example, that would allow you to get from the COPY DISC option to the COPY FILE option in Figure 5-2) are *not* provided by good software because it's an inherently unsafe thing to do and its implementation is as confusing to the programmer as its use is to the user. The safest thing is to back up the way you came to some common point, and then to go down the branch you want.

Menu tree structures are very complicated and it's possible that the program will make a lateral jump from one area to another. For example, suppose you've selected the MULTIPLE file option under COPY FILE, but only put in one file name. Then, it would not be unreasonable for the program to put you on the SINGLE branch, and for backup commands to back up along the SINGLE branch. That kind of thing is fine if it works. It's not too confusing and it may save working time.

6.3. Doing It Right

As you can see, there's more to designing menus than the creation of the individual menus. The tree must also be designed. One of the characteristics of bad software is that these trees aren't designed—they're allowed to grow wild. The designer, in order to get a competitive advantage or to meet a competitor's challenge, adds options to menus willy-nilly. A typical case is a system all of whose menus have at most 8 choices. The designer looks around for a menu with an unused choice and sticks the function in there, whether or not it makes sense. You then find "PIES," not under "DESSERTS" where you'd expect to see it, but under "SOUPS." If you saw that on a dinner menu you'd ask yourself what kind of an idiot wrote that menu, or if the chef's psychotic. Good menus are designed from the top down, with an obvious, functionally sensible, logic to them and to the way they relate to the other menus. A few "MISCELLANEOUS" menus are acceptable because it's not always possible to fit things into a rigid hierarchy. Good menu structures are simple. The trees are clean, well-pruned, and compact. Good menus don't have an enormous list of options (except for things like model numbers and other easily understood options).*

Good documentation will show each menu tree (perhaps in a simplified form if there's an essential complexity). Look at each menu, study the trees, and practice climbing around just to get the feel of the structure. It may help to draw the tree if the manuals don't show them. One of the first things I do with a new package is to learn how to get around in *that* forest. I explore all the trees, find the dead end, the lies, the traps, and the bugs, until I'm as comfortable as a software orangutan. Software that cuts the limbs out from under you, that tosses you off a branch for a hard fall to the ground, or that dies along a certain path is obvious garbage.

---

*The human mind can comprehend at most six things simultaneously, and that's only for geniuses. If you don't believe me, close your eyes and see how many individual bowling pins you can visualize without grouping them.

6

COMMAND AND CONTROL

1. SYNOPSIS

Command-driven software. Dialogues. Syntax. Mnemonic commands. Controlling commands. Changing and tailoring. Packages that learn. Sneaking into programming.

2. ANOTHER DREAM

It's midnight and I'm back at the computer, driven by righteous anger to write this section. It was a TV computer commercial which culminated in a mightly swat of an ax at the competitor's machine by a hapless soul who had succumbed to the frustration of being unable to learn how to use command-driven software. The ad implied that if only she had bought the "right" computer, then she could have been using it in hours—because that's what's claimed for menu-driven software, especially when it's iconic.

I dream of doing my countercommercial. It starts with a fat, florid, and furious boss pounding on the door: "Johnson!" he says, "Where's the Hercules diaper projection? 'Supposed to be on my desk an hour ago!''

Johnson is cringing in front of her multicolor screen with all the pretty pictures displayed on it. She goes for the mouse but it's buried under a mound of paper. She finds it. There isn't a clear spot in the room on which to maneuver that mouse so she asks the boss to bend down so that she can use his bald head as a mouse platform. She then cajoles the mouse to the right figure, gets the next menu, and then progresses from pretty menu to menu, as the boss watches it all, getting angrier by the minute. It's a cumbersome process made worse because of her nervous tremor on the mouse and the boss' increasingly heavier breathing. Finally, he can't take it any longer; he shouts: "Did they teach you that kid-stuff at Sloan, or was it Wharton?" He's too smart to ax computers. First he writes them off as a tax loss, and then cons his competitor into buying the lot. In the next scene, they're on their honeymoon, flying high above the clouds in the corporate jet, playing with two different models of the brand axed in the first commercial.

Command-driven software isn't really much harder to learn, function-for-function, than menu-driven software. It may seem that way because command-driven software is less limited and usually does more than its menu-driven counterpart. They're a lot faster to use. But it's because of these very advantages that there's more to master. And because of that apparent additional complexity (and often, very bad manuals) they can be intimidating.

One thing's often overlooked. Before you try a command-driven package, can you touch-type? If you can't, I suggest you learn, because command-driven packages work much better for people who do. How much of the intimidation is caused by the mundane problem of not knowing where the keys are, or by having to look and think for every keystroke? If you can't touch-type, menu-driven software may be easier for you to use because there are fewer keys to learn and the action is on the screen where you're usually looking anyhow.

3. COMMAND-DRIVEN SOFTWARE

3.1. Command Logic Design

One difference between menu-driven and command-driven software is that in the former, the choices are before you on the screen (unless you've deliberately suppressed them), while in the latter, the options are in your head and not on the screen unless you've asked for them. That's one reason that command-driven software is harder to learn: you must learn the commands to use the package effectively.

It's easier to learn something logical. The easiest logic to learn is that of our native language. Command-driven software that adopts that logic through the use of keywords (e.g., "STORE") is easier to learn. If (for presumably good reasons) the designers choose not to use Englishlike keywords, but adopt a code instead, then even if the code appears to be arbitrary at first, it will be easier to learn if it's consistent. There should be a method to the code so that if you learn the method, you've learned the code. Codes whose logic shifts from command to command, or whose interpretation depends on context, or which has other inconsistencies, can't be learned but must be memorized. Inconsistencies add anxiety; and then there's all the time wasted looking things up.

Good command structures, like menus, are *designed*. Bad command structures, like bad menu structures, merely accumulate. Good command structures have built-in "hooks" that allow the designers to add new features in the future without destroying the logic that's aready there and without forcing you to learn anything but the new commands. Bad command structures get worse with added features. They eventually become so arbitrary that users are faced with the choice of ignoring the new features or junking the package.

3.2. Commands Versus Dialogues

3.2.1. The Division

The bottom division on the command-driven side of Figure 5–1 distinguishes between "syntactic" and "sequential" commands. A pure **syntactic command** is one in which all the information needed to do something is typed-in before you tell the package to GO. Conversely, in pure **sequential commands** each piece of data is obtained by means of a dialogue between you and the computer.

3.2.2. Sequential Commands, Dialogues, and Menus

A sequential command is a lot like a menu-driven approach. Let's say you want to copy a file from drive A to drive B. It can be done by a dialogue. You initiate the dialogue by typing a command or hitting a command key called "COPY" (or a function key assigned to "COPY"). The dialogue follows. Italics are used to indicate the computer's responses:

⟨COPY⟩
Enter Source Drive Name: A ⟨RETURN⟩
Enter Destination Drive Name: B ⟨RETURN⟩
Enter Source File Name: MY-OLD-FILE-NAME ⟨RETURN⟩
Enter Destination File Name: MY-NEW-FILE-NAME ⟨RETURN⟩

To clarify the difference between this approach and menu-drive, in a pure menu-driven package, the dialogue would have been:
⟨COPY—the drive-select menu appears on the screen:

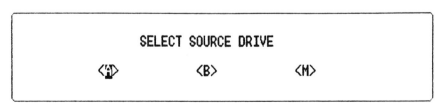

SELECT SOURCE DRIVE

⟨A⟩   ⟨B⟩   ⟨H⟩

You select the source drive and then the destination drive menu appears:

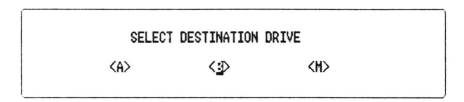

The destination drive selection is followed by the source drive directory:

```
              DIRECTORY FOR DRIVE A

 < > MY-FIRST-FILE.......................10/01/84.007
 < > MY-SECOND-FILE......................10/01/84.008
 < > MY-THIRD-FILE.......................10/14/84.002
...................................................
...................................................
 < > SAMS-FILE..........................11/01/84.001
 <█> MY-OLD-FILE........................11/02/84.001
 < > JUNK-FILE..........................11/02/84.002
```

There's no way to get a new file name without asking for it, so the last step would not be another menu, but another dialogue step.

Dialogues are midway between pure menu-driving and the purely syntactic commands discussed in the next section. You might ask, Why use menus at all?

1. Menus are safer. Only the choices which explicitly appear on the menu can be selected. Command dialogues allow you to select something meaningless—say DRIVE C—and the software must protect itself against such choices.

2. Dialogues require you to know all the possible answers. Menus give you all the answers explicitly. For example, if there were a thousand files to choose from, you might be hard put to remember the exact file name you wanted. You might be forced to quit the dialogue, fetch the directory, write the name down, and then go back to the dialogue. Conversely, scanning a list of over a thousand files names could be just as tiring.

3. Menus are slower-paced. They give you more time to think. Conversely,

it's usually faster to type a dialogue response than to make a menu selection.

4. Menus have a neat logic. Dialogues can take on a bewildering range of possibilities—as broad as human discourse. It's easier to get lost in dialogues than it is in menus. It's harder to keep track of where you are, where you've been, and where you're going. And because the same dialogue segments are used on many different paths, you might give an improper response (a cockpit error) because you became confused over which path you were on and what you were doing.

3.2.3. Syntactic Commands

Even if we improve the operator's speed by substituting command-driven dialogues for menus, there's still a lot of junk to read and it still takes time to plow through the dialogue. Things can be made even faster (but more obscure and error-prone) by compressing the dialogue into the command itself, as in the following example:

COPY A:MY-OLD-FILE-NAME TO
B:MY-NEW-FILE-NAME⟨RETURN⟩

This is faster than working through a dialogue or specifying the equivalent data by means of successive menus. But look at all the things you must know (and remember) in order to do it:

1. That the command is "COPY" and not "COPYFILE", "DUPLI-CATE", "REPRODUCE", "TRANSCRIBE", "REPLICATE", "RE-PEAT", "COPYDISK", "DISKCOPY", and so on. This seems trivial for one command, but for a complicated integrated package with hundreds of commands, it forces you to adapt to another person's (the programer's) vocabulary and usage for many, many, commands. There are so many different packages and so many different vocabularies that it's easy to get confused, or worse, to make a tragic error.
2. That the permissible drive names are what? "A", "B", "L", "R", "LEFT", "RIGHT", "M", "F"?
3. That the order must be: drive-name, file-name, drive-name, file-name.
4. That there must be a colon between the drive-name and the file-name.
5. That the source and destination specifications must be separated by the word "TO".
6. That there must be spaces between the components of the command and nowhere else. How many spaces?

119

3.2.4. The Elements of Good Syntax

A syntactic command is like a sentence in a natural language. It usually consists of a verb, possibly an adverb or two, a noun, adjectives, and so on. It has components which correspond to the parts of speech. And like natural languages, those parts must be arrayed in a standard order for the command to make sense. That order, and all the other rules (which you must know and understand) is called the command's **syntax**; which is why I've called these "syntactic commands." Natural languages have great flexibility in syntax and in the way you can say something:

> "My dog has fleas."
> "There are fleas on my dog."
> "Fleas infest my dog."
> "Is them fleas on my dog? They is!"
> "Fleas! My dog's a comely habitat to them."
> "Thou flea-beleaguered canine mine."

Computer languages don't have such flexibility (yet) so that following syntactic rules is obligatory. Designers can do two things to make your life easier:

1. Make the syntax flexible.
2. Forgive you your syntax errors.

Everyone has problems with command **delimiters**. A **delimiter** is a character or a character sequence used to separate the parts of the command. In the above example, spaces and the colon were used as delimiters. Other commonly used delimiters are: commas, periods, parentheses, brackets, hyphens, semicolons, asterisks, and dollar signs. Programmers are used to working with delimiters. Here's some typical examples:

```
PUSHR   #^M⟨R7,R8⟩ ;
MOVB    (R1)+,(R2)  ;
PRINT USING 6300; W$[V*8−7,V*];D4(V,3);D3(3,V);"JA";
```

This stuff is second nature to them and they forget that you're not attuned to writing things in which every character has meaning: maybe it's because they feel that if they must suffer, then so should you. But there's no excuse for that. Syntax can be designed so that it's easy to remember and use:

1. Good syntax is based on the rules of punctuation and delimiters of natural languages. For English, use spaces between words, commas to set off items in a list, parentheses to provide additional details, and so on. The closer to normal punctuation, the better.
2. Good syntax allows the free use of spaces and always treats more than one space in a row as if it were a single space. Furthermore, where spaces aren't really needed, it ignores them. This allows you enter commands that are closer to normal writing than would otherwise be possible.
3. Good syntax is consistent. Not just within a single command or a family of related commands, but across the entire set of commands. The verb always comes first, then the adjectives, and then the nouns.
4. The structure follows natural parlance so that the command is:

COPY FILE-A TO FILE-B

instead of:

COPY FILE-B FROM FILE-A

5. It's as flexible as possible. It doesn't pick nits. It's tolerant to obviously sensible variations.

It is possible that, because of an error you've made, what you've entered is ambiguous, incorrect, impossible, or otherwise "does not compute." It's usually possible for the software to determine that and to guess what you did wrong and where. Bad software says: "Screw you! You've made a syntax error and I'm going to make you pay for it!", whereupon the program crashes, or kicks you out of that command sequence, or gives you some other kind of grief. There's no excuse for such hostility. Good software coddles you by giving you an opportunity to correct your errors and by informative messages; and I don't mean "SYNTAX ERROR—GOODBYE DUMMY!"

1. A precise message to tell you why the command can't be executed.
2. Points to the command you've written and shows you exactly where the error was first discovered.*
3. Allows you to fetch a HELP screen that will show you the correct syntax.
4. Brings the cursor back to the command you just typed and allows you to use normal edit keys such as ⟨DELETE⟩, ⟨INSERT⟩, and ⟨BACK-SPACE⟩ to correct your entry.

---

*That's all the program can do. It may not be possible to detect what you did wrong, but only the first place where something wrong was discovered. They're not always the same thing.

5. Allows you to convert the command into a dialogue, thereby giving you the best of both worlds. I haven't seen it yet, but the action would be something like this:

⟨COPY⟩ ?   You've forgotten the COPY command's syntax and your question mark alerts the software to that fact. It responds with:
COPY
source drive?

You now remember the format and type the rest of it out:

source drive? A:MY-OLD-FILE TO B:MY-NEW-FILE⟨RET⟩

Or maybe you don't remember, so you enter the drive name and a question mark, leading to the following dialogue?

⟨COPY⟩ ?
source drive? A?
: source file name? MY-OLD FILE?
space TO space dest drive? B?
: dest file name? MY-NEW-FILE?
⟨RETURN⟩? ⟨RETURN⟩

It's expensive and takes design work, memory, foresight, and most of all, a humane concern for the people who will have to use the software. Given that, and a healthy desire to dominate the software market, most vendors should be able to justify the expense.

3.2.5. Syntax Helpers.

The designer who's decided to give you the operating speed advantages of syntactic commands has incurred responsibilities which are unfortunately too often ignored. The first responsibility is to make it work, the second is to make it good, and the third is to tell you what the syntax is before, after, and while you're using the command. Syntax is hard to learn: ask any foreigner who's trying to learn your language. Learning the syntax of a new command-driven package may be easier than learning Bulgarian, but it *is* learning a new language. How can you be expected to learn a new language without a dictionary, grammar books, or examples? You need help. Check Chapter 3 to see what good help is.

3.3. Mnemonic Commands

3.3.1. What Are They?

Up 'till now, I've used the explicit, obvious, "COPY" to designate the copy command. It's an example of a **keyword**. We could have abbreviated it as "CP", or possibly even just "C". The easiest commands to understand are mnemonic—that is, they make sense as words or as abbreviations of words. The characters you type trigger your mind for the meaning. The alternative is to be completely arbitrary, and to use letters or symbols in a code that stands for the action you want, but which otherwise has no apparent relation to it.

3.3.2. Literal Versus Keywords (and Abbreviations)

The most obvious approach is a complete keyword such as "COPY", "DIRECTORY", etc. These are defined and used in constructing commands whose external appearance is similar to English. It's a good idea. It makes things easier to learn but it does take longer to type. Most people don't find typing a complete word such as "RENAME" objectionable at first. However, as they gain proficiency and learn the commands' structure, there's a desire to take shortcuts. Because command-driven software is biased toward the experienced user, that desire is often stronger. It may seem to be a trivial thing to allow abbreviations such as "REN" and "CP", and it is for simple packages, but for complicated software, especially for integrated packages, it's almost impossible. There aren't enough letters to go around and most interesting commands begin with the same letters. For example: CANCEL, CLEAR, COPY, COUNT, CREATE, DELETE, DIRECTORY, DISPLAY, INDEX, INPUT, INSERT, READ, RECALL, REINDEX, RELEASE, RENAME, REPLACE, REPORT, RESTORE, RETURN, SEEK, SELECT, and SET. It's clear that single-character mnemonics are hopeless, that two-character mnemonics are inadequate, and that even three-character mnemonics can't distinguish between "REPlace"and "REPort". An integrated package, if it were completely command-driven, would have several hundred keywords, and even full words wouldn't suffice. There are several alternatives:

1. Use only full keywords. That loses the speed advantage.
2. Use a variable number of characters in commands—from single letters to full keywords. Allow abbreviations if the important first few characters are provided. The trouble with that approach is that you forget which parts of the keyword is meaningful and how many characters must be typed for which. The result is frustration and errors.

3. Drop the whole idea of trying to create meaningful mnemonics and go for completely arbitrary codes, such as "A1", "A2", etc. That's obviously hard to learn.
4. Use single keys, function keys, or ⟨CONTROL⟩ shifted keys for all commands.
5. Use *two* command languages—an explicit language based on full keywords and a compact language based on mnemonics, function keys, and as few as possible arbitrary codes. This can work but it's tricky because the two languages can contradict each other, and then there may be a problem with telling the computer which one you're using at the moment.

Unfortunately, there aren't any simple rules or clear-cut recommendations. Packages get out of the dilemma (to some extent) by using a combination of all the command methods. The compromise is obtained by allowing the user to define keys so that the most frequently used commands can be put on the screen, with full keywords, in one keystroke. Function keys or control-shifted ordinary keys are defined for certain (heavily used) commands. Abbreviations are allowed for others, but commands whose use is expected to be rare must be typed in detail. The programmer, by such means, tries to achieve a reasonable compromise between the novice's confusion and the master's impatience.

3.3.3. Consistency and Design

Just as the surest way to achieve an incomprehensible syntax is to let it accumulate as ideas for new commands and/or user pressure for new features arrive, so too can keyword and mnemonic selection be allowed to accumulate. The words used to denote commands must be carefully selected. If the package's complexity is such that a mnemonic scheme must be adopted, then the entire scheme must be designed from top to bottom. If it's necessary to use arbitrary letters or letter pairs (the ultimate being keyed commands) then a top-down design and complete consistency is even more important. It's the only decent thing to do. The designer has done away with natural languages because you wanted keyboard speed, so she'll give you an unnatural language. That's okay, but it doesn't have to be perverse, to have arbitrary rules, and to be inconsistent. The only way to avoid such ills is to design the whole from the top.*

---

*Before you get too harsh with designers and their apparent inability to design command languages which are as good as natural languages, remember that natural languages have been finely honed by the efforts of tens of millions of users over a period of centuries, while computer command languages have been struggled with by scant dozens for few years, and users have had almost no participation in their evolution.

3.4. Keyed Commands

3.4.1. What Are They?

The simplest keyed commands consist of one keystroke of a dedicated key, a function key, or an ordinary key when the program is ready to accept a new command. The typical keyboard is full of single-key commands. There are the obvious cursor control keys, but also many others. Here's a sample merged from five different personal computer keyboards: BOLD, CALCULATE, CLEAR, COPYDISC, DRAW, ENTER, ESCAPE, HELP, GRAPH, INDEX, INSERT, ITALICS, LINE, MAIL, MENU, PAGE, PARA, PRINT, RESET, RETRIEVE, SCHEDULE, SCROLL, SIZE, STOP, STORE, STYLE, TAB, UNDO, and WORD. Ordinary keys, used in conjunction with the ⟨CONTROL⟩ key, or alone if possible, are also used for single-key commands. If the mnemonic scheme has been reduced to single keystrokes for speed at the expense of intelligibility, it will most often be done by using the first letter of what would have been a keyword, and the ⟨CONTROL⟩ key. Alternatively, as in WORDSTAR, important keys are laid out in a pattern that makes functional sense. The closest keys are single-character moves, out from those are word moves, then paragraph, page, and finally to the beginning and ends of the document.

Single keystroke keys are fast and easy to use, but hard to learn and to remember unless there's a visual cue.

3.4.2. Fixed Versus Dynamic

Most personal computers have eight or ten keys labeled "F1," "F2," through "F10." These are the **special function keys.** They're intended to be used by package designers for any purpose which makes sense. Some computers may appear not to have such keys, but in fact do. For example, the EPSON QX-10's function keys come prelabelled with the functions used in the native mode integrated software package. But the function of those keys can be modified by software packages to mean different things.

Most modern keyboards can be redefined to do almost anything. If you wanted to go through the trouble, you could design your own keyboard, move all the permanent keys around (by lifting the keycaps), and get a keyboard which was more to your liking. And some operating systems give you the tools with which to do that. It's not only possible for the programmer to change the meaning of the function keys, but also the meaning of any key whatsoever. That is, the key's meaning is dynamic. The question you should ask is: how dynamic?

If every package redefined the entire keyboard, then the chaos would be even worse than it is now. Some designers act as if the fact that they *can* change the keyboard means that they *must*. This leads to inconsistencies and confusion. Most packages will exploit the function keys and redefine their use. The ten keys are actually 20 keys because they can be shifted. They can also be 30 keys because there's a ⟨CONTROL⟩ key shift as well. For that matter, an ⟨ALT⟩ key can give us another ten, so that there can be as many as 40 different interpretations to the function keys alone.*

The hardware manufacturer provides a keyboard. The keys have labels such as "PRINT", "DELETE", and "BACKSPACE". The labels are the manufacturer's statement of how he intends to use those keys, and how he would like those keys to be used by package builders. You might wonder, why buy package *X* from a hardware manufacturer when you can buy the same package from the software vendor at a lower price? One of the reasons for preferring the hardware manufacturer's version is that *all* the packages sold under his label, whatever their source, will (should) use the normal and function keys consistently. Conversely, the software vendor's general package, which can run on many different machines, may not use function keys at all because some hardware may not have them and they want the generalized version of the package to run on as many different computers as possible without modification.

3.4.3. Telling the Good from the Bad

The quality of single-key commands, whether they are based on function keys, redefined keys, normal keys, or on a combination of shifts, ⟨CONTROL⟩, and so on, is determined by three points: (1) Are they consistent with the key's normal use? (2) Does the key selection make sense? (3) Are they restored?

1. Good software assigns the most frequently used keys only once for the entire package. Once assigned, they always do the same thing (or very similar thing) and they always work.
2. The built-in key definitions (i.e., the ones on the keycaps) may be reinterpreted to have analogous uses. For example, the cursor control keys are used to move UP, DOWN, LEFT, and RIGHT in a word-processing package *and* in a graphics package even though a different cursor is used.
3. Any other keys which must be redefined are selected either for finger ease or for mnemonic sense. For example you'd use ⟨CONTROL⟩P for "print" and ⟨CONTROL⟩S for "store," and not the other way around.
4. Dynamic keys, that is, those keys whose functions change within a pack-

---

*And even more if you allow almost impossible combinations such as: ⟨CAPS⟩ ⟨CONTROL⟩⟨ALT⟩⟨ANYKEY⟩.

age, are minimized and used only if there's a clear legend, such as in a menu or a command line.

5. Important panic keys such as HELP, QUIT, STOP, and PAUSE, are *never* redefined.

6. However the package redefines the keys, it puts them back to where they normally are. Not doing this is a common flaw. The programmer builds a new keyboard, and when you quit, you're forced to reboot the system because the keyboard he's redefined is incompatible with the operating system.

3.4.4. Overlays and Underlays

As I wished earlier, one of these days hardware development will progress to where we can afford to buy keyboards on which every key has its own built-in display, so that when key's redefined, the legend changes to correspond. Until that day comes, though, we'll have to find ways to live with dynamic keys. The simplest method to tell you what the key is now doing is to use an **overlay** or **underlay**. An **overlay** is piece of plastic that fits over part of the keyboard, on which the temporary key assignments are printed. **Underlays** are similar except that they're strips that fit in a slot designed for the purpose. Underlays are neater, smaller, cleaner, and inherently less expensive than overlays. They'll probably become a standard feature on new keyboards in the future. For now, the world is still dominated by overlays. Good overlays (or underlays) are made of plastic to match the keyboard's color. Cheaper ones are made of hard cardboard, and really chintzy ones are made of paper. Good packages provide overlays to fit your computer, or if not, and if both the computer and the package are popular, you'll be able to buy an overlay as an after-market product. Do it! The alternative is to use grease pencils, or permanent marking pens. My keyboards tend to get sloppy because if I can't get an overlay for a package, I'll write it on the keyboard, above or alongside the key, or use small stick-on pads with the keyword written on it. I just don't know how to handle dynamic keys without some kind of reminder.

In this respect, remember that a command line which displays the functions of dynamic keys is a kind of overlay—as long as the key's value is displayed whenever you might need to use it.

4. COMMAND COMMAND AND CONTROL

4.1. A Note

Most of this section (4) applies with some obvious modification to menu-driven software and also to hybrid command methods. I've put it here because its usual context is that of keyed commands rather than that of menu selection.

4.2. Initiating the Command Mode

4.2.1. Command and Data States

At any instant, the software is either in the **command state** or the **data entry state.** The difference is most easily illustrated by word processing. If you are in the data entry state and you type the word "help," that word becomes part of the text. Conversely, in the command state, that same word will cause a help screen to appear. While this distinction is clear for word processing, it can be fuzzy for data base systems, spreadsheets, and other packages. Sometimes it is not the entire package that goes from one state to the other, but only certain keys. What's important is that keys have different meanings in the two states. Good designs try to keep the two sets of meanings analogous for all keys, but that's not always possible. What mechanisms does the software provide you with for going from the data entry state to the command state or vice-versa?

4.2.2. CONTROL and ALT Keys

When the state change is temporary and for only one keystroke, the usual practice is to use a shift, such as the ⟨CONTROL⟩ or ⟨ALT⟩ key, so that the command is actually a two-stroke command such as: "⟨CONTROL⟩X", or equivalently "^X". The shift applies only to that one command and the program returns to data entry as soon as it's executed.

4.2.3. ESCAPE Key

Many packages use the ⟨ESCAPE⟩ key for a more permanent state change. The key is struck and the program is put into the command state. Typically that's signalled by the appearance of a master menu or the first prompt of a dialogue. The use of the ⟨ESCAPE⟩ key is convenient and sounds "right" because it seems to imply "escaping" from the data entry state to the command state. As popular as this usage is, though, it's a bad method. Every key has a specific meaning and sends out a specific bit pattern. Using the ⟨ESCAPE⟩ key for this control purpose means that its bit pattern can't be used for other purposes, such as in text or in data. Unfortunately, the ⟨ESCAPE⟩ key has a longstanding use in telecommunications and more immediately, as a control signal for many popular printers. You buy a printer that can create dozens of fonts in a variety of sizes, bold, italics, and all the rest, and find that you can't exploit but a fraction of its capabilities because commands to the printer begin with the ⟨ESCAPE⟩ character and you can't use the ⟨ESCAPE⟩ because it's being used to shift to command mode.

4.2.4. Other Bad Choices

Keys that have important control functions outside of the package, such as ⟨STOP⟩, ⟨UNDO⟩, or ⟨HELP⟩ should *never* have their functions redefined for shifts between data entry and command entry, or for any other purpose, for that matter. It's lazy, bad, unnecessary, and stupid.

4.2.5. Dedicated Keys and Function Keys

The best way is to have a dedicated key for shifting to the command mode. Alternatively a *single* function key, say F10, should be assigned for consistent use in shifting from data entry to command mode. No other key should be used for that purpose and the assignment should be permanent for every phase of the package. One of the signs of a poorly designed or slapped-together integrated package is that each functional area (word processing, spreadsheet, graphics, data base, telecommunications, etc.) has a different method for getting to the command mode.

4.3. Keyboard Lockouts

The programmer can not only change the definition of keys, but can also disable keys. This takes extra effort and more software, so it's not something that happens by accident. The programmer locks the keyboard (or parts of it) in order to provide what he believes is safety. The problem with almost every keyboard lockout I've seen is that it's done stupidly. The typical method locks *all* keys, including the ⟨STOP⟩ key, or whatever else is used for that purpose. It's suicide. You initiate a long operation, such as a data-base sort, reformatting a document, or evaluating a spreadsheet. It takes longer than you expected, so you want to quit—but the keyboard's locked and the only thing you can do is turn the system off and reboot. Communications software seems to be a favorite for locking out. Three packages, on different hardware, from different software vendors, all locked the keyboard tight when it started transmitting or receiving data. It made it almost impossible to debug the interface. The best of the three provided an unlock function that would halt the data transfer, but in so doing it destroyed all records of what had been happening and restarted with a clean slate.*

I don't like keyboard lockouts. It's insulting. It implies that I'm so dumb that I'll ignore a warning that striking keys could cause problems—a warning that shouldn't have been necessary with good software. It's bad software because a good design protects itself against potentially damaging keystrokes but allows any that might be useful, such as ⟨STOP⟩ and ⟨HELP⟩. Buggy software tends to rely on lockouts more than good software. It's as if the designer doesn't know how to handle a keystroke that comes at the "wrong" time and "solves" the problem by cutting off all contact. It's the software equivalent of slamming the door and snarling: "Leave me alone, numbskull; I've got work to do!"

There are acceptable alternatives to suicidal lockouts: a master unlock key, a ⟨STOP⟩ key that unlocks and stops the ongoing process, user control over lockouts, carefully designed selective lockouts or a physical lock-and-key, such as on the IBM PC-AT.

4.4. Terminating the Command

How do you signal to the computer that you've finished entering a command? There are two main methods used:

1. No explicit signal. The last keystroke of the command initiates it. This is okay for single- or double-keystroke commands, such as dedicated keys, function keys, and so on.
2. An explicit signal, usually with the ⟨RETURN⟩/⟨ENTER⟩ key. This is mandatory for long commands with complicated syntaxes, or for command and/or data entry in which what you enter has a variable length (for example, a file name).

Both methods can be used in the same package if there's a consistency to it. Being forced to hit ⟨RETURN⟩ after *every* command changes what could be single-key commands into double-key commands, which is a pain. Immediate execution of a command with a complicated syntax (as soon as the last part of it has been entered) is as infuriating as a waiter who snatches your plate away as soon as you've taken the last bite of your steak: it denies you the opportunity to review what you've typed before you commit yourself. Good software uses both methods, but does so consistently and reasonably:

1. Only one command terminator is used throughout the package—the ⟨RETURN⟩ or ⟨ENTER⟩ key. Period!

---

*It was the programmer's way of hiding the evidence. We got around his deceit by clever techie stuff and found that indeed, he had much to hide.

2. Commands that require variable data entry (names, attributes) or that have more than one field in their syntax require an explicit terminator.
3. Dedicated keys, function keys, and single-keystroke commands require no explicit terminator. In this context the ⟨CONTROL⟩ key is a shift and therefore, ^X, say, is treated as single-key command.
4. Commands that require two or more keystrokes may or may not require an explicit terminator, but whatever method is used, the rule should be obvious. The easiest rule is to require the terminator for all commands with more than one keystroke.
5. Any potentially dangerous command has a warning prompt on the screen and requires an explicit confirmation which requires the explicit terminator.

Inconsistent use of terminators is a mark of garbage software, lack of foresight, and also hastily "integrated" software. It reveals a programming staff that doesn't talk to itself, a staff in which each designer does "her thing" without regard to the consequences or to possible inconsistencies with other parts of the software. Inconsistent use of terminators creates anxiety and is yet another barrier to learning. It is as sloppy and as bad as writing in which the scribbler has defined his own usage for punctuation so that you never know if a sentence will be ended with a period, a comma, or a dollar sign. Garbage!

4.5. Changing the Command

Any command with many parts, that is, a command with a nontrivial syntax, is error prone. The designer's compressed a dialogue or a succession of menus into one statement in order to give you a faster control method. However, that very speed improvement means that you're likelier to make mistakes. Bad software gives you no opportunity to correct these errors or to change your mind. The worst I've seen allows a multiple-file delete of the form:

DELETE FROM FIRST-FILE-NAME
TO LAST-FILE-NAME⟨RETURN⟩

Let's say you've made a mistake with the file name, so that if the command is allowed to proceed, you'll wipe out a week's work. You know you've made a mistake, and you caught it before you typed the ⟨RETURN⟩, but this rotten software won't let you correct it. You are about to execute the command, like it or not. You could pop the discs out and shut down, but the trick that usually works is to deliberately hesitate before the ⟨RETURN⟩. Look at what you've typed. If it's wrong, then deliberately screw the command up to force the software to reject it. Try it before you count on it, though.

Good software lets you use the *normal* editing keys to correct your command at any point prior to the ⟨RETURN⟩. That means the following keys: cursor control keys, DELETE, BACKSPACE, ERASE, and so on. I've seen those keys locked out in command mode, or worse, their functions are re-defined with disastrous consequences. Some junky software tries to make amends for taking away the correction keys during command mode by giving you new correction keys. You have to remember then, that backspace is done with ^$, erasures with .&*, and so on. More garbage!

4.6. Moving Around the Command Tree

Commands may be nested in a treelike structure that's analogous to the way menus nest. It's not as obvious though. Typically, the structure is re-vealed by what commands are active or inactive at any instant. Consider an integrated package that does word-processing, data-base, spreadsheet, communications, and graphics. When you're in the word processing mode, you wouldn't expect to be able to execute spreadsheet commands, say. Cer-tainly not all of them. If you're sorting records, you wouldn't expect the word-processing search-and-replace functions to work. Good integrated software does provide you with considerable overlap, and some commands, such as FETCH, STORE, and QUIT, work in all modes. However, the tree structure, although it's there, is leafier and it has many more cross-connections than an equivalent menu-driven package. But whatever that structure is, *you need exactly the same kind of tree-climbing apparatus that was discussed for menu-driven software in Section 6 of Chapter 5.*

Reread Section 6 of Chapter 5 and substitute "command" or "com-mand set" wherever you see "menu."

I just did that as a check and found that it made complete sense. The above statement is a literary **subroutine call.**

5. COMMAND STORAGE AND MACROS

5.1. Why Read This Section?

5.1.1. An Observation

You may have noticed this and the previous chapter got more technical as they progressed. I started Chapter 5 with the basics of menu-driven soft-ware, continued to greater complexities, and then went on to command-driven software. Each successive section was more technical and concerned with finer points. Also notice that as the material progressed there was a continual trade between ease of learning and speed—a shift from the novice's perspective to the master's. That shift also went from the nonprogramming user in the direction of programmers and programming. That's the way it is. Operational speed, sophistication, and flexibility usually mean that you must learn, adopt, and exploit methods and features which are ever-closer to programming. You do that if and only if by so doing you increase your productivity. Productivity increases can't be done without investment. They shouldn't be done without evaluating the return on investment. Two persons who are at the same level of expertise will have to make the same investment to increase their productivity. What differs is the payoff. If your usage of a computer is diverse, involves different packages in an unpredictable way, or if it's casual, then there's no point to learning what's in this section. But if your usage is limited to a few packages, and especially if that usage is repetitive, then this section *is* for you.

5.1.2. Creative Laziness

I said on page 7 that programmers should be creatively lazy by encapsulating frequently used processes into subroutines. Users can also do that for many packages: and this section deals with the means provided (or not) for automating repetitive work. What you can do ranges from something as simple as redefining the keys to things which are equivalent to what programmers do. Just how far you want to go depends on your mindset, the required investment, and the payoff:

1. Mindset. Some of us are natural tinkerers and there's fun and joy in learning how to use a new feature, even if it's complicated and takes effort. It's like owning a boat. For some, the joy is in the tinkering and maintenance, while for others it's in the sailing. Who's to judge who's right? But if you're a tinkerer, by sure you understand the cost, know that you're after a psychic rather than pragmatic reward, and act accordingly.

2. Investment. If you're a programmer, the investment is the familiar one of learning a new programming language, which, as you (should) know, can range from trivial to impossible. If you're not a programmer then the first investment ranges from moving toward a programmer's point of view all the way to becoming a programmer. There's also the investment of learning the specifics, telling (i.e., programming) the package what you want done and how, and debugging what you've told it to do. If the enhanced features are to be used by an operator, then there's the cost of training that operator.

3. Payoff. The payoff is increased human productivity—yours and/or an operator's. If you convert an irritating way of doing something into a method that's more pleasant for you, then even if you haven't reduced the keystrokes you may have improved your productivity because time won't be wasted bitching over how it's presently done. But be fair to yourself. How much time will you *really* save by cutting out a few keystrokes? Is this really a repetitive operation or are there small variations that can't easily be handled by the tools you have? Is the procedure you've developed really so complicated that you have to automate it or could you revise or subdivide it to reduce the complexity?

If it seems as if the above is intended to warn you away from tailoring the package (as against using it out-of-the-box), it is. I've taken that point of view not to intimidate you but because my experience is that tailoring the package is always more difficult than we expect it should be and the payoff is often disappointing. I don't tailor anything until I've used it three months or more. Then I do it by slow, small, steps and let each step stabilize for a few weeks before I take the next step. Meanwhile, my operating procedures are changing, as are my applications. This is creative procrastination and it helps me to avoid what would otherwise be a lot of tedious work with little substantive reward.

5.2. Training the Computer

5.2.1. Changing the Keys

The simplest thing you can do is to change the keyboard (if the package has the facilities for that). The most likely reason for wanting to do it is that you've got a nice keyboard with all kinds of fancy and useful keys but the package has been written for the cheapest keyboard on the market. Redefining the keys will mean that many commands which you now do by a control key shift, as in ^X, can be done with one finger or one key. Another reason for redefining keys is to make the layout more humane and to bring keys which are difficult to reach closer in. A third reason for redefining keys is to make this package more consistent with the operating system or with other packages that you use a lot.

There are many different methods used to redefine the keys and it would take too much space to describe them all. Manuals are notoriously bad in this respect and they're often written for programmers rather than users. Not only that, specifying the initial key and what it's to change to often requires you to enter the key designation in **octal** or **hexadecimal** notation and there's no explanation of what that means nor a table of the correct values. The installation software used to change keys can be terribly buggy, error prone, and vulnerable. Don't do it without several backup copies of the program. Never try this out on serious work.

The operating system (or special after-market packages) may also have facilities for changing the meaning of keys and sometimes this can be a way to tame a package's bad keyboard usage. If that's the case though, be sure that you haven't inadvertently introduced some ugly conflicts between the operating system and your package. Conversely, after you've installed a new keyboard, be sure that it's cleaned-up by the software (i.e., restored to the original values) when you quit the package; because if you don't, you might find that what had been the HELP key in another package has been converted to a key that erases your hard disc.

5.2.2. Keyed Macros

The next step beyond single key substitutions is the substitution of individual keys for sequences of keystrokes or complete commands. For example, an operation in a package requires you to key-in "^Q^Q^W^X^Y^Z". The package allows you to convert that sequence to a single keystroke, say "⟨ALT⟩Q". While there may not appear to be too many available keys on the keyboard, remember that almost any key can be modified to yield the following combinations:

LOWER CASE NORMAL	"x"
UPPER CASE NORMAL	"X"
LOWER CASE CONTROL	"^x"
UPPER CASE CONTROL	"^X"
LOWER CASE ALT	"⟨ALT⟩x"
UPPER CASE ALT	"⟨ALT⟩X"
LOWER CONTROL, ALT	"^⟨ALT⟩x"
UPPER CONTROL, ALT	"^⟨ALT⟩X".

Not all of these combinations will be available. The keyboard I'm using has over a hundred physical keys on it, but some, such as the ⟨RETURN⟩, ⟨CONTROL⟩, and number keys are duplicated. If I remove the duplicated keys there are actually only 87 different keys. The shift keys can't be counted, which brings the total to 80 keys. Multiplying by the 8 combinations above would give us 640 possibilities or **codes** for those 80 keys. However, the maximum number of possible codes is (for almost every computer) 256. Of these, 110 are in use or have been defined as part of the international character set. The same 110 codes may be used with the ⟨ALT⟩ upper and lower case to provide a graphics character set. Other codes may have been devoted to other purposes. *The bottom line of it all is that every code probably has some use someplace. If you use that code for some other* *purpose, you will be sacrificing something.* Know what it is you're giving up before you do it. If the package restores the keys for you when you quit, then sacrificing a communication code such as ⟨DC1⟩, ⟨DC2⟩, or ⟨DC3⟩ may be no problem. However, it may be a problem with a future version that now has usurped the formerly "free" code to implement a new feature. There really aren't enough codes to go around, and therefore, sharing codes among the physical keys is inevitable.

An alternative to single keys substituting for a sequence of keystrokes is to assign a command mnemonic (of your choosing) for the purpose. This is a method by which you can expand the command repertoire. You can also use this method to convert arbitrary keyed commands to mnemonic or keyword form (assuming that the word or abbreviation you want to use isn't already in use).

There are several different ways that a package can react to stored keystroke sequences and the way it reacts will affect the utility of making the change. Let's say that you want to store a document, and that there's no assigned STORE key. Function key F4 is free, and you decide to assign it to create a ⟨STORE⟩ key. If the program was menu-driven, you might have used the following keystroke sequence to store things:

⟨ESC⟩   to shift to command entry mode

"STORE"   to bring up the store menu (five strokes)

F4 will now create the sequence "⟨ESC⟩STORE". Here are two possible dialogues that follows from using the redefined F4:

⟨F4⟩

The command entry prompt appears on the screen.

The word "STORE" is typed in for you.

The STORE menu appears.

⟨F4⟩

The STORE menu appears.

The second method is nicer, faster, but also takes more software smarts. Suppose now, that you install an entire sequence of commands, which might be responses to successive menus. The first method will have all those menus appear on the screen, then for each menu, you'll see your selection made, and then the next menu appears, and so on and so on. In the second approach, only the last menu appears, or only those menus which require a selection which you've not programmed (typically the last menu).

Watching things develop according to the first approach is a pain, takes time, and probably robs you of the productivity increase you expected.

The same mechanism applies to command-driven software where a single key can be used to define a fixed sequence of commands. This is known as a **command macro** or simply **macro.** Sophisticated software will use a combination of the two methods, as follows. As long as no response is needed from the operator, screen displays are suppressed and the next command is automatically executed. When it reaches a command which requires an input, such as file name, it pauses, displays the prompt, accepts your input, and then goes on until either the next data entry point or the end of the sequence. That's nice. Nobody minds seeing essential prompts.

A word of warning to would-be macro users and definers. It's difficult to allow panic keys such as ⟨STOP⟩, ⟨HELP⟩, ⟨PAUSE⟩, or ⟨UNDO⟩ to work while in the middle of such command sequences. ⟨STOP⟩ or ⟨PAUSE⟩ may work, but there's no way to guarantee exactly where in the sequence the program will stop. Furthermore, for practical reasons, if you have a command backspace key such as ⟨UNDO⟩, it will typically ⟨UNDO⟩ only one command in the sequence and not the entire sequence. While it's possible to design the software to do that, it takes more complexity and sophistication than most of us are willing to pay for.

5.2.3. Command Sequence Capture

The designers can give you a better alternative than going through a complicated procedure which you use to convert command sequences to single keys or to command mnemonics of your choosing. The package can have a **learning mode** which captures your successive keystrokes and stores them for future use. Let's say that you've got a repetitive operation with a spreadsheet or data-base package down pat. You do this thing every day, with only a few changes. It's now so routine that an untrained operator could do it for you; but it's still a complicated, error-prone procedure, and training the operator is more trouble than it's worth.

You enter the learning mode by issuing a special command such as ''ᐱLEARN'', and every keystroke executed in the command mode thereafter is captured for you. Good software will even allow you to make such things as file names either constant or variable so that it will automatically ask for what needs to be asked for and supplies what you've written in at the right spot. For example, the master file name might be constant but you're inputting data from daily report files. When you've gotten through the entire procedure you issue another command such as (''ᐱEND-LEARN''. The package then asks you to name the sequence, and thereafter you can run it by just typing)''ᐱDAILY-BALANCE'', say.

Learning modes (whey they work) are great. One of the best I've seen is always in the learning mode. It's the only way it operates. The Q-PLOTTER graphics package captures all commands as you enter them. You store your graphics by storing the command sequence. But you can also store a command sequence, name it, and then bring it back as a figure. You can create your company logo and call it "logo." Then when you want to put the logo on a new graphics, you call for it, and it's inserted into your drawing at the cursor location. Furthermore, you can move it as unit, change its size, or rotate it at will. A plumbing contractor would create the graphic elements needed for plumbing designs (valves, pipes, etc.) An interior decorator makes top-views of furniture, doors, windows, and so on. Each user tailors the package by using the learning mode to create the graphics symbols he needs. The learning mode in Q-PLOTTER is so smooth that you hardly know you're doing it. There is a price for it, though; it's a slow package.

5.2.5. Programming Mode

The logical extension of the learning mode is to bite the bullet and recognize that the package has (or can have) a programming mode. Data-base and integrated packages may have a programming mode in addition to their normal, interactive, mode of operation. Programmability isn't restricted to data-base packages or integrated packages but can be a feature of any software package. For example, Q-PLOTTER has both an interactive mode and a programming mode. There are no fundamental differences between programming a data-base application in a language such as dBASE and programming in a language such as Basic or Pascal. The specialized language gets a lot more done with less effort but all the elements and all agonies of programming are there. Before you tackle the programming mode of any package learn something about programming a more general language such as Basic or Pascal. For one thing, these general languages are easier to learn, simpler, and a lot less buggy. For another, there are more books and training courses on the subject. Finally, some packages assume that you already know a programming language because the programming mode is an extension of that language. For example, Q-PLOTTER is an extension of Basic and if you don't know Basic, you can't exploit its programming mode. There's nothing wrong with the approach, but you should know about it. If you've never done any programming, then after you've taken an introductory programming course take a course in the specialized language (e.g., dBASE) before you tackle its programming mode.

I have gripes about programming modes and the way they're usually presented. Here's a sample:

1. You're led to believe that it's easy and that it's not programming—bull!
2. The designers give you a programming language but without the tool kit that normally comes with programming languages. Your programming facilities may be as primitive as those we had to use twenty years ago.

3. The designers don't recognize that they've created a language. Programming languages are *designed*. It's a specialty and takes a lot of skill. Many of the programming modes in use today are really awful as languages. They're hard to learn, unstructured, have huge holes, are inconsistent, and generally reflect the state of the language design art as it was twenty years ago. It's only the fact that they're so useful that we suffer with a truly lousy language. I've programmed computers in more languages than I can remember. And always, the specialized, tinker-toy languages of software packages with programming modes have been the worst.

5.2.5. Application Compilers

The packages you use are technically known as **interpreters.** They're called that because they interpret every command you type and then act on it. When you use them in the programmed mode, they internally read the commands you've stored and execute them as if they'd been typed from the keyboard. Some will suppress the dialogue, the screen changes, and the menus, but others won't and for those, you can really see your program working out. The result is that it's slow, slow, slow.

You know that there's a lot of software between you and the machine. A **compiler** takes the statements of your program and translates them into the machine's language, bypassing thereby all the intermediate software levels. The result is a new program that's a lot shorter and faster than the interpretive version. Compiled programs cannot be modified for all practical purposes. You have to go back to the program as it was before you compiled it (called the **source code**), modify it, recompile it, and try again. Interpreters are great for development, for quick-and-dirty applications, and for anything where the procedures are unpredictable or are changing a lot. Compiled code can't be beaten for raw, unchanging, production runs.

Once you're into compiled applications, though, you're up to your eyebrows in programming and no vendor's hype is going to change that fact. Welcome to the world of programming.

5.3. Editing and Debugging the Training

5.3.1. It's Programming

Training the package is programming. It may be easy programming, as when you redefine a single key, or tough programming with all its guts and glory when you use a package's programming mode. You must have, or must acquire, the mental and programming tools that any programmer needs. You must learn design principles, how to design and conduct good tests, how to verify that your program works, how to document, and all the rest. Conversely, anyone who foists a programming language off on you had better be prepared to give you all the programming and debugging tools that programmers have come to expect. I mean, those joker's wouldn't write their package without **cross-reference listings, dumps, traces, step modes, editors,** and all the rest. Why should they expect you to? Agitate for decent tools. And if true programmability is important to you, you may want to buy the simpler package with the good tools over the fancy package that leaves you naked in the wind.

5.3.2. A Good Editor

The editor is the most important part of the tool kit and the one you're likeliest to use. It's even useful (and necessary) for simple command sequence substitutions. We have erasers and word processors because we're human and make mistakes. We have editors because we make programming mistakes.

The simplest way to provide excellent editing facilities is to make the application code look like it's a document and then to do the editing with an ordinary word processing package. Otherwise you need all that any editor needs: listings, change individual characters or commands, the ability to display and print all nonprinting and/or nondisplay characters, insert commands, delete commands, insert or delete characters, move around from command to command, and all the other obvious stuff. It's not too much to ask for, is it?

5.3.3. A Tool Kit

Here's what belongs in a tool kit. If you're so heavily into application programming that you need the kit, you've learned what these terms mean so I won't apologize for being technical. If you're not into application programming, you should have skipped all of Section 5.

Interpreter Operation. A step mode with your program running under the application interpreter so that you can step through it one command at a time and check everything that happens. HALT, PAUSE, STEP, and RESUME are essential.

Trace. Trace either by declared variable changes, statement executed, subroutine calls, for individual variables, lists of variables, etc. Normal trace on/off control.

Peek and Poke. Ability to look at application level control or data variables by name **(peek)** or to change the same **(poke)**. Providing these commands in either a host language such as Basic or the operating system is *not* what I mean. The idea is to peek and poke at user variables and controls by user names and not by some awful absolute location specified in octal or hex.

Cross Reference Lists. All declared and implicit variables, alphabetically and in appearance order. Statement label lists as well as all statement (numbers or positions) which target the statement.

Program Listings. The usual source with all nonprinting characters printed, with and without macro expansion, and with decent formatting and printing controls.

7
POLITENESS COUNTS

1. SYNOPSIS

Some obnoxious friends. The user-friendly con. Software personality. Ergonomics. Software induced stress. Programmer's personality. Polite and impolite software. Robust software.

2. FALSE FRIENDS AND TRUE

2.1. Some "Friends"

The Party

You're enjoying a stimulating conversation with friends or colleagues. Your lover is on the other side of the room, flirting with someone with just enough intensity to add spice to your relation. You're suffused in a glow from the wine. It's been a pleasant evening. Then, he (or she) walks in; laughing too loud; reason and taste obscured by overindulgence, belches in your face, puts an arm around your shoulder, and professes undying friendship. Meanwhile, the boor insults your closest friend with an ethnic joke, denigrates your profession, implies that only cretins would support your political party and assaults the fundamental credos of your religion. Then the slob pukes on your new shoes and slips to floor in a coma while holding on to, and thereby destroying, your expensive new party garment. But it's all done with a smile and with the belief that because of the smile, the behavior's "friendly."

Sincerely Yours

Used-car dealers, funeral directors, and con-artists can exude an unlimited supply of syrupy sincerity as they perpetrate atrocities on your wallet. They also smile a lot. If they're really smooth, you'll buy the spiel without even realizing that you've been conned. They appeal to your vain desire to get something for nothing; or they try guilt, or pride, or whatever works. They find your special button and push it with calculable results. But whatever the spiel, it's *very* friendly and *very* sincere.

Saints and Slobs

The image of the white-coated computer guru is part of the con. Put a white coat on a programmer and elevate him to the priesthood. Give him the license to hide behind jargon. Encourage him to act out the Hollywood myths. The image is so "scientific" that there's no room for incompetence or malevolence.

Back then, forty years ago, when they were struggling with balky vacuum tubes in the Moore school's basement, or with mounds of relays at Bell Labs, or in all the other academic and semi-academic environments that gave computers birth, that puristic, selfless, image was close to the truth. Four decades have passed now. We're as far from the early computers as a jet liner is from a World War I biplane. When you take that flight to the coast, you don't have an image of the cockpit crewed by Baron Von Richoven, Eddie Rickenbacker, and Lindbergh, do you?

A more appropriate image of the people who build and sell computers is a mixture of saints and slobs and everyone between. Think of these images: pudgy Jack Tramiel chomping on a cigar, figuring how to shave pennies on production costs; Sonny Monnosson, the Boston used-computer salesman who hawks PDP-11's at the computer shows with a spiel that seems like a carny act; frenetic Crazy Eddie offering you prices on a Belchfire PC that "are insane"; Douglas Hofstadter weaving a miraculous tapestry of computer science, art, and Bach; Jim Kidder bearing his and an industry's soul; a smooth-talking fake mesmerizing a group of gullible dentists from duBuque; a hacker breaking into credit rating files for the hell of it; a Cosa Nostra hoodlum with a computer science Ph.D. breaking into the same files with a more serious purpose; a careful craftsman who fiddles with her printout until it's perfect; a sociopathic programmer who builds a time bomb into the control software of an oil refinery: these are closer to the truth than the stereotypes.

2.2. The "User Friendly" Con

There's as much con to the personal computer sales game as there is to any expensive consumer product. That much is obvious to the millions of disappointed buyers of home computers which now lie rotting on the top shelf of the hall closet. It's obvious to the kid who flunked math because he was busy learning elementary programming from incoherent manuals. But it's less obvious to serious users of personal computers.

The worst con is the "user friendly" myth, and its little brother, "ergonomic." It's such a pervasive con, and so sincerely put, that the con-artists have conned not only buyers, but themselves. And who can doubt the depths of their sincerity. Pathological liars such as used-car salesmen actually believe their own spiels. It's a defense mechanism because without it they'd be consumed by guilt. They're so sincere that they could pass a lie detector test that showed that the last ten lemons they sold had indeed been driven only by the parson's wife to church on Sunday.

The most incompetent customer service department I've ever dealt with (Coddler) was the most sincere, most polite, and friendliest. But don't expect a generalization. There's no correlation, inverse or otherwise, between social graces and computer competence. I've gotten good service from gruff, taciturn, anti-social monsters—and bad. I've gotten both useful data and drivel with a smile.

What do you expect from your hardware or software? It isn't love or friendship—it's work. Do you expect friendliness from your car, washing machine, or other appliances? No! You expect them to work—and work reliably.

2.3. Software Vices and Virtues

You may accuse me of anthropomorphizing software—and so I do, even though I rank that as a sin: but we don't have a vocabulary for describing those aspects of software behavior which are analogous to human behavior. Software can't be virtuous or sinful, only programmers can: but we must bear the pain of their sins, or delight in the products of their virtue. So it's natural (albeit, improper) to ascribe sin and virtue to the software. We have no special words to describe machine behavior; so we borrow from psychology and human relation. Finally, it's cumbersome to always remind you, that in this context, it's not "insulting software", but "software produced by insulting programmers."

I reckon seven deadly software sins and seven cardinal software virtues. This chapter will help you recognize which are which and to understand why:

Not Working. Good software works; bad software doesn't. There is no greater sin than not working.

Lying. Bad software lies to you, plagues you with half truths, and misleads you in many other ways—sometimes, with the intention of making things "easier" or "friendlier." Bad news is bad news and better gotten over with.

Rigidity. Computers *are* rigid and so is software, but that has nothing to do with how rigid that software's *behavior* is while interacting with humans. Good software behavior is flexible, robust, and can tolerate human imprecision. There is no contradiction (as we'll see in Section 4.3).

Illogical. Good software is logical, predictable, self-consistent, and consistent with the job it's designed to do.

Patronizing. This has nothing to do with software, actually: it's an unwanted insertion of the programmer's personality.

Insulting. Insulting, impolite behavior is never correct.

Anthropomorphisms. Good software doesn't mimic humans. It doesn't use personal pronouns or your name.

There's one class of software for which almost all sins are acceptable—entertainment software. If the software is for a game, of if it's designed to let you participate in an adventure or a story, then all but the first of the sins can be delightful. But truly skillful entertainment software will, in its peculiar way, follow the above rules. It will work, although it may not seem to; it may lie and cheat;* it may be rigid and unforgiving, but not about trivial things like miskeying; there may be an off-the-wall logic and the game's purpose is to discover it; and snide remarks, sympathy, insults, anthropomorphisms, and the programmer's personality are just part of the game.

3. SOFTWARE PERSONALITY

3.1. What and Why

Many software packages, unfortunately, have personalities—the designer's. The programmer's personality may be so deeply imbedded that it's not only

---

*I played a fun blackjack game that not only cheated, but also moralized. Optimum strategy did better than expected at the "dollar" table, but the "dealer" became more crooked the higher the stakes. You could lose millions in minutes at the thousand dollar table. And what was worse, it had a built-in hustle that tempted you to the higher stakes.

manifested in the way the program works with the user, but in the program's very structure. Although it's technical, illogical behavior (from the user's point of view) is often caused by illogical internal structures. The best software tends to be internally clean, and externally it exhibits no obvious personality at all.

We expect the programmer's personality in games software just as we expect a writer's personality to come through in a book or a director's in a movie. But what about serious software? Personality gets in the way. You paid for word processing, not for the programmer's ego. Unwanted personality gets into serious software, because for many programmers, software is a game. Personality injection is immaturity rampant—of programmers and of the software industry.

We've accepted the insinuation of the programmer's personality because it's an industry tradition. It's encouraged by the stereotypes, the exploits of hackers, the hyped-up press, and academe. So pervasive is this myth, that not only do users believe that the programmer's personality *must* be part of software, but so do programmers, software designers, vendors, and computer manufacturers. We are all conning ourselves, brothers and sisters.

The tradition began in the early days of software when the field was dominated by (very young) mathematicians. They were a good source of talent for this new field. Early programming was brutal. It required the kind of mental discipline that at that time was taught mostly in mathematics departments. And what's more, most of early software concerned problems that had a high mathematical content. Mathematics is not science, it's not engineering, and it's certainly not psychology. It is an exquisitely pure art form that may occasionally be useful—but most mathematicians couldn't care less. They treasure elegance and brilliance far above utility: and the greatest utility to mathematicians is the possibility of applying a mathematical result to mathematics itself. Above all, because the doing of mathematics is a pure art, it is an essentially egotistical process.

Early programming was brutal, as I said, and the resources into which the programs were placed, the early computers, were inadequate. Cramming a program into the computer's pitifully small memory, and then getting it to work, often took dazzling insights. There was no room for discipline of the kind on which we now insist because such disciplinary constraints squelched the kind of creativity that was then so essential to getting the job done. And the pressure didn't relax. They'd program a job ten times larger than any one could imagine that computer could handle but when they got a new computer that had ten times the power, the problems had escalated a hundredfold. That kind of pressure continued into the early seventies.

The programs, like mathematics, were dominated by the efforts of individuals, rather than by cooperative efforts of hundreds of programmers. It was only when the programs started to take hundreds or thousands of work years to build that the industry started to shed the cult of the individual. Personal computer software has followed exactly the same course. It started with kitchen-table efforts by one or two clever programmers, lone hackers, and all the rest, and only recently have the programs which the users want reached the complexity of mainframe software.

But what has it left us? We have managers who grew up in the free-for-all atmosphere of early software, who now look back longingly at their early acts of clever egotism. We talk about "brilliant programmers" rather than craftsmanship. I've heard managers complain with pride about their uncontrollable, sociopathic, "software geniuses"—it seems as if every software department needs at least one like that. The press and Hollywood, always two decades behind reality, reinforce the myths of egotistical software. So with all of that going for them, is it any wonder that we must suffer the intrusion of the programmer's personality?

3.2. What's Really Giving You Those Headaches

3.2.1. Do they Get Headaches?

Computers, especially personal computers, have been blamed for everything from Addison's disease to zoophilism: but headaches are the most common complaint. I'll squelch the protests up front by asserting that some computer operators *do* get headaches and that some suffer from even more serious symptoms. We shouldn't poo-poo these symptoms, whatever their cause, or as some neandertals* have done, attribute the phenomenon to "female complaints" because so many computer and word-processing operators are women. The symptoms are real; the discomforts are real; and if you've no concern for human dignity and suffering, then at least the productivity loss attending such widespread complaints should be a concern.

3.2.2. Physical Causes

The physical situation in computer use can be a problem for new users; but it's less of a problem than most people think, and far less of a problem

---

*My wife tells me that I'm perpetuating the malignment of Neandertal man—there's no evidence that they were of subhuman intelligence or as brutish as some modern day sexists.

than the hawkers of **ergonomic** doo-dads would have you believe. Every new technology brings a rash of physical complaints and putative cures for them. Look through 19th century literature for examples: trains, cars, electricity, running water, indoor plumbing, and other innovations are blamed by hysterical muckraking writers for spontaneous abortions, gout, and yellow fever: while on the next page, electricity and magnetism are hawked by quacks as the cure for the self-same problems. We're seeing a replay of all that now. Most of the complaints will not be solved by varying the screens' tilt or reducing the glare. The physical problems, for the most part, are caused by an unfamiliar physical situation. Here are some examples:

Eyestrain. For many new users, the computer is not only a major change in the way they work, but a sudden escalation of eye usage. My ophthalmologist friends tell of frequent eye complaints by new computer users. Their previous way of working was not as demanding on their eyes. They had needed glasses all along, but never knew it until they started heavy computer use. Fixing the screen's color, intensity, glare, tilt, and all the rest, will help, but won't solve the problem if new glasses is what you need. Have your eyes checked before you buy the ergonomic what's its.

Backaches. The manager who used to spend hours looking *down* at papers on his desk is now spending the same time at a keyboard, which is often at desk height, and he's looking *up* at a screen. Furthermore, he does it while sitting on the same chair he's been using for years. The keyboard is too high—look at any typist's desk: the typewriter is on a return unit that's two inches lower than the desk. The chair height is probably wrong, and the CRT may be poorly positioned. I've used a receptionist's desk with a proper height return piece for years. And, when my back has acted up, I've swiped one of those really comfortable secretarial chairs with a good lumbar support.

Computer use tends to keep us in a limited set of postures. The more we use the computer, the more time we spend in such postures, and the more important comfort becomes. But before you spend thousands on "ergonomic" furniture, see if the old-fashioned secretarial furniture that's been in use for decades will do the trick. And don't be chintzy—if you spend a few thousand on the computer, you can afford to spend a few hundred on using it in comfort.

Bad Designs. The most notorious (but not the worst) piece of bad hardware design was the first IBM PC keyboard. The main problems with that keyboard was the smallness of the most heavily used key of all, ⟨RETURN⟩, and the confusing placement of the shift keys. Both of these deficiencies invited keystroke errors. A bad keyboard will increase your typing error rate. A fuzzy screen will contribute to errors in addition to eyestrain. Every physical characteristic of a system, including the noise made by the fan, can contribute to error reduction or error increase. And the more errors you make, the more likely you are to have a headache. If you don't touch-type yourself, have the keyboard and system tried out as a word processor by someone who does. There is almost no cost difference between a good, comfortable, design and a piece of junk that's impossible to use for hours at a time. And, because "ergonomics" has been such a popular bandwagon, almost every new system is acceptable or rapidly becoming so.

3.2.3. Social and Organizational Causes

The computer's use is new. It would be silly to think that with its use there's no shift in organizational structure or the responsibilities of individuals. Word-processing departments are good example. Before word-processing, the typical job is that of a secretary-typist who reports to one supervisor or who services a small department. Word processing equipment is brought in, and now the operators of this newly centralized department have to deal with many different departments. They are forever barraged by conflicting priorities and requirements. Furthermore, the scope of their job has narrowed. The combination of these factors is enough to give anybody headaches, no matter how good or bad the hardware is. Any person who goes from noncomputer methods to computer methods has changed his product. Your new product may increase or decrease the scope of your work and interactions. It may increase or decrease your responsibilities and/or your authority. Whatever the change is, it is often profound for you and your organization. All such changes induce stress. Headaches and physical symptoms often accompany stress. Talk these changes over with a human resources expert before you buy the ergonomic whatchamacallits.

3.2.4. The Cause No One Talks About

I shared the word-processing department with experienced operators for about two months. I had been directing the test design of a large software system. Because the software specification had changed, we had to change thousands of pages of test documents. I was also responsible for quality assurance over the test process itself, so it was my job to review those thousands of pages of documentation. The easiest way to do the job was to read, review, check, edit, modify, and all the rest that had to be done with that massive document, directly on the word-processor. At the same time, I was polishing the manuscript of my latest book, *Software Testing Techniques,* which had also been put on the word-processor. Once I had become a proficient word-processing operator, it was easier for me to correct and edit directly, rather than to have an intermediary operator between me and my work. The result of both of these efforts was that I was spending 60 hours a week at the word-processor.

There were two operators: Pat and Helen. Pat was the senior operator: an exceptionally intelligent older woman with a fine command of English and no technological phobias. Helen was younger, but also intelligent and diligent. They had taken the training courses, they'd read the instruction manuals, and they had headaches: but I didn't—and neither did Linda, a professional programmer who did almost as much work at the word-processor on that document as I did. We'd been through all the physical stuff. The lighting was good, the furniture problems had been corrected, we had the anti-glare stuff on the screens; and those of us who needed them had new eyeglasses.

What Linda and I were doing was more complicated than the typical word-processing work, and as a result, we came up against Coddler's many bugs more often than did the word processing operators. Yet, word-processing operators got headaches and programmers didn't (much). It took several weeks, but the headaches began to diminish when Linda and I were present—the gurus' laying on of the hand? No! It was our (the programmers') continual reassurances that the problem of the moment was caused by a bug in that software and not by anything that the operator had done. There'd be a muttered curse from the other side of the room, and then "Linda?" or "Boris?", and one of us would examine the situation, try a few keys, and pronounce: "Dumbass software! Idiot programmer!" or some other equally reassuring statement. Linda and me, as software test and quality assurance experts, had a better than average sensitivity to bugs and their effects. It would never occur to us to doubt ourselves. We *knew* that we had not struck the key that could wipe the disc. We *knew* that a crash could never be our fault, no matter what key we'd struck. We *knew* that the cryptic message on the screen was a programmer's cop-out. *We* were completely immune to the continual psychological debilitation brought about by buggy software. We were immune to **software-induced stress.**

I've combed the computer and psychology literature for some recognition of software-induced stress and have found none. I have tried to interest hardware and software vendors and others in this subject, but I've gotten a reception which is slightly less polite than that given to software quality assurance.* It's not a deep thing—it's common sense. Bad software insults the user and induces stress. Because most users view computers (and their programmers) as infallible, they emotionally accept the blame for crashes and misbehavior, even if intellectually they know it's not their fault. My psychologist friends tell me that the effect is cumulative: every time you're insulted by a prompt or otherwise abused, no matter how small the abuse, it leaves a scar. When the accumulated pain reaches some level it can express itself in headaches and even worse physical symptoms. Very bad software even gives me a headache. I have been insulted, patronized, lied to, mislead, and had my head twisted about by "logic" that could have only been created during a psychedelic trance.

What's the real purpose of this long harangue, the above anecdotes, this chapter, and much of this book? It's an inoculation against software-induced stress. It won't cure the software, but recognizing junk, and achieving self-confidence in the use of computers and in calling garbage software what it is, will help you achieve the immunity which programmers have against software induced stress—the same immunity which blinds them to the unfortunate side effects of their bad software.

3.2.5. Psychological Software Screening

There's been a lot of good research done on the psychology of programming. It's aimed at finding the psychological barriers to software quality and productivity. It's good research and as a result, we know more about what makes a programmer tick than ever before—and probably than is known about most other occupations except astronauts, test pilots, and football players. But we know almost nothing about the psychological impact on the user of the programmer's product. They're not at all the same. What turns a person into a comedian is different from what makes people laugh. For every programmer, there are thousands of users. Who, in the grand scheme of things, is more important? Who should accommodate to whom?

---

*Hardware vendors sell hardware, so it's never been in their interest to provide efficient software, except when forced to it by competition. Similarly, software vendors have no interest in publicly expressing concern of the possibly harmful effect of their software. For now, they'd rather make believe that the problem doesn't exist.

As of 1985, there has been almost no research done on the psychological impact of software (especially bad software). Software producers don't screen their products for psychological correctness. There's a lot of talky-talk about "user-friendly software," but none about the hostility lurking just beneath that "friendliness." The entire question is not now part of the scheme of doing software things: it won't become part of software design until you express your righteous anger over abusive software.

3.3. The Programmer's Personality

3.3.1. Mainframe Programmers and Programming

Mainframe software is big and complicated. It's the product of many pro-grammers over a long period of time. There are packages in use today which were started more than twenty years ago. Such programs have gone through many modifications and have migrated from one computer model to an-other. But for all their complexity, only a tiny part of mainframe software interacts with humans, and when they do, the human is often a technician or software specialist who has a high tolerance for computer abuse. Some-times the software *is* abusive to operators, but because it's private affair, completely controlled by the operating entity, it's easier to tell the operator to "take it" than it is to change the software. After all, who cares if a few hundred clerks in an insurance office go bananas. But because of their lon-gevity, the complaints filter through and eventually, the rough edges are worn off.

3.3.2. Personal Computer Programmers and Programming

Much personal computer software, especially some of the earlier packages, was produced (and is still produced) by programmers who are not in the mainstream of software development. Some software authors went directly from a university (or no formal training at all) to form their own company armed only with a good idea and lots of guts: they never learned the dis-cipline which the rest of the industry has found to be so essential to quality software. There is more ego per instruction in personal computer software than in any other kind of software. The personal computer software field has been going through a replay of the general computer field as it was twenty years ago. They are relearning the old mistakes. And while main-frame programmers have learned to keep software as personality neutral as possible, much of personal computer software's abusive behavior is the result of being new and unpolished and of being written by programmers who do not have a tradition of *not* inserting their ego into the software.

3.3.3. What's Wrong With a Programmer's Ego?

What is really wrong with a programmer's personality crashing through the software in prompts and messages? After all, we allow, even expect, the author's personality to come through in a book—even in technical books such as this one. There are several things wrong with it, even though software has many parallels to literary works:

1. *It's Not What You Paid For.* You paid for word-processing, spreadsheet, data-base management, or something else that works and not a game.
2. *Personality Conflicts.* You have a personality and the way you use the package is a reflection of your personality. Good software becomes an extension of your personality. It's hard to achieve that kind of rapport if the programmer's personality intrudes. There are tens of thousands of users for every programmer, so it's likelier that the programmer's and user's personalities will clash than it is that their personalities will be compatible. A personality blank-slate is best for software because it gives you the greatest freedom, as a user, for self-expression.
3. *It's Badly Done.* I could accept the intrusion of the programmer's personality if it were done with skill and sensitivity. But it's *so* badly done. Most of the personality intrusions are accidental. There's no point to it. It's not to instruct, or to make it easier to learn, or fun to use. It doesn't fit into a plan. It doesn't complement the package's work, but detracts from it. It's gross, obvious, and usually childish.

3.4. What to Do About Boorish Software

3.4.1. Complain

Don't buy boorish software if you can help it, and tell the dealer why. But if you're stuck with it, the only thing you can do is complain. You must take a statistical attitude. Don't expect your letter to accomplish anything by itself: but every letter is powerful because less than one out of a thousand users will take the trouble to document their complaints. Therefore, your letter has a thousand times the weight you think that it might have. If enough users took the trouble to complain, we'd all have better software sooner.

3.4.2. Dos and Don'ts About Complaints

1. Don't complain about missing features—that belongs in a positive letter of suggested improvements. Unless of course, the missing features are essential and you were led to believe that they existed.
2. Document all bugs and technical problems.
3. Group your complaints into bugs, manuals, insults, clumsiness, cockpit error induction, misleading, etc. Use screen dumps and specific examples for each case.
4. Avoid generalized bitches. Be as specific as possible. It's better to have a twenty-page letter of specific gripes than a two-page letter of generalized complaints. Put yourself in software developer's place. He'd rather respond to substantive specifics than to generalized philosophy.
5. Do make specific suggestions for improvement or corrections. If a prompt is misleading, give them an alternate, more precise prompt to use. If the program's response is insulting, show them how to say it better.
6. Don't wave the competitor in their face. They know all about the competitive products and understand their strengths and weaknesses better than you do.
7. Be realistic. Don't expect satisfaction and compensation for consequential damages.
8. Don't expect gratitude, credit, or feedback. Consider yourself lucky if you get a form-letter back that acknowledges that you sent them something. If the package is changed, you'll know if your letter had an impact. It's not that the vendors are ungrateful, but that their legal position makes it almost impossible for them to safely acknowledge your contribution.
9. Insist on a no-cost update and/or upgrade. Ask when the revised version will be available.
10. Don't whine.
11. Be sure the problem is theirs, rather than yours. All you need is to complain about one cockpit error which is your fault (unless you can clearly show how the package misled you into the error) to have the whole letter dumped into the wastebasket.

12. Dont' threaten a lawsuit. If it's that serious, let your lawyer write the letter.

3.4.3. To Whom Should You Complain?

I use two documents: a cover letter and a report. The letter is tailored to the recipient, but contains almost no technical material. It's purpose is to get the report acted upon. The report has the technical material. With word-processing you can send letters to *all* of the following. You'll want to tailor the cover letter for each recipient—"In your review of the Belchfire package you said . . . but the following is the truth." "You have been advertising a product whose deficiencies, as outlined in the accompanying technical report, border on fraud;" and so on. It's a multiprong attack intended to get the complaints and suggestion to responsible individuals, no matter who along the line chooses to block it.

The Purchasing Chain:
1. The retailer who sold you the package—he's a powerful force for quality, but needs ammunition. He doesn't have the time or resources to document your verbal comments. A written list makes his job easy. He'll take your report and slap his own cover letter on it.
2. Your own purchasing agent and any others responsible for software buys such as the data processing department or the corporate personal computer guru.

The Hardware Vendor:
3. The vice president of software quality assurance. Although it may not be their package, it's often sold under their label and it has their tacit approval. Also, some of the things you're complaining about may be peculiar to that version and the way it was tailored for that computer.
4. Public relations VP.
5. Executive in charge of the personal computer division.
6. Director of customer technical service.
7. The regional sales and service organization.

The Software Vendor:
8. VP of public relations.
9. VP of software QA.

10. VP of technical development.
11. VP of customer service and support.
12. The chief programmer and any person whose name appears in the documentation or on the disc.
13. Any designated ombudsman.

The Press:
14. The editor of hardware and/or software user's group journals—especially the independents.
15. Reviewers and editors of big-ticket journals such as *BYTE, PC-WORLD,* etc.
16. For vertical packages, letters to the appropriate industry journals.

The Image Makers:
17. Independent review and testing organizations such as *Software Digest—* especially if they've published a review.
18. Letters to any reviewer or author whose words of praise may have influenced you to buy the product.
19. The business sections of your local newspaper, business magazines, *The Wall Street Journal,* or any other publication in which ads for the product appeared—ads which may have influenced you to buy the product.
20. Letters to anybody who endorsed the product.
21. Computer technical and trade organizations such as ACM, DPMA, and IEEE.

4. SOFTWARE MANNERS

4.1. General

This section is a catalog of ill-mannered software with examples of how good software might do the same thing. Crashes, which are the ultimate in bad manners, are discussed in Chapter 4.

4.2. Lying

4.2.1. Why Do They Lie?

I call any untruth or misleading statement a "lie" in this context. A lie is expressed in a program's message. The typical lies deal with the status of

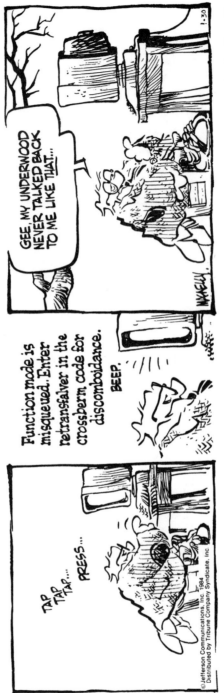

something, the results of processing, or in a response to your command or command error. There are several reasons for lying software:

1.Wrong Message. The programmer has inadvertantly used the wrong message. It's a rare case, but a common excuse.

2. Bad Logic. In a misguided attempt to save memory, the programmer miscategorizes the situation and merges it with the message for a different error. For example, your actual error was a keying error while entering a file name, but because it involved retrieval, the message says "FILE NOT FOUND" instead of "FILENAME SYNTAX ERROR."

3. Laziness. Messages are written by programmers. The same message is used in different parts of the package: consequently, the messages are stored in a message list. Any new message must be added to that list. The programmer meant to say that there was a disc error but there is no such message on the list, so instead of installing the correct message he utilizes "NO SUCH FILE."

4. Memory. As above, but the new message is not installed because there isn't enough memory. A version designed for a larger memory might not lie.

5. Cop-Out. This is the most common cause of all lies. The programmer doesn't know how to handle a situation which the software has detected. The cause may be complicated and not easily categorized—instead of doing the work required to specify the situation precisely, he cops out by using a convenient message, such as "USER INPUT ERROR," thereby making you feel that you're to blame.

6. Illogicals. Internal checks have conclusively shown that there is an unrecoverable problem (know to programmers as an **illogical**). The programmer (and program) knows that there's trouble but hasn't the foggiest notion of what or how. A correct message in that case, would be: "PROBLEM OR UNKNOWN CASE—ABORTING." Instead of admitting to his justifiable perplexity, the programmer lies—"USER INPUT ERROR," "NO SUCH FILE," and "DIRECTORY ERROR—ALL FILES LOST" are three of the more hostile responses around.

7. Misguided Kindness. I hate this lie above all others. Something bad has happened, such as a lost file or scrambled data, and instead of telling you outright so that you can do something about it, the program lies by giving you half truths and hiding the bad news.

8. Guilt. The programmer suffers either from deserved or undeserved guilt, but usually, it's a reflection of corporate policy. It often happens in conjunction with misguided kindness. So a misleading or ambiguous message is provided ostensibly in order to make you feel better, but really it's to make the programmer feel better.

Notice how the sources of lies reflect the programmer's personality and also the personality of the organization that created the software. Programs lie because people lie—either to others or to themselves. I don't know why people lie.

4.2.2. Generic Lies

Sometimes I think that programmers take a course in lying, or else there's a very popular underground text circulating the industry, which somehow, I haven't yet seen. The following generic lies cover almost all the lies you're likely to be fed. Couldn't they at least come up with some originals once in a while?

It's Our Secret. The archetype is an undocumented message or coded gobbledegook. Don't accept that kind of garbage, please. You have a right to know and to understand *anything* which appears on *your* screen, which results from *your* actions, on *your* data. This is a terrible lie because it's confusing, it doesn't tell you what you can or should do about it, and it's as patronizing as software can get.

Syntax Error. This message should only occur in response to a user input, and only after the command terminator key (say ⟨RETURN⟩) has been struck. If the message is just "SYNTAX ERROR," it's a half lie. Something's wrong with what you typed. You should be given some hint of what you did wrong. Here are the components of a truthful syntax error message:

1. Display exactly what you did type and point to the place at which the error was detected.
2. Display the correct syntax.
3. Display the reference manual page.
4. Reassure that no damage has been done (if true) and then repeat the prompt that led to the message. A statement of the form "REENTER COMMAND" is sufficient reassurance.
5. Any other information which can help identify the specific syntax error. For example, "FILE NAME TOO LONG," "FILE NAME CANNOT START WITH NUMBER," "MISSING COLON," "MISSING COMMA," and so on.

Too Big—Too Many. This is often used as a cop-out. The generic form is: "DISC FULL," "DOCUMENT TOO BIG," "TOO MANY REC-

ORDS," "INDEX FULL," and so on. Merging "DISC READ ERROR," "DISC FULL," and "TOO MANY FILES," which are not at all the same things, is the most common lie.

A "TOO BIG" message means that you've hit a limit of some sort. It's not a lie to tell you that. It becomes a lie when either it isn't true, or worse, when the program doesn't check the limits before starting the process, starts it, and then after the fact, after destroying your data, it tells you that the job can't be done. Approach all limits with care, and if you must operate there, be sure you have a backup. Then, when you get the "TOO BIG" message, check to see if anything's been destroyed as a result.

No Such—Can't Find. This is an easy one to confirm as a lie. Most often, this message is not a lie because you *did* type in the wrong filename, say. It is a half lie if you can't see what it is you did type in. The correct, truthful, form of this message is: FILE yourfilename NOT FOUND", or some other indication that will tell you what you did. If the package doesn't display what you typed, repeat it, very carefully. Also, for files, check the directory by some independent means such as the operating system's directory command. There is always some way to confirm if what you asked for does or doesn't exist.

Invalid—Wrong Type. This message is often used where a syntax error message should be used and vice-versa. It is also used where a CAN'T FIND message should have been used. An INVALID message means that although what you typed is syntactically correct, it exceeds some limit or is in some other way incorrect. For example, you might have asked for an overly large record number, or named an index file when you wanted a data file. The truthfulness principles that applied to syntax errors apply here also: what was wrong, specific field, specific limit or form, reference manual reference, and so on.

Hardware Status Problem. The status of hardware is not valid. For example: printer not ready, disc drive door open, no paper in printer, things turned off. The truthfulness of most hardware status problems can be easily checked. However, status related lies abound in communications software. Most of the problems I've had with communications software has involved hardware status lies. My solution has been to put a low-cost **status monitor** on the line so that I can get a independent confirmation of the line's status.

Data Status Problem. Like hardware, but for files and records. For example: "FILE NOT OPEN," "MUST CLOSE FILE FIRST," "DUPLICATE FILE." The prompts that result in such messages have the same problems as the prompts that lead to INVALID messages: they are inherently prone to cockpit errors. Truthful software will display exactly what you typed.

Program Status Problem. You've entered a syntactically valid command with valid fields and options but the command can't be executed in that program state. For example: "PITCH CHANGE NOT ALLOWED WHILE PRINTING," "EDIT NOT ALLOWED DURING DATA ENTRY." Truthful software, especially for complicated integrated packages, will always let you know what state you're in by something displayed on the screen, such as in a status line. Really terrible software actually lies. The command is denied, but something is nevertheless executed.

No Can Do. There are many reasons why a program can't execute a valid command. The file type could be wrong, other prerequisites might not be satisifed. Furthermore, it's not always possible to determine that fact until the command is attempted. For example, you command the package to merge incompatible files. It has to fetch the files before it can check compatibility. So it's partway into the command before it tells you there's a problem. NO CAN DO situations are cockpit error prone, so such messages should say "NO CAN DO because. . . . " Anything less is a half-truth. Furthermore, if there is a possibility of a NO CAN DO which can only be detected after the processing has started, then it's imperative that the program work on a copy of the data rather than on the actual data.

False Hopes. An error condition is detected and you're given an unambiguous message about it. Then you're offered a recovery procedure—which doesn't work. For example: the program tells you that the directory is lost and offers to reconstruct it. You agree. You try it again, and the same error message appears. I've had this kind of thing dangled in front of me with disc read errors, write errors, directory failures, searches, data inserts, and all the rest. What makes it a lie is that there do exist very specific circumstances in which the recovery procedure will work, but there's no sensible documentation of that. The lie exists because you assume that whatever is offered will work, but the programmer knows that it will not always work. If false hopes are to be avoided, then manuals must tell you how likely recovery will be and not offer it at all if the odds exceed 3 : 1. The worst false hopes are those that lull you into believing that there has been a successful recovery, usually by a message of the form "DONE." Be a cynic. Never assume that it works, and confirm its correctness many times before you rely on it.

4.3. Rigidity

4.3.1. The Rigidity-Robustness Pseudo-Paradox

Computers take things literally. They're monomoniacal. They do precisely what they're commanded to do; nothing more, and nothing less. Software, because it is written in a programming language which is analogous to the hardware's operation, is similarly rigid. It will do exactly what the program statements say and no more or less. It seems therefore, paradoxical to talk about robust, forgiving, software, that's tolerant of human imprecision. There is no conflict and there is no paradox. The programmer, albeit with much thought and work, can exploit the computer's prissy exactitude to create tolerant software.

As examples of how that might be done, consider the selection of one of several choices from a menu. Intolerant software forces you to enter a number to select the choice, but good software uses several different methods simultaneously:

1. *A Number.* The program checks to see that it is a number and that it is one of the valid numbers.
2. *The First Letter of the Choice.* It wasn't a number, so the program checks to see if it's a letter, and if the letter corresponds to one of the first letters of the choices.
3. *The Cursor Keys.* The program keeps track of where the cursor is. It also knows that it's in a command entry mode, and consequently, the action of the cursor keys will be different. Each cursor keystroke is programmed to land the cursor on one of the valid choices.
4. ⟨*CONTROL*⟩ *Key.* If the keystrokes starts with the ⟨CONTROL⟩ key, then that is the mode being used. The next keystroke is checked for a valid command letter, which furthermore corresponds to one of the choices on the screen.

There's more to it than I've shown above. Its obvious, even if you know nothing about programming, that handling all of those variations and options takes work. A very robust package might use twice as many instructions to do things because of that flexibility. As another example, an intolerant package will insist on all file names, say in upper case, with no preceding or following blanks. A good package strips off the preceding and following blanks and then converts your lower-case letters (if any) to upper case, and proceeds from there. Even though each component of the program is itself rigid and uncompromising, the collection of options is robust and flexible.

The key to robust designs is thought. Designers must think through not only all the valid ways of doing things, but also all the errors which the user might make at every point. If robustness is designed in from the beginning, then these variations fall into patterns which allow the creation and use of generalized software segments: then, the extra cost is not severe.

4.3.2. Weak and Robust Option Selection

Let's for the moment, think like a good programmer would when she designs a menu selection method. The focus isn't on the valid things the user might do, but on invalid things:

1. A valid choice.
2. A syntactically correct choice that doesn't exist: e.g., option 7 out of 5.
3. A syntactically invalid choice: e.g., a letter instead of a number.
4. A nonchoice: e.g., hitting the RETURN key without making a selection, the UNDO key, the STOP key, etc.
5. Too many choices: e.g., choice "1234567890."
6. An off-the wall choice: "⟨CONROL⟩ &."
7. Abort or change state: e.g., ⟨ESCAPE⟩, ⟨HELP⟩, ⟨QUIT⟩.

The same principle, with variations, applies to letter choices, keywords, cursor selection, and all the rest. Each selection method has an equivalent set of considerations. If the software is really robust, then several different methods can be used, and the programmer must not only think in terms of potential errors for each method alone, but for combinations of methods. It is as complicated as it sounds and it can twist your head around to think about it, but that's what programmers are paid to do.

4.3.3. Weak and Robust Syntax and Format Tolerance

Anything you enter which requires a specific format is error-prone. The worst software quits (and crashes) on the least input error. Programmers should be sympathetic to the problems of user syntax errors, because programmers make so many of them while writing programs. I've seen bad programmers who wouldn't put in a smidgin of tolerance to a user input error squeal like a stuck pig when the compiler rejected their program over a minor error. Bad software has absolutely no tolerance. If you don't follow (the often undocumented) rules with exquisite precision, then bye-bye birdy. Total intolerance to user errors requires the least effort on the programmer's part. Here are various ways in which polite software can be tolerant (and impolite software, intolerant):

1. Upper-case/lower case. Good software accepts either in any mix or order.
2. Spaces. Good software always allows spaces wherever they make sense and as many as you might want to insert.
3. Alternate punctuations. Allows different kinds of punctuations between fields—spaces, commas, colons, dashes, and so on.

4. Alternate forms. Numbers, especially, can be entered in many different formats. For example: "4000", "4000.", "4000.0", "4000.000", "4,000", and "4.0E3" all represent the same number. It's no big deal these days to accept all those variations and more. Similar tolerance can be built into the formats of other fields.
5. Field order variations. This one is tough and could be confusing. Flexible software permits some variations.
6. Synonyms. Common Synonyms are allowed: DISC and DISK, DELETE and DESTROY, CLEAR and ERASE, GET and FETCH, EXIT and QUIT.
7. Abbreviations. Allowed where it makes sense and it's safe: DES, DEL, CLE, FET, EX, and so on.
8. Filler words. These words aren't essential but are more natural: STORE ⟨filename⟩ *TO . . .*, FETCH ⟨filename⟩ *FROM*. Filler words can change a mechanistic command language into something which is closer to normal parlance. Filler words can also be used to separate fields instead of using artificial punctuation.
9. Patient. Good software lets you change you mind as often as you want to, up to the last keystroke (⟨RETURN⟩, say), which actually activates the command.

4.3.4. *Value Tolerance*

Anything you enter has a range of permissible values. That's obvious for numbers, but it also applies to other fields, such as **keys.** For example: there is a first and last record; the first key in your file may be "ALPHONSE" and the last "ZBIGNEW." There is an implied order to things, of which numerical and alphabetical are the most common. We can compact the discussion by treating everything as if it were a number. For each thing, there is a minimum and maximum value which the system can handle, and a minimum and maximum value in the object—a file, say. There may also be forbidden values or missing values in between. For example, you start pagination with page 205. The valid page numbers for your document are 205 through 221, say. The valid page numbers of the system are 1 through 999.

No program should bomb for incorrect values—the least that a program must do is tell you that your entry is out of range and allow you to try again. But that's not enough to claim tolerance.

1. Lower limit tolerance. The program's lower limit is 10, say, and the file's least value is 20. Accept lower values than 10 or 20 and default to the lower value but give the user an opportunity to reject the default.
2. Lower value tolerance. For example, a command to print from page 1

of a document whose first page number is 10 will be interpreted to mean to print the first page, or page 10.

3. Upper limit. As with lower limit, default to the highest value. For example, accept page number 5000, but treat it as page 221 or "END".

4. Forbidden and nonexistent values. It's difficult to select a consistently useful default for these cases. For example, a communication package allows 75, 150, 300, 600, 1200, 2400, 4800, and 9600 baud. It's not clear what the user intends with an entry of 900 baud. The best thing to do is to reject the command. If a default is used, then the program must give you the opportunity to reject the default.

Value tolerance can be complicated when several values interact. For example, in word-processing, left and right margins, tab placements, and letter pitch are not independent. Similarly, setting up a communication link can require a dozen or more parameters whose values are interrelated. The validity of an entry depends on the entries already installed. Rotten software doesn't give you a hint as to what the conflict might be and simply rejects the current value, and all the previous values you've entered. Another alternative for bad software is to accept the values, even though they conflict, resulting in strange processing, data loss, and who knows what else. Robust software behaves as it would for individual, independent numbers (to the extent that it's possible), gives you the opportunity to accept or reject default values, and also tells you exactly what appears to be conflicting with what. It takes a lot of extra software. In complicated cases, the software required to validate all the values and their combination can be much more complicated than the software that actually does the work. In communications systems, for example, the software that checks the setup is four times larger than the software that does the setup. Because this situation occurs often during installation, it's one of the reasons that installation software is so intolerant and buggy.

4.3.5. Idiot and Malicious Idiot Proofing

Good software is idiot proof, but that's not enough. It must be **malicious idiot proof.*** The most malicious idiots of all should be software quality assurance independent testers. The idea behind idiot proofing is to try to predict *all* the incorrect actions which a user might take. That goes beyond striking incorrect keys, double keys, and so on. Let's say that the vendor sells 50,000 copies of the package. That's a potential for 50,000 different

---

*I confess that that's how we programmers tend to talk about users—"idiots", "malicious idiots", "apes", and other, unprintable, epithets. Does that tell you something?

sets of errors. The kinds of errors I make in using a computer are totally different from the errors you make—not fewer, nor better, nor worse, just different. Idiot proofing means being smart and forgiving over not only common user errors, but uncommon ones. Here's a sample:

Disc. Wrong kind (hard sector instead of soft sector), single-sided rather than dual-sided, the cleaning disc, write-protect tab on instead of off and vice-versa, wrong density, formatted for a different computer, not formatted, wrong-way in, dirty, scratched, torn.

Disc Drive. Door open, not changing the disc, changing the wrong disc, wrong drive, opening the door while running, drive turned off, drive doesn't exist.

Printer. Printer doesn't match installation parameters, off-line, busy, broken, out of paper (ribbon, ink, etc.), wrong interface cable.

Communications. Wrong speed, code, mode, protocol, message length, interrupted communications, noise on the line, breaks, voice, modem turned off, playing with the modem keys, the other party is haywire.

Configuration Parameters. All possible incompatibilities between the stored version of the system's configuration parameter values (e.g., amount of memory) and the actual values.

Files. Wrong type, no such file, no such type, empty file, files with everything deleted (not the same as empty).

Idiot proofing the software consists of making it invulnerable to the above user errors and many more. So many more that it takes several chapters of a book to list them—and even that's only a larger sample. By invulnerable, I don't mean that the program will do what you intended, because that would require telepathic software, but that:

1. It doesn't crap up data or lose it.
2. It doesn't crash.
3. It asks for a new command or action.

Malicious idiot proofing goes beyond that because it's based on detailed knowledge of the program's structure, its weak points, and the kinds of design bugs which programmers are likely to make. The malicious idiot, usually an independent tester, uses combinations of the above potential user errors to create more complicated error conditions and malfunctions. One of the marks of good software is the difficulty an experienced tester will have in "breaking" it. Garbage software is so easy to break that its pathetic.

4.4. Patronizing

The same outfit that publishes the textbook on computer lies also runs a school for snots. Before computers, they ran three-day seminars for waiters in pretentious French restaurants, especially for the sommelier—"Ze Chateau Haut-Brion dix-neuf quarante-sept (at $500 a pop) is, of course more appropriate to your selection of angoustine-aux-cravat, but if you can't afford it, we can send ze boy out for a jug of Thunder-Fizz, which might be more to your taste!" I know several nurses and they all swear that "And how are *we* feeling today" is not essential to the practice of medicine. There must be a large, sick, segment of the population with a need to be patronized—why else would it be so common among waiters, hairdressers, real estate agents, nurses, elementary school teachers, interior decorators, and programmers?

Patronizing behavior has nothing to do with computers. *A* patronizes *B* by setting himself up as superior to *B* by virtue of his specialized knowledge. The purpose of it is to make *B* feel small, worthless, and vulnerable—and therefore manageable. If *B* accepts it, *A* has gained control. In some cases, *A*'s patronizing behavior is a method of self-aggrandizement. *A* has so little self-worth that only by making *B* squirm can he gain something to be superior about. There's no possible polite response to patronization—you might as well object clearly and bluntly because it is the only thing such people understand. In the very best French restaurants, such as Philadelphia's Bec Fin, there's not a hint of patronizing remarks. The sommelier does have extensive, specialized knowledge, which he's pleased to share with you, and does it with a grace and tact that helps you to choose a wine that's a fair compromise between your palate and your budget.

Patronizing behavior when there's a real human interaction involved, although annoying, is understandable. What about patronizing programmers—when the patronizee is far removed from the patronizer? It's a symptom of unsure programmers with little self-worth. It's also the arrogant belief that if a person doesn't know a whole lot about computers, then they're to be treated as children. Note, however, that there's an inverse correlation between a programmer's knowledge and the frequency of patronizing behavior. Programmer trainees on their first assignment are the likeliest to insert a patronizing prompt. Helen, my human-resources resource, tells me that most technical people don't intend to be patronizing and that they don't really know that they're doing it—just as it's not always obvious that you've been patronized. Here's a sample:

Talking Down. This is the most common form, and it appears most often in software that's touted as "user-friendly." Look for it in manuals, especially in the introductory, or "getting started" manuals. Manuals for word-processing packages are notorious for being sexist, and if not that, for attempting to avoid sexism by changing it to patronizing.

Jargon. Jargon, when it's not necessary, is patronizing. The worst is jargon which is peculiar to the package and which has not been generally accepted in the industry. The index/glossary at the back of this book lists almost all of the acceptable jargon for personal computers. I may have missed a few, but most other terms you'll find in manuals and prompts are peculiar to that vendor and make false claims of universality.

Belaboring the Obvious. Repeating the definition of things, such as "file," not once, but many times, in the manuals, in the prompts, and so on. Redundant definition of terms is okay, within limits. Once when the term is first used, a second time for reinforcement, and perhaps again in a glossary, or again in sections which might be read independently. But if the same thing is defined on every other page, the writer must think you're an idiot. If the definition appears in a prompt, say, then it will appear whenever the prompt appears, and the program is inadvertantly patronizing. It's better to define terms in a HELP file, rather than in the working messages.

Misjudging Prerequisites and Knowledge. The programmer has to assume that you know something about the package's application. If the programmer (or manual writer) has underestimated what you know, then his explanations and tone will seem to be patronizing. It's not unreasonable to expect a secretary to know what a form letter is—he probably typed thousands of them before the word-processing package was bought. If the manual tells him what a form letter is, it's patronizing. A sophisticated statistics package, say, shouldn't try to explain elementary statistics, but should rather provide references to a good text.

Here's What I Mean. This kind of patronization often occurs with specialized software or for vertical packages. The programmer is a programming specialist who doesn't know a whole lot about the application although she does know programming. The flower business is as new to her as software is to a florist. Learning a new business, be it retailing or mathematics, can be exciting—so the programmer communicates that excitement to the user in manuals and prompts. The programmer is really groping for reassurance that her understanding of a new (to her) field is correct—but to the application expert, the florist say, it sounds patronizing.

Ain't It Great. This kind of patronizing is, thankfully, becoming less frequent. Sometimes it's an attempt to allay the user's supposed fear of computers. The writer in the manuals, and the programmers in the prompts, are constantly selling you on how great the package is.

4.5. Insults and Injury

Patronizing is only one of many ways in which a program can be abusive. The highest insult frequency occurs in messages, especially responses to possible user input errors. I used one sorry data base management package whose error messages were so strident that they must have been written by a former SS officer who had defected to the KGB: "NO SPACES ALLOWED!!!", "TERMINATE WITH A CARRIAGE RETURN AND EXTREME PREJUDICE!!!", "WRONG COMMAND!!!", "TOO MANY ENTRIES—ALL HAVE BEEN DESTROYED!!!", and so on. That programmer loved exclamation points, upper case letters, and boldface. Every little mistake resulted in one of those hostile messages. After a few hours, I was timid about hitting the ⟨RETURN⟩ key. It was really intimidating and my overactive imagination conjured images of sadistic Nazis deep in a bunker programming things like: "We have *ways* to make you conform to input formats!!!"

It doesn't take many bad messages or prompts to establish the relation between you and the software. Take "INPUT ERROR" and think of all the ways in which you might say it:

"Input Error"—an emotionally neutral, factual statement.
"INPUT ERROR!!"—Aha! I gotcha!!
"INPUT ERROR???"—My God! You've started World War III.
"input? error?"—It's cool, man. Don't sweat it.

It isn't always the prompt that's insulting or injurious but how you interpret it; and the interpretation is biased by the first few prompts you see. Let's try to be fair. If you're insulted, who created the insult? Was it the programmer or your reaction to the program? Ask around and see if others have the same reaction. Their initial use was different from yours and consequently, they received different prompts in a different order so that the software you love, they despise, and vice-versa. Good software avoids those problems by using emotionally neutral terminology and prompts, and by screening all prompts for potential insults and misinterpretation.

4.6. Illogical

Good software is logical and bad software isn't. There are at least two sets of logic involved: the internal, technical logic of software and the external logic of the application. Logic in this context isn't the formal logic of mathematicians and logicians, even though that's at the heart of it. Logic means common sense, common usage, and predictability. The opposite of logic in this context is arbitrariness. Arbitrary behavior is most often a consequence of patching in new features not originally planned for the package. Predictability means that you can deduce the structure of most commands once you know a few of them. It means that the fact that you thought of doing something with a specified option means that you can expect to find that option. For example, a word-processing package allows word search and replace in either the forward or the backward direction. An illogical package allows a single word search in the reverse direction but not a search and replace. A logical package allows thirty-character names for all files while an illogical package has different name length rules for each file type. A logical package consistently ignores leading and trailing spaces in a name but an illogical package has specialized rules for different name types and different situations.

Don't expect to find the rules when they're arbitrary. They won't be in the manual and you'll be lucky if they're in the error messages. Don't expect to find those rules because the programmer doesn't know them either. The rules are arbitrary because the package is a slapped-up piece of junk. You know it's that kind of package when you find yourself muttering: "If it's Tuesday and there's a full moon. . . . "

Conversely, a package can be completely logical but it's not an obvious logic. If that's the case, good software will document the logic by a few simple rules, up front. Once you know the rules, you know the logic and the program is a snap to learn.

4.7. Anthropomorphism

Personal pronouns don't belong in a programmer's lexicon:

"Which file do you want me to retrieve?"
"I don't understand your command."
"We cannot execute that command."
"The printer he is busy and the disc, she is full."
"I'm sorry ⟨username⟩, ⟨filename⟩ is not on my disc."
"All right now, ⟨username⟩, try to . . . "
"Please enter the file name."
"Thank you."

I junk packages which ask me for my name in order to use it in prompts and messages. It's as convincing as a "personal" letter addressed to "occupant"—"Dear Ms. Occupant. You have been selected for this award because . . . " You chuck such letters before reading because you know that they're as personal as an IRS form letter. You should also chuck such software. The first few times you saw a "personalized" letter produced by a computer you might have been fooled or even impressed: but then it wears thin and hardly anyone over the age of twelve is fooled into thinking that it's a letter from a real person.

What's wrong with the above "friendly" and "polite" prompts? What could possibly be objectionable about a "please" or "thank you" now and then in software? What's wrong is that they're simulation of interactions between humans. Machine "politeness" is well-conceived, properly functioning, robust software and not the artificial insinuation of polite words to mask profound functional deficiencies. Polite language is an inherently human activity—evolved by humans, for humans, to facilitate their relation with one another. A computer simulation thereof robs us of our dignity. It blurs the distinction between man and mere objects. It cheapens us and robs us of our souls. And it's a lie. A polite phrase and the use of pronouns implies a human on both sides and human intelligence. Despite sci-fi movies, computers are incalculably far from intelligence today. And when machine intelligence *is* achieved, it will be no more like human intelligence than an eagle is onto a 747. It will not be the anthropomorphic HAL of 2001 but something which none of us can now foresee. I'm sure of one thing, though: whatever the shape and function of machine intelligence will become, the current fad for simulated polite behavior, the use of personal pronouns, and other such, will seem as quaint to our descendants as those first (and failed) feathered wing-flapping attempts at flying machines seem to us today.

8
PERFORMANCE COUNTS

1. SYNOPSIS

What is performance. How much do you need. How to be happy with inadequate performance. The hardware, system, and software factors that affect performance and what they cost. Reasonable expectations. Measuring and comparing performance. Benchmarks.

2. HOW FAST IS FAST ENOUGH?

2.1. The Difference Between Big and Small Computers

One of the most noteworthy contributions to computer science was made by the English logician, Alan Turing, a decade before the first computer was built. He "designed" a simple conceptual machine which he proved could do any calculations done by any computing machine at all. Turing's "computer" consists of a long piece of tape on which the machine can print at least two different symbols. The machine can read a symbol and, depending on its internal state, either print a new symbol and/or move to the left or right. That's the jist of it.

A Turing machine's theoretical power is limited only by the length of its tape, which, for the Turing machine, combines the function of keyboard, screen, printer, internal memory, and disc. There's a caveat though: "assuming the tape is long enough and you can wait for the answer." For example, a Turing machine tape that simulated the operation of a calculator might be several hundred meters long and the time needed to add two numbers would be measured in days.

If you don't care how long it takes to get results, then there's no difference between what the cheapest home computer can do and what can be done by multi-million dollar supercomputers. Except for speed, the $99 computer is *exactly* as powerful as all the rest of the computers in the world combined. So it isn't that you can't calculate a 50 by 100 spreadsheet in the cheap computer—you can—but that you wouldn't want to. Just because the ZIPZAP package *can* run on a cheap computer, you're encouraged to believe that the cheapy is equivalent to one costing ten times as much. It *is* equivalent in the theoretical sense that they can both execute equivalent programs, but if it takes two weeks of processing to run through the spreadsheets for your weekly report, equivalent or not, it's useless.

2.2. Objective Performance Needs

We are an impatient lot. Our brains are much faster than our computers. We tend to confuse our subjective performance needs (see below) with objective needs. There are objective performance needs for computers in general, but relatively few for personal computers. If the computer that controls a nuclear reactor isn't fast enough, there might be a meltdown. If a communications computer is too slow, messages may be lost. It is, for most large-scale computer applications, straightforward to determine objective performance needs based on technical and/or financial considerations. It's more difficult to do that kind of analysis for personal computers. And because the cost of the analysis itself is usually higher than the cost of the equipment, it's easier (and wiser) to overbuy than it is to analyze and agonize. Furthermore, it's almost impossible to determine your objective needs before you've used your first computer—that's something that you can understand only after you're dissatisfied with the performance you've got and you're ready to get your second computer. It's only after you've used a computer for a while that your usage pattern settles and that you know how your time is spent. Here are some guidelines that will help you assess what your objective performance needs might be:

1. Assume that you can buy a new computer which is infinitely fast. It still takes time to key in data, to evaluate results, and to think about what you want to do next. The infinitely fast computer doesn't help with that time but it does eliminate all waiting time.
2. Use a stopwatch to accumulate all the time you spent waiting for results during a typical day: an infinitely fast computer can't be more valuable than the cost of that time.
3. Will you be able to exploit the time you save or are there factors that will limit your productivity even if the computer isn't the bottleneck?
4. Will the infinitely fast computer make your work more timely and therefore more valuable, or is timeliness not a factor in your work? How much are people willing to pay for a more timely product?

5. Are you making effective use of the time you spend waiting now (think, plan, make telephone calls, read, review documents, proofread, and do other things during long computer runs)? Will a faster computer chop into such simultaneous activities, so that there's a net productivity decrease instead of an increase?

6. To what extent will the higher speed allow you to do things which you can't do now? Distinguish between what you *might* do, or would *like* to do, and what you could realistically do. Will anyone want those products if you do produce them?

Assume that the hypothetical infinitely fast computer costs some small amount—a few hundred dollars, say. If you can't justify the cost of that additional performance, then you certainly can't justify a real computer that's faster than the one you have now; at least not on objective performance grounds. But that doesn't mean that there aren't objective reasons other than performance or valid subjective reasons. Most personal computer users can't justify the additional performance of the hypothetical infinitely fast computer. If you can justify it, then get more realistic by using the following rule of thumb:

A 30% cost increase generally doubles the computer's processing speed. The same rule applies to most other components such as printers and modems.

You know how much time you could save with the infinitely fast computer and how much time you're waiting now. Double the computer's speed and the waiting time is at best cut in half. From that, you can establish a value, which can be compared to a cost. The above rule of thumb is a starting point. Later, assuming the payoff warrants it, you can put in the cost of specific hardware and/or software upgrades to see how much better things might be. It generally doesn't pay to bother with anything that won't at least double the speed or equivalently, cut your waiting time in half. When I upgrade systems, I typically look for a five- to ten-fold performance improvement. An alternative to replacing a computer with a faster model (if you can really gainfully employ the additional speed) is to use *two* computers. You do the routine stuff, such as writing reports and keeping records on one computer and do the processing-intensive work on the other. The combination is far more powerful than either alone, and the trade-in value of used computers is so low, that the additional cost isn't that high.

The objective reason for upgrading computer hardware is rarely performance alone, but includes other factors such as:

1. Your computer is no longer in production and service is impossible to get—it's **orphanware.**
2. It has memory limitations and the newer (and more useful) software requires the larger memory.
3. The speed improvement is incidental to many other new features offered such as: better graphics, more compact storage, more reliable, easier to use, and less desk space.

2.3. Subjective Performance Needs

The need for computational speed in personal computers is almost completely subjective. Just because it's subjective, though, doesn't mean it's an invalid need. There is only one *subjectively* satisfactory speed—instantaneous. We work personal computers in a dialogue. Type a command and the response appears on the screen. We're ready to issue a new command as soon as we think of it and any delay in accepting that next command is irksome. Such subjective needs, if satisfied, would mean that we would all have supercomputers on our desks. Let's rationalize these subjective needs:

1. The screen is refreshed thirty times each second because that's as fast a change as the human eye-brain combination can discern. Therefore, anything that takes less than 1/30th of a second is fast enough. Our subjectivity, however, is unfair—we expect to sort five-thousand records, evaluate a 50 by 100 spreadsheet, and spell-check a 50 page memo all in the same 30th of a second.
2. There's **think time** needed to understand the result of the previous work: it's a few seconds for most people.
3. We think ahead three or four steps.
4. We hate being blocked by anything whose outcome is routine. For example, there are no surprises in printing so we're ready to go on to the next step as soon as we give the print command.
5. We like progress reports. We want displays to start as soon as possible. That way, we can overlap our reading and thinking time with the computer's processing time.
6. Time is measured on a subjective scale which is proportioned to what we can do with the waiting time:
   a. 0–0.05 seconds—effectively instantaneous.
   b. 0.05–0.5 seconds—sluggish but acceptable.
   c. 0.5–2.0 seconds—slow.
   d. 2–4 seconds—very slow. Time to get angry.
   e. 4 seconds to one minute—intolerable waste of time.

   f. 1–5 minutes—acceptable. Glance at a memo or make a telephone call.

   g. 5–20 minutes—useful time, no effective delay.

   h. 20–120 minutes—very slow.

   i. 2–8 hours—might as well be 24 hours.

2.4. Living with the Performance You Can Afford

When, after almost three decades in the computer business, I find myself repeatedly doing something pointless and dumb, and furthermore, when I find my better-wrapped colleagues doing the same, then I figure it's worth thinking about, and more important, worth talking about to my readers so that if I can't make them not feel guilty about it, then at least they'll know that they're in good company. Which brings me to just about the dumbest thing I (and everybody else) do—staring at the printer.

You get a new printer, say, and the first document you print out, you stare at as it comes out—line by line. I do it with new computers, new software, new anything. I stare at the printer, or at the screen, or at whatever else is giving me a tangible indication of work. Confess it! Don't deny that you've done it—and be assured that it won't make you blind and that eventually, you'll outgrow it.

What has the above confession to do with performance? It's an illustration of both how subjective we are about performance and also of how to better live with the performance you can afford. When you're in the printer-staring mode of life, no printer is fast enough—you want a thousand, ten-thousand characters a second and anything slower is too slow: but when you've reached the state where deep down, you know that the printing will get done, without error, with or without your staring, then you can get on with other things and that previously "slow" printer is now fast enough.

The key to living with the performance you've got is to find something useful to do while you're waiting. Evolve a working relation with your computer so that while it's doing its thing, you're doing yours. Then the waiting time isn't wasted at all and you can live with less performance than seemed reasonable at first. But you can't do that until you've gotten beyond staring at the printer, which can take weeks or months of steady use. Here are some ideas that may help you utilize the waiting time:

1. Don't put the computer on your desk—put it on a separate stand or on a return piece. If you share your desk with it, you've blocked the ability to do something useful with the waiting time and have condemned yourself to printer staring.

2. Keep track of how long the computer takes to do things and try to schedule little stuff in while you're waiting. Pattern your coffee breaks, telephone calls, and administrative work to long runs.
3. Do very long runs (of hours) overnight or at lunchtime, or while you're at a meeting.
4. Use pin-feed paper, sheet feeders, buffered printers, multi-strike ribbons, and anything else that minimizes the need for your attention.
5. Learn how to use the operating system's and package's automation facilities, such as command files and macros to reduce hands-on attention.
6. Either break up the tasks so that the individual delays are subjectively tolerable (under a few seconds), or alternatively, do the opposite: combine the tasks so that the delays can be gainfully employed.
7. Don't stare at the printer.

3. THE HARDWARE, SYSTEM, AND SOFTWARE FACTORS

3.1. Binding Factors

Performance is determined by a combination of four things: hardware, the operating system, the software you're running, and the data you're processing. A system, meaning the agglomeration of hardware and software that you use, is no faster than the slowest of its elements. The slowest element is called the **binding element** or **binding factor.** If a system can't compute fast enough, we say that it's **computer bound** or **processor bound.** If it can't print fast enough, it's **print bound.** And if it can't fetch things from disc fast enough, it's **disc bound.** If your system is print bound and you install a faster computer, it won't help because a print bound system can only be improved by a faster printer. Performance improvements can only be achieved by improving the binding factors. Therefore, prior to purchasing any hardware or software intended to improve performance, you must have identified the binding factors, and must be sure that the new thing will improve them, and not something else.

Think of performance as a set of curtains. You can only see the curtain that's directly in front of you. You want to get the stage's back wall (maximum performance) and in order to do so, you raise the first curtain (e.g., you buy a faster printer). Raising that curtain does not necessarily reveal the back wall, but only another curtain, which could be disappointingly close to the one you just raised. So now you buy a hard disc, and reveal yet another curtain, which you raise by buying more memory. . . .

3.2. Performance Predictions

If it were just a matter of lifting consecutive curtains, then performance evaluation would be simple. Unfortunately, each change rearranges the curtains yet to be lifted, and sometimes drops previously lifted curtains down again. Can you depend on the retailer or on brochures for guidance? Not really. The number of combinations is so great, and everything is so dependent on the specifics, that the manufacturers and retailers can only guess about your situation. I don't want to mislead you into thinking that computer and software designers can't predict the performance of new systems or software: they can and do. Performance can be determined theoretically or experimentally. But whatever method is used, the analyst has to make assumptions about hardware, software, the operating system, the data to be processed, and the user's behavior. If your situation matches those assumptions reasonably well, then the predictions might be satisfactory for you; but how do you know if the analyst's assumptions fit? You can only know that by making meticulous measurements over a long period of time and then crunching the data through statistical packages. This kind of thing is routinely done for mainframe systems where the performance issues are valued in thousands of dollars a day and the hardware costs millions. While it could be done for personal computers, so far, the cost of analysis has been, and probably will remain for a long time in the future, much higher than the possible benefits. Consequently, a formal analysis can only be justified by the vendor, who's dealing with average characteristics, or by a multiple unit buyer—and I mean *hundreds* and *thousands* of units.

3.3. Be Fair

You've heard about a new after-market whiz-bang that promises dramatic performance improvements, and you think that you could gainfully employ the added performance. You talk to the retailers, say, and you get a spectrum of responses, most of which seem to be evasive. Some foolish vendors will confidently assert that you'll get all kinds of improvements, but most will hedge, refuse to put things in writing, or they'll waffle in some other way. Here are some of the things that may be going through the dealer's mind:

1. I've never seen that precise hardware configuration before. I hope it works the way it did on ours.
2. Should I tell him about the performance problems of release 2.33. Nah! Nobody uses 2.33 anymore.

3. I wonder if he knows how badly the system slows down when you use that feature? But if I tell him that, he might not want to buy it.
4. So far, nobody's complained.
5. I hate to tell him that he also has to buy X if he's going to get the full performance improvement.
6. Well even if it isn't faster for him, it's more reliable, more convenient, easier to use, flexible; he'll be getting his money's worth.
7. How did the manufacturer establish those claims? I can't get that kind of performance out of it.
8. What was that reviewer in *BYTE* smoking? I couldn't make it work that slowly if I tried.
9. She seems to be knowledgeable—I'll just give her the raw numbers and test results and let her sell herself.

So it's the blind leading the blind in a fog. I say "be fair" because in the context of a typical purchase, there's no realistic way, short of an exact demonstration, of predicting the true performance impacts and improvements. You're being fair if you accept that as a fact of life and reinterpret the vendor's action, not as evasiveness or waffling, but as a real attempt to help you make the right decision based on complex, interacting, and imperfectly understood factors.

3.4. Should You Read Further?

For most personal computer users, raw performance is less important than convenience and features so there's no need to read the rest of this chapter. If performance is a real issue for you and you're thinking of a heavy purchase in order to improve it, or it you're just interested in the factors that determine a system's performance and want some insight into how those factors work, then read on.

4. THE HARDWARE FACTORS

4.1. Technology Trends

Hardware speed is the ultimate determinant of performance. Everything else being equal (a rare situation), faster hardware means proportionately better performance. Hardware speeds have been improving dramatically for decades. The last great hardware speed improvement came when very large scale integration (VLSI), which permitted the construction of an entire computer on a chip, came into common practice. Technology moves in spurts and we're still integrating the hardware performance improvements that

VLSI provided. It's not likely that the present hardware generation will allow more than another twofold performance increase. Hardware which is now in the laboratories seems to be pushing up against the limits of the present technology. But that doesn't imply that performance limits have been reached. For one thing, hardware costs are still tumbling, so that the unit which was prohibitively expensive a year ago is now in reach. For another, there are new technologies afoot. Of the two trends, you can expect your next performance improvements to come almost completely from hardware price reductions rather than from technological breakthroughs. So if you want to see what your personal computer might look like in few years, look at the engineering work stations that now cost ten to twenty times as much as a personal computer. Think in terms of a 30% compounded price cut each year for the next several years.

4.2. The Microprocessor(s)

The microprocessor chip is the most important determinant of the system's speed. There is a range of speeds for these and even the same chip can operate at different speeds. Those factors are discussed in the next section. This section deals with a higher level look at things—especially the number of microprocessors in the system.

Don't assume that there's only one microprocessor chip in a personal computer system. There could be only one, as in a programmable calculator or in a home computer, but usually, there are several. The number of processor chips in personal computers has been steadily increasing over the years and promise to increase even more in the future. Some processor chips are so cheap that it's cost-effective to dedicate a microprocessor to a mundane function such as controlling a printer. Most of these supporting microprocessors are loafing most of the time, and there's no effective way their full power can be utilized. So just because you have five microprocessors in your configuration doesn't mean that it will be five times faster than one which has only one: it might only be twice as fast. Here's a roster of the kinds of uses to which microprocessors are put to in personal computer systems and the likely performance improvements you can get from them (see Figure 8-1):

1. Central Processor. Every system has at least one. It usually works full tilt at all times and it is the most important performance determinant.

2. Display Processor. This processor takes care of displaying things on the screen. Some kind of processor is needed because loading the work onto the central processor could consume half of its power. But there's a wide variability here, especially when you consider graphics, different type fonts,

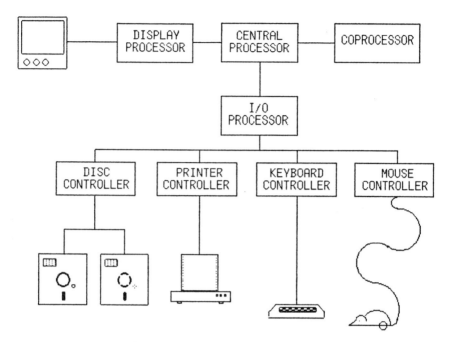

Figure 8–1. Personal computer processors.

boldface, italics, and other fancy operations. Cheap home computers use a TV set as display unit, which of course doesn't have its own display processor. So the work must be done by the central processor.

3. Disc Controllers. These may or may not use actual microprocessors. Smart controllers can be dramatically faster than dumb controllers and smart controllers usually require a dedicated microprocessor of some kind. The impact is usually more obvious for multi-user systems, especially those which are used to play with large data bases. For single-user, personal computers, which manipulate relatively small data bases of a few thousand records, the use of a dedicated microprocessor for disc control is an engineering economics issue rather than a performance issue.

4. Printer Controller. At least one microprocessor is common nowadays. A microprocessor can speed things up by optimizing the printer's operation. It can also be used to provide a built-in spooler, multiple copies, font changes, and other goodies. Except for the spooling, though, there's no big performance improvement.

5. Spooler Controller. Most after-market spoolers have a dedicated microprocessor. Spoolers can give you a dramatic performance improvement, especially if you have to do a lot of printing and your system doesn't do concurrent printing and processing. Spoolers allow the central processor to dump the data to be printed at a far higher speed than the printer can print. Even personal computers that provide concurrent printing and processing are improved by a spooler. Spoolers can similarly improve communications. Spoolers can be installed in one of the following three places, or all three: inside the computer itself as part of the printer controller, as a separate unit, or in the printer itself.

6. *Input/Output Processor.* A system may reduce the load on the central processor by using a specialized input/output processor to do some of the routine input/output work. In some systems, this function is on the central processor chip.

7. *Keyboard Controller.* A microprocessor dedicated to controlling the keyboard is becoming increasingly popular. It gives users and designers flexibility over keyboard layout and key uses, and it provides a more responsive keyboard that can store hundreds of keystrokes.

8. *Modem Controller.* Very much like printer controller and print spoolers. A microprocessor here can slightly reduce the load on the main computer while transmitting or receiving data. It can also be used for multiple copies, sending copies of data to lists of addresses, and so on.

9. *Coprocessors.* The most common coprocessor is an **arithmetic coprocessor.** This unit is a special chip designed to do arithmetic at blitzkrieg speeds, and not much else. It can, especially if you're in the number crunching business, say a heavy spreadsheet user, increase the spreadsheet calculation speed by a factor ranging from two to fifty. It has almost no effect on operations such as a data-base work, word-processing, or printing. Other kinds of specialized coprocessors exist for processing voice and other signals.

4.3. Words, Busses, and Clocks

4.3.1. Microprocessor Families

Microprocessor chips are developed in families. The business is dominated by three families today: Intel 8xxxx (used in most IBM PC's), Motorola M68xxx, and Zilog Z-8xxxx. The three families compete across the board so that there's a comparable model from each vendor at any performance level. The performance difference between members of a family centers on three numbers: the **word length,** the **bus width,** and the **clock speed.** In general, bigger (word length, bus width, and clock rate) is faster, and the effect is not additive, but multiplicative.

4.3.2. Word Length

Numbers in computers are represented by a bit pattern in memory, usually 64 bits, or 8 bytes long. The instructions the computer executes to do something, say addition, are also stored in memory. The length of instructions ranges from one byte (or eight bits) to as many as 8 bytes or longer. The **word length** is a measure of the number of bits which the processor can simultaneously handle. For example, in addition, an 8-bit processor (i.e., a processor which has an 8-bit word length), must do the addition of two 64-bit numbers as 8 additions on each of the 8 bit segments of the full 64 bits. A processor with a 32-bit word length can do it in only two steps, while a 64-bit computer does it in one step.

Microprocessor word lengths include: 4, 8, 16, and 32 bits. Calculators generally use a 4 bit word, but some expensive programmable calculators use 8 bits. Most personal computers use 8 or 16, but high-end machines such as work stations and the newer systems use 32 bits.* Minicomputers generally use 16 bits (on the low end) and 32 on the high end. Mainframe computers use 32- or 64-bit word lengths and supercomputers use 64-bit words or greater. The first commercial home computers had 4-bit word lengths. This was rapidly followed by the dominance of 8-bit machines, soon to be replaced by the IBM PC (and clones), which has a 16-bit processor. The cost difference between 8, 16, and 32 bit processor chips is roughly $10, $40, $400. But it's not only the cost of the processor chip, but the cost of all the other hardware that must be there to make a 16-bit computer, say, work like it was intended to. Don't assume that because a system boasts a 16-bit microprocessor that it will run like a 16-bit system. It won't do that unless the supporting hardware is geared to 16-bit operation.

4.3.3. Bus Width

Figure 8–2 is a more accurate representation of the internal structure of a typical personal computer. All the elements are connected to a **bus.** The bus is a communications highway used by the parts to talk to one another. The computer gets its instructions and data from the memory via the bus. Data are moved from the memory to the disc or printer over the bus. Just as the word length determines how many bits can be processed simultaneously, the **bus width** determines how many bits are hauled simultaneously. All else being equal, a 16-bit bus hauls data twice as fast as 8-bit bus. Calculators use 1, 2, 4, and 8 bit busses. Personal computers use 8, 16, and 32. Minicomputers use 16 and 32. Mainframes typically use 32 or 64, and supercom-

---

*The IBM PC-2 family uses 8, 16, and 32-bit busses with 16 and 32-bit word lengths.

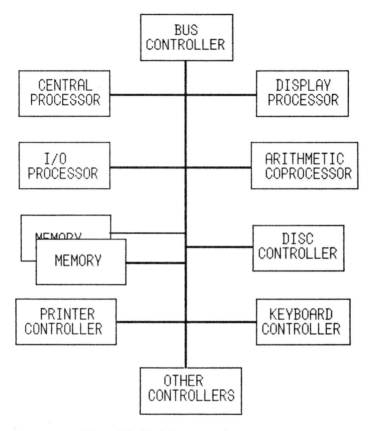

Figure 8–2. Typical computer bus structure.

puters use 64 or 128. Bus bits are expensive. The difference between an 8-bit and 16-bit bus could be 30% of the computer's cost. Again, it's not just the wires that make up the bus itself that matters, but the entire set of supporting chips, the internal connectors, solder joints, and all the rest. Because the bus is so expensive, the chip manufacturer provides different versions of the microprocessor, so that a 16-bit (word length) processor might be available with either an 8-bit or a 16-bit bus. The nomenclature used is: "8/8" (or "eight-by-eight") means an 8-bit word with an 8-bit bus; "16/8" means a 16-bit word with an 8-bit bus, while "16/16" means a 16-bit machine with an 16-bit bus. The typical configurations are: 8/8, 16/8, 16/16, 32/16, 32/32, with a rough speed doubling for each one.

4.3.4. Clock Speed

The operations you're aware of, such as adding numbers, are themselves executed as a sequence of many computer instructions. The instructions, in turn, take many steps to do—from a few to a few dozen, depending on the instruction and the data. The rate at which the steps take place is controlled by a **clock.** Typical clock rates range from 2 MHz (two million clock cycles per second), to 20 MHz. It's clear that the 20 MHz clock is ten times faster than the 2 MHz clock and, consequently, so is the computer. A given chip, say a 16/16 may have a top clock speed of 20 MHz, but the computer vendor can run it slower than that. Why wouldn't a designer always run things at the fastest possible rate?

Speed costs. A given chip, a memory chip say, may be available in several different versions. The slowest version may cost a dollar or two, and the fastest version, ten to twenty dollars. The same applies to all components in the computer. The ubiquitous 30% rule (30% more cost to double the speed) applies here also. If the top speed of the 16/16 is 20 MHz, it can only achieve that speed if *all* the chips run at that speed, and if all the connectors, cables, and circuit boards are designed for that speed. Otherwise, it'll run no faster than the slowest component in the bag. Sometimes, the difference between a clone and the clonee may be that although the processor is the same, the clock rate isn't. Another possibility is more nefarious. Often the only difference between high-speed and low-speed components is testing and inspection—both are made on the same production line, and they're sorted according to speed. The high-speed components that don't quite make it are marketed as lower-speed components at a lower price under a different number. Another possibility is that there is no difference between the low-and high-speed components, except that the manufacturer does not do extensive testing on the low-speed version and thereby can sell them at a lower price. That means that 80 or 90% of those lower priced components can run at the top speed—but not all of them. The unscrupulous vendor knows that he can run the "low-speed" component at the faster rate. Most operations will be okay, but here and there, things will get bollixed. So you lose data—but quickly. Playing games with clock rates can vary the computer's effective speed over a five-to-one range, and the processing reliability over a much greater range. Furthermore, low-speed components can usually be "pushed" by more power, which is cheap. But more power is more heat and more heat is more failures. *Caveat Emptor.*

The obverse side to the unscrupulous vendor is the conservative designer. The conservative designer knows that the system can't be faster than its slowest component and still be reliable. Consequently, the system's speed is deliberately held back by a slower clock so that all component speeds can match. For example, IBM used a slower than theoretically possible clock rate for its PC-AT, because an arithmetic coprocessor with matching speed was not yet available.

The impact of clock rate is the easiest of all factors to understand—everything else being equal, processing speed is proportional to clock rate. Unfortunately, it's the factor which can be played with best. You can't tell (unless it's really awful hardware) how fast things operate without putting the product on a test bench and looking at it with instruments. You can measure the clock rate on the bench, but that won't tell you much about reliability. My suggestion is to be conservative. Small vendors, pirate vendors, and the like cannot, popular myths to the contrary, achieve the economies of scale that the giants can. They really can't produce the same product at a lower cost. They can sell it at a lower price, though, because of lower overhead, less support, much less R&D, and fewer options. They can temporarily offer a lower price because they're working to a much smaller, short-term dominated, margin. But they can also achieve the lower price by clock games and chancy engineering. A two-to-one performance advantage stretches the limits of credibility. Three decades of an industry competing with IBM has shown that the runner-up vendors could at best achieve a 30% improvement in performance versus price (i.e., 30% better performance at IBM's price or the same performance for 30% less). Well-established manufacturers such as DEC, Hewlett Packard, and other giants such as AT&T, can also achieve economies of scale comparable to IBM.

4.3.5. Putting it Together

Table 8-1 is a comparison of how an 8/8, a 16/8, and 16/16 microprocessor operating at the same clock rate might do the same addition of a 64-bit number. It isn't exact, and the techies might object, but the purpose is to show you how word length and bus size have a multiplicative impact. The numbers are time periods which are proportional to the clock rate. The process consists of fetching the first number, fetching the second number, doing the addition, and then storing the partial result. The process must be repeated several times: the 8-bit machine repeats it 8 times in order to add the full 64-bit number; the 16-bit machines only have to repeat it four times. There are also some instructions needed to take care of the repetitions, which I've lumped together. Note that there are two steps involved in each operation. The computer must fetch the instructions from memory before it can execute them. That also takes time. On the basis of this example, it would seem that there's an almost two-to-one speed difference for each machine. That could be the case for raw addition, but relatively little of

Table 8-1 Performance Impact of Word Length and Bus Size.

	8/8	16/8	16/16
Fetch FETCH instruction	4	4	2
Fetch first number part	2	3	2
Fetch FETCH instruction	4	4	2
Fetch second number part	2	3	2
Fetch ADD instruction	4	4	2
Do Addition	1	1	1
Fetch STORE instruction	4	4	2
Store result part	2	3	2
Fetch REPEAT instructions	10	10	5
Execute REPEAT instructions	5	5	4
SUBTOTALS	38	41	24
REPEAT multiplier	8	4	4
TOTAL TIME	304	164	96

the computer's time is spent doing that and many instructions, such as those used for handling keystrokes and updating the display, take about the same time in all three machines.

The 16/16 doesn't tell the whole story because there can be substantial variations within a group as well. For example, some microprocessor models arrange things so that the fetching of the next instruction and the execution of the present instruction take place simultaneously. That kind of thing can further double the 16/16 speed.

4.4. Memories

4.4.1. How Much Memory is Enough?

Speed is performance and memory is speed. The first computer I used had only 8k bytes of memory, which is less than what's in my calculator today. The only way to do big problems was to break the data up into chunks that could fit into that tiny memory. But even that wasn't enough because the software was itself much bigger than the memory—the software also had to be broken down into small steps. If the data was divided into ten segments, and the software into twenty segments, then each segment of data had to be massaged by each program segment. That meant that the program segments had to be shuttled into memory two hundred times in order to complete the processing. It takes time to move programs into memory, and while that's underway, the computer isn't processing. What's more, because things couldn't fit, it was necessary to store many intermediate results so that the various parts of the program could pick up from the previous processing phase. The bottom line is that the entire processing was about a thousand times slower than it could have been had all the data and all the programs been in memory simultaneously.

The speed improvements that come from big memory are no less dramatic today. Double the memory, for large jobs, typically means double or better the speed; but there's almost no difference for small jobs. Big memory has a big impact on word-processing, spreadsheet, and data-base software. Many integrated software packages require a lot of memory. That isn't quite true, because it would be (theoretically) possible to put the largest integrated package into a very small memory. However, the package would be constantly shuttling data and programs to and from the disc, with the result that it would be unacceptably slow. You can see how dramatic the effect of memory size is by running any package which can be configured for different memory sizes. Compare the package's operation with a 64k memory and a 256k memory. The memory-speed trade-off is one of the fundamentals of computer performance.

One of the happiest consequences of VLSI is that memory is really cheap and getting cheaper by the month. Computer and software designers are taking advantage of this. Big memory means faster, simpler, more reliable, software in addition to better performance. As a consequence, we've seen the minimum memory configuration increasing steadily (both for hardware and software), so that while 64k was the standard a few years ago, nobody can compete with less than 256k, and 640k is rapidly becoming the norm. By the decade's end, 2 or 4 megabytes will probably be standard for personal computers.*

DON'T BE CHINTZY WITH MEMORY. BUY TWICE AS MUCH AS YOU THINK YOU NEED, AND THEN SOME. IT'S THE BEST BUY THERE IS.

4.4.2. Uses for Memory

Memory has many uses. Here are some of them, and how they affect performance:

Operating System Storage. The operating system is a large program. It is used by all packages. Only the most commonly used functions remain in memory at all times—the other stuff has to be shuttled from disc every time it's needed. A big memory means that more of the operating system can be in memory at all times and that means less time wasted getting the program

---

*High-end PC's *need* 4 megabytes.

from disc and setting it up to run. It also means less wear and tear on the disc drives, and the floppy diskette itself.

Program Storage. The same applies to packages, especially integrated packages. An integrated package designed to run completely in memory is not only much faster, but about half as complicated as one that's segmented to operate in a small memory. Wear and tear on drives and floppies is also reduced.

Directory Storage. A big memory means that the directory for files can be in memory at all times. Therefore, one more disc operation is eliminated whenever you have to fetch or store anything on disc.

Index Storage. This is especially important for data-base software. Big memory allows big, easily accessible indexes. This can, for a large database, improve retrieval and storage time by a factor from two to ten.

General Data Storage. Big memory means that intermediate results don't have to be stored on disc. It means that almost any part of a document, say, can be accessed almost instantaneously. This is especially noticeable in word-processing operations such as search-and-replace, reformatting, and spell checking.

Reference Data Storage. The most obvious example is a word processing spell checker. A big memory allows the entire dictionary to be in memory simultaneously. A twenty to hundred-fold speed improvement is possible compared to a small memory.

RAM Disc. Big memory means that part of it can be used to simulate the operation of a disc. You pay a few seconds of time to move data and programs from the floppy to the simulated floppy (RAM "disc") which can access programs and data thousands of times faster than the floppy. The performance improvement can be impressive.

Internal Buffers/Spoolers. A big memory means that part of it can be devoted to provide buffering for printers and data communications. It allows greater concurrency in the system's operation. It permits data transfers by more efficient means which are not as processing intensive.

4.4.3. RAM AND ROM

Memory comes in two main flavors: **random access memory (RAM)** and **read-only memory (ROM)**. ROM memory can't be changed by software means. It's used to store fixed parts of the program that must always be available. The typical things stored in ROM are: the software used to load other software, control software for discs, the monitor, the keyboard, and printers, and also parts of the operating system. In some computers, such as the Hewlett-Packard 80 series, the entire operating system is stored in ROM. RAM memory isn't dedicated to anything special. When vendors talk about memory, they usually mean RAM, and not ROM. Consider two computers, each with 128k of RAM, but one computer has an additional 128k of ROM which is used to store the operating system. 32k of that operating system must (for the sake of this discussion) be resident at all times in order to do anything. The all-RAM system has only 96k of memory available for program and data storage while the ROM-RAM system has a full 128k. Compare the real memory capacity of two systems by adding half of the ROM size to the RAM size. Nothing is free, though. Note that although a big ROM can give you more bangs for your buck, ROM changes can't be done by slipping in a new disc. ROM can only be used for very stable software. Upgrading an operating system which is totally stored in RAM takes a few minutes and costs a few dollars. The same for a ROM stored program takes a few hours and can cost a hundred dollars or more.

4.5. Discs—Hard and Soft

We have **soft** or **floppy discs** and **hard discs**. Floppies have capacities which range from a low of 180k to a high of 2 megabytes per drive. Hard discs range in size from a few megabytes to hundreds of megabytes. In either type, double the price usually means four times the capacity. The bigger the disc capacity, the fewer discs you need to store data or programs, and the less disc popping you'll have to do. Think of yourself as an extension of the system's hardware in which your relation to the disc drives is analogous to the relation between the disc drives and the internal memory. The bin in which you store your floppies is yet another memory, and you're the (very slow) mechanism that provides access to that memory. Think of it that way, and all the speed improvements which resulted from a large internal memory also apply to large discs. As with internal memory, big disc memory is a bargain. Two drives are more than four times better than one drive. Don't buy **single-sided** (drives in which data is stored on only one side of the floppy) if **double-sided** drives are available. Don't buy **single-density** (96k bytes per side) if **dual density** (192k bytes per side) are available. Don't buy dual density if **quad density** (384k or higher per side) can be bought. But high-capacity discs also mean that more of your data is vulnerable at any one time.

Hard discs, with their huge capacity, extend the argument used for double-sided, high density floppies. Most users can gainfully employ a 10 megabyte hard disc—if only to store the programs in daily use. Beyond 10 megabytes it depends on what you're doing with the computer. Hard discs not only save wear and tear on drives and floppies, but they are also (typically) ten times faster—there is almost no perceptible delay in getting things to and from disc.

The price is even greater vulnerability to failures, and good backup practices are mandatory.

4.6. The Rest of the Gear

Almost every piece of computer gear follows the 30% rule—a 30% price increase means roughly double the speed. The rule applies to printers, modems, plotters, and will probably apply to devices we haven't thought of yet. Start the rational selection of devices for their performance by getting price and performance data. Plot the price versus speed for all contenders and keep the 30% rule in mind. The next step is to put an upper and a lower limit on the speed you need, after having taken into account all the things you might be able to do to live with less speed and what features you're willing to sacrifice for speed.

The simplest case, which almost every user faces, and faces early in the game, is selecting a printer. There's huge quality range available at any given speed. Quality for printers includes: type font quality (e.g., draft versus letter quality), continuous versus intermittent operation, paper feed options, carriage width, internal buffering, and graphics. Selecting the printer that meets your performance needs is good training for future purchases, such as modems, where the issues are murkier and more technical.

5. THE SOFTWARE FACTORS

5.1. The Operating System

5.1.1. Efficiency

The **operating system*** is a program that manages all of the system's hardware and all the software that's run. You don't need to know in detail what it does or how, beyond that. However, management can be efficient or inefficient. The simplest instance of efficient management is providing concurrency, especially of printing and processing. The printer accepts one line of print at a time, prints it, and then requests the next line. By human

---

*At the time of writing (January 1988), few personal computer operating systems had all the feature's discussed in this section. Those features were then more typical of minicomputer operating systems. But history has shown a steady migration of features from mainframes to minis and from minis to micros, of which the adoption of the UNIX operating system and its derivatives is an archetype. Over the useful lifetime of this book, most personal computers will have sophisticated operating systems for which everything discussed here will be germane. Compare, for example, OS/2 to PC-DOS.

standards, the time wasted by the computer while it's waiting for the printer is imperceptible—a few tenths of a second. For computers, which can execute a million instructions a second, that's a huge block of time. There are always several things going on simultaneously: putting new stuff on the screen, getting your next keystroke from the keyboard, fetching or storing a record from disc, printing a line, or accepting data from the modem. Although you may touch-type the keys at olympic speed, those pauses every few seconds and the time between keystrokes are opportunities for the computer to do more work. An unacceptable operating system would only do one thing at a time and force everything to wait for the next step. Although the time loss for any one operation would be small, the bottom line would be a useless system. A good operating system hops about from task to task like a juggler—fire up the next line to print—did he strike that key yet?—get the next record—oops, the screen needs refreshing—set up the next print line—here's the keystroke, does it make sense—no time now, look at it later, printer's ready—is this the last line?—running out of things to print, fetch the next record from disc—that keystroke's dumb, give him an error message—fetch it from disc—got the next record, move it to the print buffer—another keystroke. . . .

Good management is hard for people to achieve and no less difficult to program. It's bug prone, and consequently, it needs a lot of testing. An efficient operating system is complicated and it needs a lot of memory. The same operating system (from the point of view of external appearances) may be made to fit in different memory sizes, but the difference may be how efficiently it manages the system's resources. The operating system can swing performance over a four- or five-to-one range.

5.1.2. Optimization

Keeping a dozen balls juggling in the air isn't all there is to it. There's a higher level of efficiency which can be obtained by employing effective strategies. Let's use word-processing as an example. Say that the document you're editing is too big to hold in memory. A dumb program fetches the next segment only when you call for it so that there's a time lag every time you need a new segment. A smart program keeps track of the direction in which you're moving and fetches two or three segments ahead for you. Also, while you pause to think, it stores the revised version without an explicit command from you. The programmer has built some smarts into the software. It's similar for the operating system. It can, within limits, rearrange the order in which things are done to achieve higher efficiency. This is especially true for managing the disc. Simultaneous disc operations may be needed to fetch and/or store programs, data, directories, indexes, temporary work space, and to support the printer. Optimization means not only that the operating system keeps track of what's up in the air, but also that it schedules things so that the least time is wasted.

5.1.3. Memory Management

Even a huge memory isn't enough for everything at once. The operating system constantly juggles programs and data in and out of memory. This kind of thing can be really frenetic for integrated packages with windowing. The memory must be shared, and therefore, its use must be managed. Management of memory means giving each program what it needs, when it needs it, in accordance to a scheme which is globally optimum. If too much memory is given to one process, then some other process must suffer. While effective memory management was not a big issue in early personal computer operating systems, as application complexity has increased, so has the importance of memory management.

5.1.4. Tuning

Tuning is the act of matching the computer and its operating system to best fit the workload. Tuning is a technical operation. For mini- and mainframe computers, which are normally attended by a professional staff, tuning is done regularly as the nature of the work changes. Personal computers (for the most part) are pretuned, but there are some things you can do: how you partition a hard disc between data and programs; how you partition main memory for printer use; how you allocate memory to service the disc; the order in which things are read from and written to the disc (interlace). As personal computer operating systems become more sophisticated, there will be even more opportunities for fiddling with the system and for tuning it to match your needs. *However, I know of no personal computer for which tuning is required in order to run things.* Tuning is required only if you want to squeeze every last bit of performance out of the system. Designers of **vertical packages** (i.e., bundled hardware/software packages intended to serve a specific application) will normally tune the system to an optimum configuration for that application—we say that they are **sharply tuned.** General-purpose personal computers, conversely, are **broadly tuned:** the combination of hardware and operating system is tuned *to what the designer believes is an optimum for an assumed mix of work.* The system will be out of tune for any mix other than the assumed mix. A broadly tuned system has fair performance for most applications. A sharply tuned system has great performance for very specific jobs, and lousy performance elsewhere. All other factors being equal, tuning can swing performance over a two-to-one range. An unscrupulous but clever vendor can make his system appear to be much faster by tuning the hell out of it for the demonstration programs!

5.2. The Software

5.2.1. Good Algorithms and Bad

The final performance factor is the software package and the **algorithms** on which it's based. Consider how you might look up the word "poke-berry" in the dictionary. If you were pathologically stupid, you'd start with "aardvark" and crawl halfway through the dictionary, word-by-word, until you reached "pokeberry". A more sensible procedure is to jump to "P," skip to "pr", back to "poke," and then to "pokeberry." The above was an example of how two different algorithms can have vastly different per-formances. As incredible as it may seem, there's a lot of software that looks things up in a manner that's not much better than the first approach. The proper choice of algorithm can swing the performance over a range mea-sured in millions. The kinds of processes which are very sensitive to the algorithm used include: sorting, searching, spell-checking, and solving equations. Very good algorithms may be proprietary, unpublished, and kept as trade secrets. Sometimes it's the algorithm which makes a package pos-sible. A justifiable claim of a thousandfold improvement in performance is not impossible, especially if the work is processing-intensive.

5.2.2. Tuning and Problem Assumptions

The efficiency of any algorithm is based on the assumed characteristics of the problem. If our dictionary consisted of only 10 words, then the "stu-pid" serial approach described above is actually faster than the more com-plicated skipping algorithm. Similarly, if we had to deal with a dictionary of several million words, then the skipping algorithm is stupid compared to what can be done by better algorithms.

Just as the operating system must be tuned to the assumed workload, the package designer must select and tune an algorithm to the assumed data characteristics. So both vendors claim to use the Belchfire algorithm, but one vendor has a better tuning match to your problem set. Then there's the vendor whose very convincing demonstration is convincing only because the problem exactly matches the characteristics which the algorithm handles best. Tuning can swing performance over a four- or five-to-one range.

Because no one algorithm can be best everywhere, really sophisticated search, sort, and solve software uses a mix of algorithms and has an automatic transmission to shift gears between them: it's complicated, bug-prone, and takes a lot of memory. The development cost for such software, if brought to an acceptable quality level, is obviously higher.

5.2.3. The Source Language Impact

Programs are written in a language, called the **source language.** For our purpose, we can distinguish between three different ways a program can be written: **interpreter, compiled,** and **assembly language.**

An **interpreter** is a program that translates statements in the source language into instructions which can be executed by the computer. The translation is done on-the-fly, as processing progresses. Therefore, in addition to the actual processing that has to be done, there's the additional time required to do the translation: that time must be expended whenever the program is run. The advantage of interpreted software is that it's easy to check, modify, and create. The disadvantage is that it's slow. Few commercially successful programs run in interpreter mode—not just because it's slow, but more important, because it's too easy to steal. Public domain software, by contrast, is often written in an interpreter language. The most used interpreter language is Basic.

The same program that ran under an interpreter can be translated from the source language to computer instructions once and for all, or **compiled.** The translation, or compilation, is done by the vendor. Compiled software can't be easily changed or stolen unless you have the original or **source** program. The translation process can itself either introduce efficiency or slow things down terribly. A good translator can produce machine code that's better on an average than a human, while a bad translator can create ludicrously slow software. Sometimes, a vendor can improve a package's performance just by using a better translator.

The most efficient (and error prone) software is written in **assembly language.** Assembly language is a way of writing programs whose instructions match one-for-one the instructions which the hardware uses. Function-for-function, programs written in assembly language are efficient, but far more labor intensive than the equivalent program written in a **higher-order language** such as FORTRAN or Pascal. At one time, the whole operating system was written in assembly language, but this practice is dying out with the introduction of languages such as C which are suited to such jobs. However, performance-critical segments of the operating system or packages may be written in assembly language. A dedicated programmer working in assembly language can beat the best translator and can optimize a small program segment so that it can outperform the same routine written in an HOL by a factor of two or three to one. A slow package may be improved by just this strategem.

5.3. Performance Laws

Humans have a linear mentality when it comes to performance. We intuitively expect that if it takes *n* seconds to process *y* objects, then it will take twice as long to process twice as many objects. While that's true for some things, it's not true for all: and the fact that it's not true is a source of confusion, anger, and frustration where performance is involved. Figure 8-3 shows several families of performance laws. In all cases, we show the time to process versus the number of things processed. Note that the lines cross each other, which means that if one algorithm follows one curve, and another follows a different law, then there is a region in which the first is superior, and another region in which the opposite is true. If your job in life is designing algorithms, then understanding these laws is an essential part of your tool kit. But why should a personal computer user bother? You should bother because knowing which laws apply to which process helps you to have realistic performance expectations. If you think linearly, then a process which follows a cube law will seem to have suffered a catastrophic performance loss when you went from 5 items to 10. Knowing that it's a cube law process won't make it go any faster but it will help you accept the nature of things and will make the wait more bearable. There are five main groups of processing laws. They are in the order of increasing work: logarithmic, linear, *N*log*N*, polynomial and exponential. Typical cases of each are discussed below:

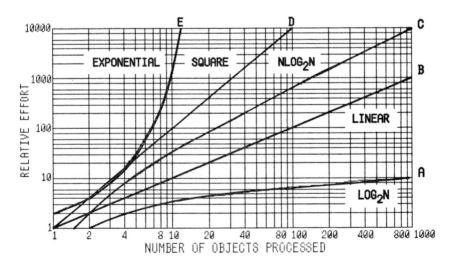

Figure 8-3. Behavior of different processing laws (note use of log-log scale; logs and exponents to base 2).

Logarithmic. This is the curve labeled *A* in figure 8-3. The work is proportional to the logarithm of number of objects manipulated. The primary example of this law is searching an ordered or indexed file. The work is proportional to the logarithm of the number of items in the file. Poor search algorithms will be linear with respect to the number of items in the file. Very few processes are better than logarithmic and most logarithmic processes are dominated by some kind of searching.

Linear. This is the curve labeled *B*. The work is proportional to the number of objects involved. This kind of law dominates simple processes. Typical linear processes include: sorting things into categories, finding the biggest or the smallest, searching for a specific word in text, searching an unordered file, picking a good stock out of *n* possible stocks, shuffling a deck of cards, finding the median of a set of n numbers.

NlogN. This is curve *C*. The work is proportional to the product of the logarithm of the number of objects and the number of objects (i.e., *NlogN*). Efficient sorting is a typical *NlogN* process, but naive algorithms go as *n*-squared. Other *NlogN* processes are: finding the shortest path, analyzing a PERT chart, and many optimization problems.

Polynomial. This is a family of laws, of which the first is the square-law which is shown as curve *D*. Polynomial processes go as the square, cube, or higher, of the number of objects involved. Polynomial laws can give you a bad shock. The primary example of a polynomial process is a stupid sort algorithm. Simultaneous equation solving goes as the cube or higher.

Exponential. How long it would take the million monkeys to type out Shakespeare's work, playing chess, or an equivalently complex business game such as analyzing decision trees, picking a good portfolio. Processes that follow exponential laws could have simple programs that seem to behave decently on toy and demonstration problems but that require all the supercomputers in the world combined for realistic cases.

6. MEASURES, COMPARISONS, AND BENCHMARKING

6.1. Measuring Versus Comparing

Performance can be measured, but even the act of measurement costs more than any possible benefit for a single personal computer. Measurements are made by vendors, their competitors, the designers, and reviewers. It's rare, though, in the context of personal computer use, that you need to know the actual performance. What you typically want to do is to compare competing solutions to your problem: two different computers, operating systems, or packages. If actual performance figures are important, because you're involved in a multiple-unit purchase that's going to be used for a

very narrow set of well-defined tasks, then you're beyond this book and into performance analysis of a type that's little different than the kind of thing you would have to do for a mainframe computer—because the modern personal computer is not much less complex than a mainframe, only slower.

6.2. Benchmarks

The primary method used to compare different systems is called **"benchmarking."** A **benchmark** is a simple problem which is representative of what you want to do. For example, if you wanted to test the speed of a spell-checking program, you might create an awful document with many misspellings in it. You compare the performance of different spell-checkers by testing them against this document. You time how long it takes from start to finish with a stopwatch. If that document is really representative of what you intend to do, then the benchmark test is valid. It's not possible to evaluate an entire system, or even a package with a single benchmark. Not only isn't it possible, but it's misleading because no one benchmark covers everything you want to do. You'll need several benchmarks for each package or system you test.

There are, in the literature, "standard" benchmarks, the most popular of which is the procedure used to check prime numbers, known as "the sieve of Eratosthenes." Other "standard" benchmarks include: evaluating a fixed spreadsheet; some raw calculations such as addition, subtraction, multiplication, and division; formatting and copying discs; sorting a fixed list of numbers. There's nothing wrong with the "standard" benchmarks, and using them as a basis for starting a comparison and selection is better than nothing. If something showed a ten-to one performance advantage on the standard benchmarks, I *might* be inclined to bet that it was faster—but at two-to-one, I'd ask for favorable odds. The problem with "standard" benchmarks is that they're intended to satisfy all users in all situations, which means that they're so general that they can't really give a specific comparison. For example, multiplying a million numbers tells you a lot about multiplication, which might be 1% of my work, 5% of yours, and 0.05% of hers.

Use published benchmarks as a general guide and starting point, or if you don't have time to go deeper—but recognize the limitations, and that their validity is based on assumptions and situations that you can't control and which may have no relation to what you're doing.

6.3. Doing Your Own Benchmarks

It's unlikely that you'll be able to do your own benchmarks until you have a computer and have used it for a while. The benchmark exercise, then, is most likely to be used for a new computer or to compare a new package against one you're already using. There are two benchmarks you should be interested in: (1) a benchmark that's typical of the average work you do, and (2) one that characterizes the time-consuming, annoying work—the work for which you would welcome a performance improvement.

Benchmarks work best when they're simple, clean, and easily understood. For example, if you're interested in the performance of a spreadsheet package, a benchmark that just adds successive columns and totals from column to column is as useful as a more realistic benchmark. If you use a narrow set of spreadsheets, then use one of them as a benchmark. Alternatively, estimate the average number of additions or subtractions, multiplications, and divisions in your spreadsheets and build a spreadsheet that reflects those numbers. Because the evaluation may be very fast, if at all possible, arrange to automatically reevaluate the same set of figures a hundred, a thousand, or ten thousand times. Keep the processing laws in mind—most laws aren't linear and as a consequence, it's essential to measure at least three points to get a valid handle on the performance. For example, sort 100 records, 200, 500, and 1000. You can use duplication commands to build files of whatever size you need.

Word processing benchmarks can be based on a long standard document. You create the document by writing a short test-piece and then reproducing it with the block copy command. Then you can do several thousand search and replaces, spell checking, reformatting, and other time-consuming operations. For data-base management packages, the useful benchmarks include: searching for a record, inserting a record, deleting a record, and most important of all, sorting a file.

Don't take the results of benchmarking too seriously. Don't let performance be the end-all and be-all of your evaluation. Look for things over a two-to-one range. Don't be trapped into making comparisons based on figures worked to ten decimal places when the underlying assumptions are dubious in the first place.

GETTING STARTED—HARDWARE, SOFTWARE, and WHY

Hardware is the physical stuff you buy. A computer's hardware typically consists of the **keyboard,** a screen or **monitor,** one or two **disc drives,** and a **printer.** The keyboard is used to enter data, commands, words, or numbers. The screen lets you see things such as words, numbers, or pictures. The disc drives are what you put the discs (also **"diskettes"** or **"floppies"**) into. The diskettes are used to store **programs** or **data** or both.

The hardware is like a blank slate. It can't do anything by itself, but it can, with the proper software, do almost anything. **Software** is a set of instructions that converts that blank slate into the special kind of thing you want the system to do for you—for example, type form letters, do income tax calculations, pull customer lists, and so on. Every user wants to do different things with a computer. While it is possible to build everything into the hardware, it isn't done. It isn't done because the hardware required to meet all possible customers' needs would fill a house. It's cheaper, these days, to build a generalized piece of hardware that can do anything, and let the user tailor that hardware by specialized software, than it would be to build the do-all hardware. Furthermore, it also means more flexibility and freedom from obsolescence than fixed hardware could ever provide.

The three most commonly used pieces of software are: **word-processor, spreadsheet,** and **data-base.** A **word-processing software package** converts your computer into a world-class typewriter, form letter producer, mailing list handler, and almost anything else you might want to do with words. A **spreadsheet program** or **package** is used to do almost any kind of complicated, repetitive calculations, such as financial proposals, construction planning, cash flow analyses, and so on. A **data base package** is used to handle large files of data, from lists of telephone numbers to complicated customer records which you design to suit your purpose. There are, in addition to these three main kinds of packages, hundreds of specialized packages, such as all the common accounting functions (general ledger, accounts receivable, accounts payable), inventory, pricing, mathematical—

you name it—if it can be done by a personal computer, there's probably a package available for it. There are, of course, games and entertainment software, ranging from blackjack to a pretty good aircraft training-simulator for new pilots.

Most work starts by putting a special software package, called the **operating system,** into the left-hand disc drive. There's more on what the operating system does in other parts of this book, but for now, you might as well think of it as if it were part of the hardware. You put the operating system disc into the drive, the computer does its thing, and then the following (typically) appears on the screen:

A⟩

The next step is (usually) to remove the operating system disc and to replace it with the disc for the package you want to run now—(the word processor, say). You may have to type something such as "GO", followed by hitting the carriage return key. The package is then loaded into the computer, which has then become a word-processing system, say. The right-hand drive is usually used to store data, such as letters, address lists, form letters, records, calculations, and so on.

The operating system software is often included in the computer's price: but expect to pay about $250–500 for each additional software package you want. You may find that a dealer is reluctant to cut the hardware price below a certain point, but he may be willing to toss a few useful packages in to sweeten the deal.

THE AUDIO MONITOR

1. IN THE OLD DAYS

Computers are silent. They do things, but there's no sign that anything is actually happening. Old computers weren't like that. Some of the first computers were constructed of the same kind of hardware that was used in pinball machines. The room would resound with impressive clicks and clacks at the slightest excuse. When electronic computers came along in the early '50s some of them made impressive noises, but most of them worked in eerie silence. While this was technically reasonable, it was psychologically bad. So we put lights on the console and had their blinking as a substitute for the sound. The movie and TV industries understood the psychology better than computer designers did—TV computers blinked and beeped like the granddaddy of all pinball machines. Today's computers, though, from supercomputer to personal, are silent. Oh, there's the occasional chirp of a disc drive, a printer clatter now and then, and of course, the whir of the fans; but all that tells you very little about what's happening inside. And the huge panels of blinking lights are gone and have been replaced by unimpressive CRTs.

2. THE AUDIO MONITOR

I don't know what genius dreamed up the **audio monitor.** It's a loudspeaker connected to the computer in such a way that what the computer's doing is translated into an audible sound. It was part of most mainframe computers, but it's out style now. An experienced operator could tell what the computer was doing, which program was running, if everything was okay, or if there had been a malfunction. The audio monitor was as useful to a sensitive operator as a stethoscope is to a physician.

When sophisticated operating systems arrived in the early '70s, they took over much of the intelligence that had been exercised by the operators, and the few manufacturers that had had audio monitors no longer offered them. I know of no commerical computer today that has an audio monitor. Alas, it went with the blinking lights, the rocking tapes, the card reader's tattoo, and all the other things that made computers fun to watch and listen.

3. YOUR OWN AUDIO MONITOR

Those of us who had learned to depend on audio monitors mourned the loss of this valuable diagnostic tool, but our entreaties to the computer manufacturers didn't help. So another genius discovered that a cheap transistor radio placed near the computer, could do all that an audio monitor ever did, and better.

The **audio monitor** is a *cheap* AM/FM transistor radio with an extendible antenna. It needs the antenna to pick up the sound. It should be a cheap radio because an expensive radio might suppress the very interference you're trying to pick up. Place the radio with the antenna extended across the top of the computer (not the monitor). Tune it to 54 on the AM dial to start with. Move the radio until you get a clear, pleasant, sound. Tune around and listen for a regular, one second beep, or a steady tone interrupted with a short pause or click every second. This may not happen on all computers. In any case, find an area in which there are relatively clean beeps and tones in response to what you do at the keyboard. AM works best for most computers but some will do better on FM.

4. USING THE AUDIO MONITOR

The audio monitor makes your computer come to life. Almost every keystroke results in a beep, click, whistle, or change to the sound pattern. Sometimes, an innocent keystroke, for a simple operation, will yield an impressive concert. You can mystify your friends and amaze your colleagues and supervisors. Hide the radio so that your boss doesn't see it and if she asks, tell her that it's the latest option. Leave it on while you work. The more you use it the more you learn; the more you'll be able to tell if there's been a crash. You'll appreciate how complicated seemingly simple operations can be. And it will give you insight.

Word processing packages are a good place to start to interpret the audio monitor, but almost any package you use, and any normal operation is beneficial. Here's a beginning to interpreting what's happening:

1. *One-Second Beep, Click, or Pause.* This is the program that updates the clock every second. You may also hear additional work on the minute and on the hour.
2. *Do-Nothing Pattern.* Computers have to execute instructions even when they have nothing to do. This usually produces a clear, steady tone, or

a tone interrupted by beeps, clicks, or pauses or some other kind of repetitive pattern. It could be more complicated. High-quality operating systems are programmed to check the system's health when there's nothing else to do, and that results in a more complicated do-nothing pattern.

3. *Start-Up Pattern.* Turn your audio monitor on *before* you turn the computer on and listen to the start-up and bootstrap procedure. It should be the same whenever you use it. You'll soon be able to spot anything out of the ordinary.

4. *Normal Operation.* Most operations produce clicks or have a raspy quality. Pure tones are rare, although some things can play a really nice tune.

5. *High-Pitched Scream or Whistle.* This is typically a crash. The tone for a crash is often clear, pure, and it has none of the raspy qualities you'll soon associate with normal operation. It can usually be heard everywhere on the dial.

6. *Silence.* That's probably a crash.

7. *Other.* Go through your normal routine and listen to what happens when: you touch the RETURN key, any special keys, store, fetch, copy, get a directory listing, move the cursor, give a print command, change discs, format a disc, copy a disc, copy a file, erase a file, and rename a file.

CONNECTORS, CABLES, AND SWITCHES

1. THE PROBLEM

Something as mundane as connectors and cables can give you big head-aches. It's also another place in which you might think to save a few bucks only to pay for it in hours of frustration and wasted time. Connectors and cables range from those that have one or two wires in them to those that have a few dozen. There's almost never a problem with the first type: they either work or they don't. The problems occur with the multiwire cables and their connectors. A related source of problems are such things as **ABC** and **X switches,** which you can use to switch between several printers or to share a printer among several computers. The three most common multi-wire connectors are those used for RS-232, Centronics-Parallel, and IEEE-488 interfaces. There's a wide variety of prices for seemingly identical ca-bles, and as usual, you get what you pay for.

2. FULL WIRING, PARTIAL WIRING, AND LENGTH

An **interface,** such as the commonly used Centronics parallel printer inter-face, has many wires (36). Each wire has a purpose, but not all of them have to be connected to work properly. The first difference between cheap and expensive cables is the number of connected wires. Cheap cables will have the minimum number of connected wires, while high-quality cables will have most or *all* of the wires connected, whether they seem to be needed or not. I only (knowingly) use fully-connected cables and connectors, not because they're necessary, but because they're likelier to avoid problems than to create them. It's insurance. Partially wired connectors and cables can give you mysterious problems, especially when used with switching de-vices.

Use the shortest cable that will do the job. Never connect two cables to make a longer one. If the short cable doesn't reach, buy a longer one. Also, follow the equipment manufacturer's limits on the longest allowable cable—keep well short of that length.

3. CONSTRUCTION AND TYPE

I don't like the flat ribbon cables. They may be okay for some uses, but they're subject to abrasion, tearing, and they're often not electrically shielded so that they tend to pick up more noise than a properly shielded round cable. Good cables have an armored shield that protects them physically and electrically. The shield is also brought out of the connector and has an attached grounding lug. It's a good idea to make the ground connection if one is provided. Cheap cables may be round, but not shielded, or if shielded, the shield is not properly connected.

Good connectors have a positive locking mechanism (such as the spring clips on Centronics connectors, the screws on RS-232 and IEEE-488 connectors, or the clip on telephone connectors). Good hardware has those locks, while garbage hardware saves a few cents by leaving the locks out, for which you pay. Use the locks if they're there. It makes a more positive connection and prevents connectors from coming loose. Loose connectors can be another source of mysterious problems—jiggle the connectors and make sure that they're properly plugged in before you call for service.

Good connectors can be opened without damage so that you can check the connections, or remove unwanted ones. They also use gold-plated contacts.

4. COMPATIBILITY

Because not all cables are fully wired, all cables are not compatible. If you put two cables in series, or through a switching device, it is possible that, because of a difference in the wires that are not connected, a necessary connection will not be made from end to end. This can be frustrating because either cable may work alone, with or without the switch, but the combination will not work. Using fully wired (and therefore more expensive) cables and switches avoids this problem.

Sometimes, certain wires should *not* be connected. In such cases, a fully-connected cable will get you into trouble. It's not good design, but you may have to live with it. If it's a high-quality cable and connectors, then you can undo the connector and remove the connection that you don't need. If you do that, label the connector; for example: "pin 14 disconnected". This won't usually be a problem unless you're using switching devices. Another alternative is to always use the manufacturer's cable—but this can be confusing because, say, the printer manufacturer's notion of a proper cable doesn't match the computer manufacturer's idea. Compatibility isn't something to be taken for granted.

Good installation manuals will specify exactly which wires must, and which *must not* be connected. Good designs will work so that all pins can be connected, thereby avoiding the compatibility problems.

Connector incompatibilities can have subtle effects. It can be very difficult to determine if the problem is caused by the software, a hardware malfunction, a cockpit error on your part, the wrong connectors, or incompatible connectors. Furthermore, such incompatibilities may not show up for all packages. If you suspect a problem, reduce the configuration to the minimum required to run the package. Then add one thing at a time, until the problems show up. You may have to employ test gear, connector and cable checkers, or alternatively, get a knowledgeable technician to check things for you. I've had trouble with about half of new hardware installations and connector and cable incompatibilities were most often the culprits.

POWER

1. CLEAN AND DIRTY POWER

Don't expect reliable work from your computer if you don't have clean, reliable, power. Clean power means a good line, proper outlets, the right voltage, and the removal of electrical crud. One of the common causes of unreliable operation and crashes is the power used. Converting dirty power into clean power is cheap and easy, and one of your best investments.

2. A GOOD LINE AND OUTLETS

Start with the outlet. It should be a properly wired, three-prong, grounded outlet. Don't use converter plugs; rather, replace the outlet if it's not correct. Just because the outlet itself is correct does not mean that it's wired correctly. Incorrect outlet wiring is another source of trouble: it's common in many older homes and office buildings. You don't have to take the outlet apart or be an electrician to check the wiring. You can buy a tester for under ten dollars at electrical supply houses, hardware stores, and electronics stores. Plug the tester in. It'll tell you if anything is wrong and just what. Get it fixed before you go on.

Most outlets are double and that's not enough for most computers. You need an extension cord combined with a grounded outlet strip. Four outlets will suffice for most computers. Don't use junk. Buy a proper extension strip or one combined with a **filter** (see below).

I recommend that each computer have its own power line tied back directly to the fuse or circuit breaker box. It should be wired with number 12 wire. Most offices are not wired for the power consumption of computers and as a consequence, you may find too many computers on the same line—which is a source of trouble. I like computer outlets high on the wall. It's more convenient, and less likely to be slopped up with water by the cleaning people. If you have a hard disc that has to be kept plugged in, or if you do long overnight runs, then have a separate outlet labeled "vacuum cleaner" so that the cleaning people won't unplug your system or use your power strip. That's what happened to my brother and that's how he solved a recurring series of mysterious crashes. So before you call the computer manufacturer, abuse the software vendors, or invest money in power conditioning equipment, make sure that not only is the system plugged in, but that it stays plugged in when you're away.

3. ELECTRICAL CRUD

A good source of power with a plug that doesn't pop out of the wall is not always enough. The system must be protected against a variety of electrical crud that comes down the power line. Most good computers have some crud filtering built-in that's designed to handle moderate amounts and it may be adequate in your case. Cheap hardware saves a few dollars by leaving out the crud filters—but you'll pay for it one way or the other in the end.

Electrical crud is cause by many things: lightning, electric motors, fluorescent lights, cars crashing into power poles, air conditioners, and so on. Having a separate line helps to cut the crud down. Electrical crud (or **noise**, as it's called) comes in two flavors—fast and slow. Fast crud is short surges or drops in voltage under a thousandth of a second long. Slow crud is a drop or surge in voltage longer than a thousandth, typically a few hundredths of a second long. A filter that works on short crud doesn't work on long crud and vice-versa. Short crud filters are cheap. You can buy a combined extension cords, power strips, filter, and circuit breaker for under $100, such as those made by ISOBAR and SGL-Waber, to name two. But your computer may have a good built-in filter—ask. If you use a filter strip when you don't need one, it won't hurt the system but it's a more expensive way to buy extension cords and power strips.

Slow crud is more expensive to filter out and is more persistent. Proper filtering may require a **regulator** or in extreme cases an **UPS** (see below).

4. REGULATORS

Filtering high-speed crud and even low-speed crud is no help if the voltage is incorrect. This becomes a problem in the summertime when some urban areas have brownouts. The nominal voltage, which should be between 115 and 120 volts, can drop when many air conditioners are in use. The computer's power supply can handle things down to about 105 volts, but below that, you can expect problems. If your area has brownouts (a drop of 10% or more from the nominal voltage) or if you're forced to share a power line with many other users, then invest in a **regulator** transformer. This is a big box (25 to 50 pounds is typical). A good one will accept voltages as low as 80 or 90 volts and put out a clean 120 volts from which all low-speed crud has been removed. It may or may not include high-speed filters. Such regulators cost between $300 and $800 and are available from companies such as SOLA and most computer equipment suppliers.

5. UNINTERRUPTIBLE POWER SUPPLY (UPS)

The ultimate in filtering and regulation is an **uninterruptible power supply (UPS)**. They're a little bigger than a regulator but more expensive ($400 to $1200). They have a battery that will allow you to operate for 10 to 30 minutes even if there's a total blackout. Many of them do all of the above jobs: extension cord, power strip, high and low filters, and regulation. The cost therefore, is not as high as it might seem at first. If your installation has more than one blackout a month or frequent brownouts, and especially if you have a hard disc, you should add the cost of an UPS to your system cost. You don't need a whole lot of time. All you need is enough time to store your work, possibly do a backup, and quit clean. If you need more time than that, some of these units can be provided with auxiliary batteries that could let you work for hours (in total darkness?).

Make a proper comparison of different models by calculating how long you can expect to operate without power. The units are all rated in terms of how much power they can put out (watts), for how long (minutes). If the unit can output 200 watts for 30 minutes, then that's a total available power of 100 watt hours. If your equipment draws 200 watts, you've got a half hour. If your hard disc draws 20 watts, you'll be safe for 10 hours, assuming that you shut everything off but the disc. One of the big differences I found between units was in the total watt-hours available. One $400 unit gave only 25 watt hours while the $750 unit gave 250 watt hours: or five minutes versus an hour for the typical computer.

Some units do a fine job of switching from the power line to the battery and keeping things going during the blackout; but when the power's restored, *they throw in their own nasty piece of electrical crud,* thereby creating the very problem you were trying to avoid. It's something you want to ask about. The safest thing to do is to shut down cleanly and read a book by candlelight, or find some other form of entertainment until the power's restored. Another thing you can do is not to buy hardware whose turn-off instructions seem to be as complicated as shutting down the local utility.

INSTALLATION

1. WHY AND WHAT

Installation is the process of adapting a package to:

1. The hardware.
2. The operating system.
3. Options in using the package.
4. They way you want to work.

Installation procedures can, from the user's point of view, be simple or complicated. They can be complicated because: (1) the package is flexible and can be adapted to your needs, or (2) it's poorly written and it has only primitive installation software. Conversely, an installation procedure may be simple because: (1) there are no tailoring options, or (2) the installation procedure is automated.

It's hard to generalize which is which, so that a simple or complicated installation procedure is not in and of itself a valid criterion for judging quality. If, however, the procedure is complicated, for whatever reason, then it must be designed with the following in mind:

1. A step-by-step (possibly laborious) process with matching instructions.
2. Built-in, safe, options (these are called **default options** or **default values**).
3. A fail-safe procedure—because we make mistakes.
4. The best possible writing and graphics.

2. INSTALLATION COMPONENTS

2.1. Hardware Installation

Hardware installation consists of:

1. Plugging things in.

2. Setting switches.
3. Telling the operating system what you've done.

It's possible to automate most of what's usually done in hardware installation, but besides the additional cost of the supporting software, every piece of hardware, including **after-market** hardware would have to conform to unrealistically stringent standards. The safe approach, taken by most vendors, is to have the user tell the operating system exactly what's connected to what and what hardware there is. The vendor assumes a minimum **default hardware configuration.** Typically, the default configuration is the minimum amount of memory, one standard disc drive, a popular printer, and a standard monitor. The default hardware configuration is also assumed by the operating system. If you don't go through the installation procedure, the operating system will assume that you have the minimal configuration and as a consequence, the packages you use will not exploit the hardware you actually have; it may not be possible to run some packages, or even to load the packages into memory.

Dip switches are used to specify such things as the amount of memory, if there is or isn't a coprocessor, number and type of disc drive, printer interface type, light-pen, mouse, and so on. Dip switches may be conveniently located on the back panel, beneath the front panel, or deliberately placed inside the cabinet. A logical designer puts all dip switches that must be changed when you plug in different devices on the back panel, and all dip switches that must be changed only when you add an extension or **option board** inside the computer.

2.2. Operating System Installation

2.2.1. Phases

The operating system must be told what hardware is plugged in and how the dip switches are set. Operating system installation consists of three phases: (1) mandatory, (2) options, and (3) tailoring.

2.2.2. Mandatory

The mandatory phase is mainly concerned with specifying the hardware configuration. A good hardware installation procedure will step you through a series of questions, most of which can be answered with a "yes" or "no," a choice of several numbers (e.g., amount of memory installed), or the selection of specific models (or printers, say). Some installation programs determine these values and asks you to confirm them. The following order is typical: installed memory, processor options (e.g., arithmetic coprocessor), number and type of disc drives, printer. Each device has its own installation procedure. A menu allows you to choose the order in which things are installed (except for memory). You can also review what's been done before you make it permanent.

2.2.3. Special Hardware Options

Installing hardware options can be complicated because there are so many different options. There are two ways to handle it:

1. The possibility has been included in the main installation program. This is typical for printers, monitors, light-pens, communications, and mice.
2. A separate installation program for each device.

The first approach is safe but limited because it's not possible to predict what (after-market, say) devices will be available and how they're to be installed. The second option is flexible, but there can be conflicting installation requirements. For example, if you install device X and then later install device Y, and both have their own installation procedure, you have no assurance that the X installation and the Y installation are compatible. If they're not compatible, the system might work with either X or Y installed alone, but not with both. A more bizarre situation can occur in which a third hardware option is bollixed as a result of the conflict between X and Y. So X and Y work fine, but the printer you've been using all along now doesn't work. One of the advantages of buying optional hardware only from the computer manufacturer is the reduction (but not the elimination) of such conflicts. The price is: higher cost, fewer features, and a longer time to wait. If you intend to use a nonstandard configuration with many options, then be sure to have the technical expertise needed on tap.

Devices with inherently complicated installations include: almost any communication device (such as a modem), after-market hard-disc drives, printers with graphics options, special keyboards, and high-resolution monitors.

2.2.4. Tailoring

The designer of a complicated package, such as an operating system, has many choices which affect the way users will work. The choices are often not between "right" and "wrong" but between individual preferences. Early personal computer operating systems provided no facilities for tailoring the package to the user's preferences. As a result, operating system designers had to contend with a multitude of comments and suggestions along the lines of "Why didn't you do such-and-such?", or "Wouldn't it be nice if you did . . . ?" The modern approach to operating system design is to provide tailoring facilities. This allows the user to make the operating system appear completely different from "normal." Each change must be installed. The kinds of things that can be changed include: keyboard "click" on or off, screen colors, clock display on or off, time of day and date format, assignment of memory to **ramdisc,** the name of disc drives, automatic startup procedures, assignment of keys, operating system prompt, verification of disc operations, monitor screen format, disc format.

Only the most common forms of tailoring are provided with an explicit installation program. Less common variations are installed by executing operating system commands, and the most complicated (and least used) variations are installed by writing programs or by direct (and dangerous) modification of the operating system's data. Both of these are best left to experts. So actually, operating system tailoring methods are spread from fully automatic procedures at one end to raw programming at the other. Item for item, all else being equal, the operating system that provides an installation program for a feature is better than one that requires you to program the change.

2.3. Package Installation

2.3.1. General

Installing a package is similar to installing the operating system, which after all, is just another program. The main difference is that almost all package installation is done using an installation program or package commands. There are three aspects to package installation: (1) prerequisites, (2) mandatory phase, and (3) optional or tailoring phase.

2.3.2. Prerequisites

The prerequisites of a software package are the hardware and software you need to run it. It may be necessary to repeat much of the installation process that had been used with the operating system, and for complicated packages, there can be overlap and conflicts. It may seem silly to repeat parts of the operating system installation, but the package has been designed to work with many different hardware and configurations, *and operating systems.* Repeating the installation is a way to assure that the package will have the essential information even if the host computer or operating system doesn't. Hardware prerequisites can include: the amount of memory, types and number of discs, printer specifications, communications, and any other special hardware used by the package. Typically, hardware prerequisites installation is the first part of the installation.

Software prerequisites almost always assume a specific operating system and version. For example, "Version 3.1 or *later*." Some poor packages may set an upper limit to the operating system version and/or also a limit to the maximum amount of memory installed. Software prerequisites may also include another package in addition to the operating system. For example, an **application package** consists of a set of predefined spreadsheets—the spreadsheet software package is then a prerequisite. Spell-checking programs may have a word-processing package as a prerequisite, and many applications are constructed using a data-base management package for a base. There is rarely any installation required for such prerequisite packages, except for the sequence in which things must be loaded, or the requirement that the prerequisite software and the package be loaded onto the same disc using a specified operating system command sequence.

2.3.3. Mandatory Phase

The mandatory installation phase is that part which all users must go through. Installation actions required for prerequisites are part of the mandatory phase. Mandatory installation procedures may include creating a working copy of the program—often, this is done in conjunction with a **copy protection** scheme.

2.3.4. Optional Phase

The optional phase of package installation corresponds to tailoring for the operating system. It is usually the most complicated part of installation, but fortunately (for a good package) it can often be avoided at first. The optional phase is concerned with the available variations in the way you want to work. For example, multi-keystroke commands can be converted to single-keystroke commands by using the **function keys.** A printer can be directed to follow a specific format. The program can be directed to "awaken" in a specified state. A good package has a copious optional phase. It may be very complicated and its instruction manual could be as big as the working instruction manual.

2.3.5. Operating System and Package Conflicts

It's possible that the options you select during the operating system's installation and the options you select for the package differ—either by intent or by accident. A good package always keeps track of how things were set up by the operating system and restores those values when it quits. A bad package leaves its values installed instead of reinstalling the operating system's values. For example, you normally use 10 pitch on your printer, but for spreadsheet work, you direct the package to shift to condensed print at 15 pitch. The bad package leaves the 15 pitch set up after you quit. That kind of conflict is obvious and there's an easy, albeit annoying, way around it. Unfortunately, some of the inconsistencies are more complicated and not obvious. Many bugs have this origin. Note that often, the symptoms don't show up in the package that was responsible, but in whatever package you use next.

3. THE INSTALLATION PROCESS

3.1. "Before You Start"

Finding and reading the "Before You Start" notice (if there is one) is the most important part of the installation procedure. The part of the installation process discussed in such a notice can include complicated, vulnerable procedures. There is only one way to follow such instructions—keystroke-by-keystroke, point-by-point, exactly as specified, no matter how silly it may seem. Following arbitrary directions precisely takes training and experience: most first-time, would-be installers can't do it. The possible difficulties of installation is one of the best reasons for buying from a retailer rather than mail-order. You let the retailer do it for you—it's included in the higher price you paid.

3.2. Parameter Values

Installation consists of giving a program the information it needs to do its job. Most of these data are numbers, but they could also be device names or models, answers to yes/no questions, and so on. Three values are possible for any piece of information used during an installation:

1. The built-in value—also called the **default** value.
2. The previous value—because this could be the second or later time that you're installing the program.
3. The new value—what you are changing it to.

   A good installation program displays default values, the previous values, and the new values at all times that you might need to see it: especially when you're about to enter a new value. For example:

INSTALL PAGE SIZE:
Default size = 8.5 × 11 inches
Present size = 8.5 × 14 inches
New size = ???

There's also a simple command that you can use to display the current set-up and default options. For example:

Report Format Summary:

	CURRENT	PREVIOUS	DEFAULT
page width	8.0	8.5	8.5
page height	14.0	11.0	11.0
lines/inch	8.0	6.0	6.0
chars/inch	12.0	15.0	10.0
justified	yes	yes	no
left margin	15	20	10
right margin	90	120	70

Every number you enter is checked for validity by itself, and for consistency with previously entered numbers. In the above example, an 8-inch page width at 12 characters per inch allows a maximum right margin position of 96. Any number greater than 96 entered for the right margin option would be questioned by the program. You're then allowed to correct the value or to keep it, despite possible problems.

The installation procedure goes step by step. At the conclusion of a step, you're given the opportunity to:

1. Review the current entry.
2. Correct or change the new entry.
3. Install the change.
4. Quit (leaving things as they were).

Good procedures allow you to restart the installation at any sensible step. Bad procedures force you through the whole thing, even for minor changes.

3.3. Assumed (Default) Options and Option Selection

A good package can be extensively tailored. Many of the ways in which the package can be tailored may involve technicalities that are not obvious to the first-time user. It might not be possible to appreciate those features until you've gained some experience with the package. For example, WORD-STAR provides user control over how much of the **command menu** is present on the screen. You can select options that will display anything from the entire menu (appropriate at that point in time) to nothing at all. The more you display, the less room there is on the screen for text. Consequently, as you gain familiarity with the commands, you tend to choose smaller displays. VALDOCS has user levels ranging from "novice" to "expert." The "novice" selection blocks commands that might cause problems for inexperienced users. The "expert" has no restrictions.

Whatever the installation parameters are, be it in the mandatory or the optional phase of installation, the designers can (should) assume typical values, which are then built into the program as **default** options. Default options are essential to quality. The optional phase may allow you to change hundreds of options, of which you initially understand only a few. A good installation procedure will start with all such values installed. That way, although you may not be fully exploiting the package's features, you'll at least be working with reasonable values.

3.4. Filling in Details

Installing a package may require detailed data which are generally not known by the user. For example, printers can have a bewildering variety of parameters to specify. Designers should not expect nontechnical users to know these numbers, nor even to know where those numbers can be gotten. The ideal procedure gives the user a choice of several dozen name-brand printers, say. The detailed information is included in the program and automatically installed when that printer model is selected. The same applies to **modems,** discs, and other devices. If, for some technical reason it is not possible to have the installation program insert the details automatically, then the installation manual should list the details for enough popular devices to cover most users. The same principle of handling the details also applies to nonphysical things such as **communication protocols.**

3.5. Handling "Other"

Although automatic installation is provided for the most common name-brand devices or protocols there must still be an installation procedure for "other" situations or devices. If there is no such procedure, morality demands that the manual clearly exclude all devices and situations not explicitly covered. For example, it should say: "Printers which do not appear in the following list may not be usable with this package." I haven't seen such warnings.

It's usually possible to install devices and programs for situations and parameters not covered by the automatically selected methods (e.g., by naming a model number). This part of the installation process is concerned with covering the remaining few percent not covered elsewhere. Consequently, it tends to be more technical, less well designed, more error prone, and more complicated than normal installations.

3.6. Help Screens

A **help screen** contains information, explanations, and instructions which are pertinent to the task at hand. It's nice when there's a HELP key, such as on the Epson QX-10, but often its done by designating a special key or keystroke sequence (e.g., F1, ^H) for the purpose. Whatever method is used, the same method (e.g., key) should be used throughout the installation procedure and throughout the package. Touching the HELP key brings up a screenful of explanatory material or sometimes corrections of the installation manual's errors. I routinely fetch every HELP screen there is in the installation program the first time I do it. Of course, fetching the HELP screen doesn't destroy what you've already done. Typically, touching any key or the RETURN key brings you back to the installation procedure without harm.

The HELP screen defines terminology, states alternatives, suggests values, tells you how to undo a mess you've made, and all the rest. I've used some excellent installation procedures in which there was no installation manual but rather, a well-crafted sequence of questions, HELP screens, and summaries. The actual installation manual was a single page that told you how to start the installation program. This method of handling things has the advantage that it's easier to control and to assure that few mistakes will be made by the installer. Conversely, it may force you through the reinstallation or confirmation of things that you don't intend to change.

3.7. Recovery

We make mistakes, and in the especially vulnerable installation phase, first-time users of a package (be they computer novices or experts) make many mistakes. Therefore, some simple method for recovering the situation as it existed prior to installation is essential. Such recovery procedures should be invocable at every stage. They should restore either the default values or the previous values on choice. And there should always be a method for quitting without prejudice.

HYPE, PITCH, AND DATA

1. WRITTEN HYPE

I've yet to see a manual that doesn't try to sell me the package I've already bought. I suppose that if a publisher has as sweet piece of software he should be allowed to boast in the preface, but how about it when every other paragraph tells me how marvelous this or that is? Who are they trying to sell? Themselves?

One way to rate an instruction manual is to go through it with a felt marker pen and obliterate every word of hype. I took a two-hundred page manual and reduced it to sixty pages that way. Try it: especially if you're considering buying many copies. The army rates the effectiveness of a combat unit by its "fat to muscle ratio." "Fat" is headquarters, support, and overhead. "Muscle" is the troops that fight. Do the same for the information package:

PROCEDURE: Evaluate the "fat" (hype) to "muscle" (information) ratio* of the package before you buy. Rank as follows:

99%–100% Muscle		—excellent
97%–99%	"	—good
94%–97%	"	—fair
90%–94%	"	—marginally bearable
85%–90%	"	—only if there's nothing else
under 85%	"	—garbage

2. PICTORIAL HYPE

Hype isn't necessarily written. Graphics can also be hype. A vendor who ranks high in my esteem for good information packages, took an introductory manual for their operating system and crapped it up with cartoon

---

*Actually calculate it as: (information)/(information + hype).

characters. On page one there's a lion, tiger, and leopard being trained by an obnoxious yellow bird that looks like a cross between a canary and a parrot, and which is in desperate need of a nose job. And there's a mouse in the corner shivering with fear. Big-nose-yellow-bird appears ad nauseam doing things which have nothing to do with the subject, or which confused me. I've seen more mature stuff on Saturday morning TV cartoon shows. What was worse, I never saw either the cats or the mouse again. What happened to the mouse, Big Blue? Apply the "fat" to "muscle" criterion to this one and it slips from excellent to unbearable.

Graphics are an important teaching tool. Cartoons (if suited to the maturity of the audience) can also be useful. Cartoons, like humor, in technical material must be incisive, illustrative, and meaningful. Usually, the cartoons are mere filler and a distraction that masks the manual's mediocrity. Rank the pointless cartoons with the hype and factor their area into your evaluation of the fat/muscle ratio.

3. DEMONSTRATION PROGRAMS

Demonstration programs are useful but also the most insidious pieces of software hype there are. Demonstration programs (**demos**) can give you a good overview of a program's or computer's capabilities. Often, it's the demo that does the selling; but demo programs have the same relation to reality as TV commercials do. They are hard sell all the way. They razzle and they dazzle; they walk and they talk and they crawl on their bellies like reptiles. And they're easy to use. Pop in the disc, hit two keys and go-go-go! I've *never* had trouble getting a demo to run.* Let's look at demos from the inside.

A competent programmer can cook up a convincing demonstration of how a program will behave for a fraction of the cost of doing the actual software. Programmers have been writing mickey-mouse demos as long as they've been writing software. You've seen the TV pitchman use a glass cutter to snip out a silhouette of the "Charge of the Light Brigade" in a couple of seconds—and you know that it took him ten years of practice to get there. You know that if you buy the Flim Flam cutter that you'll cut your own wrist with it sooner than you'll cut glass. Did you think that software demos are different?

The demo is possible because 90% of software is concerned with strange situations, limitations, differences in hardware, memory, large data-bases, and thousands of records. The demo deals with a fiercely confined set of

---

*And sometimes it was the only part that ran.

circumstances which are easy to program. Furthermore, demo bugs are fixed by blocking the embarrassing cases. Honest demos, which are based on real software, do exist—but there aren't any easy rules that would help you tell which is which. If you know how to use the package then you can try big files, big numbers, oddball cases and see how many messages like these you get:

"Feature not implemented in this demonstration"
"Parameter beyond installed limits"
"See your dealer for a more thorough explanation"
"FATAL ERROR 060 AT USER UUO 45671"
"Go 'way kid! You bother me!"

But most demos won't let you try even that because for all their apparent pizzazz, they're nothing more than animated storyboards that may have nothing to do with the package's actual software. If you can't interact with it, it's of no more value than a slide show except in a multi-unit buy or a bulk license agreement where you can insist that every feature you saw during the demo be included as a contractual line-item.

4. USEFUL HYPE

Some hype is useful before you buy. There should be informative brochures (even if they do lie). Published reviews are part of the pitch as are published ratings by outfits such as *Software Digest*. Try to get all the brochures you can get before making a decision. Compare earlier brochures with later ones to see what new features are claimed and what old features have been dropped.

COPY PROTECTION

Software vendors spend lots of money developing and marketing their products, so it's natural that they want to protect their investment. Software piracy *is* probably a serious problem: I say "probably" because there are no real statistics on it other than the self-serving cries of anguish from some software vendors who claim that but for piracy, their income would have equalled the gross national product of Luxemburg. The long-term solution to piracy will not be in software gadgetry, but in using the existing copyright legislation, and in vigorous, unmerciful, public, prosecution of pirates. There's a good technical solution that would make piracy almost impossible, without inconveniencing the user, but it would take cooperation between hardware vendors, who for the most part, have winked at software piracy (as long as it wasn't of their software). If every personal computer had a built-in serial number that could be examined by the software, it would then be possible to fix things so that a package, or any copies of that package, would run only on that specific computer. There are cute cryptographic things that can be done so that the scheme would frustrate all but the most dedicated hacker and raise the cost of breaking the security scheme to well beyond the selling price of the package, which is all anybody can (and should do).

Because we don't have industry-wide standard that would help prevent illicit copying, many software vendors have tried various methods of **copy protection.** Copy protection is any means that prevents you from making unrestricted copies of the package. For every copy protection scheme on the market, there's a countermeasures program available (openly advertised) that will make copies for you. The biggest contribution to the software industry which copy protection schemes appear to have made has been the impetus it's given to the sale of such lockpicking software. Most copy protection schemes are easy to circumvent if you're an expert (which many pirates are) or if you have several computers (also typical of professional pirates).

The trouble with copy protection is that it's inconvenient to the point of absurdity. It's not unusual to go through four or five copies of a heavily used program a year. Copy protection can make that impossible. Here are some of the schemes and policies in use, in order of increasing obnoxiousness:

1. Master Required. You can make a working copy if and only if you have the master disc in the left drive: there's no restriction on the number of copies made. Slightly inconvenient, but acceptable. The scheme is vulnerable to bugs introduced during the copy or installation process.

2. Restricted Number of Copies. Typically combined with the above, but the master retains a record of the total number of copies made. Unfortunately, sometimes it's a record of the copies attempted and the counter is too low. Also, I've seen no package that give you a running tally of which copy you're using. A decent thing to do it you're restricting the number of allowed copies is to tell the user at startup time that this is "COPY 17 of 25". Not only don't they tell you how many copies you've made, but often, they don't tell you how many you're allowed. It's software Russian roulette. Can you deal with that kind of anxiety?

3. Restricted Number of Installations. This isn't quite the same as the above. I tried one package which seemed to have a very high counter, but whenever I switched from my draft quality to letter quality printer, it counted as another installation, with the result that the count was run out in two days—useless.

4. No Copies. The vendor gives you a master and one working copy. This policy can make a good package unusable.

Most vendors will provide an unlimited number of replacements at nominal cost if you send in the old one. Whatever the nominal cost is, be it $5.00 or $10.00, the time required to send the letter, to reinstall, and do all the rest can often exceed the cost (and the value) of the package. Another problem with many of the implementations of the above methods is that they do not permit operation with a hard disc, or force you to have the master copy in a floppy drive when using the hard disc copy. The master still gets beat, and many of the speed advantages of a hard disc may be lost.

Preventing copies is only half the story. You have to ask what the program does when you attempt to make a copy and are refused. The policies range from reasonable to criminal:

5. Refusal with Reason. This is the only acceptable policy. The copy request is not honored and you're told why—"INSTALL MASTER IN LEFT

DRIVE TO MAKE COPY,'' ''COPY FROM MASTER ONLY,'' ''YOU ARE PERMITTED ONLY *n* COPIES.''

6. Cryptic Refusal or Lie. The typical thing is an operating system prompt, a vaguely related message such as ''DISC READ ERROR,'' a crash.

7. Self-Destruct. The master and the copy destroys itself. This is a really hard-nosed approach which may be illegal, but which certainly warrants a class-action suit.

8. Data Destruct. The package self-destructs and then takes whatever else may be around with it.

9. A Worm. This is a deliberate bug that the package introduces into the operating system software or itself. The worm pollutes other packages, other data, and it may be self-replicating. Things appear to work correctly—for a while. Worms are technically possible. The stories one hears about them are mostly apocryphal. Any vendor insane enough to put a worm into a package will probably find that the legal fees required to fight suits for consequential damages far exceed the cost of prosecuting pirates.

APPLICATIONS

Applications are examples of the use of a package. They can be printed in a manual or be installed on a disc. Applications are useful in and of themselves. A word-processing package might have an application that does simple bulk mailings. A spreadsheet package might have prepared spreadsheets that can be useful for financial calculations. A data-base package might have a telephone directory, a recipe file (including the author's favorite recipes), or a tickler file. When provided by the publisher at no charge, applications tend to be simple and are more illustrative than they are useful. If you're lucky, you can use them without change. You might also be able to modify them to your purpose with less effort than if you had to design your application from scratch.

Some applications are sufficiently complex and useful to warrant marketing them as a product. This is especially common for applications written over data-base and integrated packages. Such applications may be provided by the publisher or by a third, independent party. It's important that these applications exist because it means that the package is in wide use and unlikely to become orphanware. It also increases the likelihood that you'll be able to find what you need. Applications typically sell for a fourth or less of the cost of the package on which they are based. They usually have the base package as a prerequisite.

Part of the information package, therefore, should include either application examples (printed or on disc) which serve a tutorial purpose, references to available applications supplied by the publisher, or references to third party applications.

UPDATES

1. CHANGING MODELS

The idea of an immutable software package is as inaccurate as the idea of a one-model automobile. A responsible auto manufacturer makes changes to a car as soon as a deficiency has been found, solved, and its correction introduced into the assembly line. A responsible software or computer vendor does the same. Each batch of computers that comes off the assembly line is slightly different from the previous batch. The hardware could be changed. Sometimes, the change is in ROM-stored firmware. Most often, the change is in software. Your copy of the package, however, does not change: you must *act* if you want the latest version.

Good software progresses by version numbers (1, 2, 3, etc.) and by release numbers between version numbers (1.17, 1.20, 1.68, etc.) A typical package consists of a dozen programs. Each of these have their own version and release numbers. Publishers don't change the package's release number unless several programs have been changed, or unless there have been major changes to one program. Consequently, not all package releases, 1.68, say, are identical. You find the subsidiary release numbers by finding the document file or program that lists the individual programs and their release dates—assuming that it's on your disc.

2. IS THERE AN UPDATE AND SHOULD YOU BOTHER?

You don't know if you should bother unless you know what's been changed. You can't know what's been changed unless you know there's been a change. Here are several ways you can find out if there's been an update worth going after, listed in the order of decreasing likelihood:

1. Word-of-mouth, especially at user group meetings.
2. Ask the retailer from whom you've bought the package.
3. Call the software publisher's customer service hot line and angrily de-

mand if the "lost-file problem" (say) has been solved by an interim release.

4. Letters to the editor and short notes in *independent* user-group newsletters.
5. Letters to editor, letters to reviewers, reviews, and notes in *BYTE* or *InfoWorld*—e.g., Jerry Pournelle's column.
6. A note in a *captive* user-group newsletter.
7. An advertisement by the publisher (for new versions only; I've never seen this for a release.)
8. A letter mailed to registered owners of the package by the publisher. This is yet another one of the great lies of the Western World.

Knowing that there's a new release doesn't tell you what's in it. That information usually comes with the release software; typically on the disc which contains the new version or release.

As far as bothering is concerned, that depends on what you're after. If you want to have the latest release for the sake of having the latest, then bother, whatever the cost. Otherwise, if the release's only meaning is better functioning and fewer bugs, use the following guide:

1. If it's easy to get a new release (e.g., a telephone call, a letter, a blank disc, or a few bucks)—do it.
2. If the new release has changes to areas you use heavily or if it fixes a bug that's bothered you, do it.
3. Always get the new version if you intend to continue using the package. The competitor's most important advantages are usually incorporated into new versions. A new version, whatever the price, is always cheaper (all costs honestly considered) than learning a new package.

3. UPDATE COSTS

New releases are usually available to registered buyers from a retailer or the publisher at cost. Another alternative is that you're required to send in your master disc and you'll receive the new release disc and update pages for the manuals (if any) for a nominal fee. By nominal, I mean anything from 1% to 10% of the original package price. Versions are essentially new packages and usually have new features. Typically, you must supply the original disc (as proof of purchase) to get the trade-in price. That leaves pirates out in the cold. A typical price for a new version as a trade-in ranges from 10% to 75% of the original price. But if the new version is a big improvement, the publisher may not give you a trade-in. Before you call this "unfair," realize that you're still ahead of the game because you don't have to spend much time learning the new version, and there should be no translation needed to use your existing data.

4. GETTING AND DOING SOFTWARE UPDATES

New versions are usually totally new and on a new disc. The only workable procedure is to reinstall the package, and to redo any tailoring that you want done. If only because the new version will have new installation options that may be useful to you, you should redo the installation—based on the new installation procedure. Don't assume that you know how to do the installation because you've done it before: it might have changed. Another thing to watch out for is the possibility that you will no longer be satisfied with the default cases—for that matter, the possibility that the default case will no longer work for you. For example, you were able to use Version 2.0 "out-of-the-box" without any special installation. The configuration you had (memory, disc, printer, etc.) was standard when you bought Version 2.0, but hardware and operating systems have progressed in the interim and your configuration is now the exception. Always start fresh, as if you knew nothing and as if this was the first time you installed the package. Your knowledge will allow you to do the installation much faster than before, and this "naive" approach could save you heartache.

With new releases, the procedure could be theoretically simplified. For example, it may be that the new release involves changes to only one out of twenty programs. Furthermore, the publisher may state or imply that only that program need be changed and that reinstallation isn't necessary. Don't believe it! That's yet another great lie. Here's where being knowledgeable can hurt. Because only program X is affected, and because there's nothing in the installation that (seems to) affect or be affected by program X, there's a temptation to just replace program X and to not bother with the tedium of installation. I've tried that approach, when I was told it would work, but it never does. There's always a buried "gotcha" that the programers forgot, that wasn't documented, that only comes out after several hundred unlucky users try the "simplified" installation procedure. Treat new releases as if they were new versions. Insist on a complete copy of the package, and work it accordingly.

5. INFORMATION UPDATES

The likeliest source of information updates is a packet of additional pages that comes with the basic information package. If the information package is bound in a loose-leaf notebook, then when there are changes to that information, such as might be necessitated by a new release, supplementary sheets are provided for you to install. Don't complain about a publisher who makes you spend an hour putting pages in a loose-leaf book before you read the manual, be thankful. The alternative is an information package that gets increasingly out of kilter with the software it's supposed to describe. When you buy a package, be sure to ask (both the retailer and the publisher's customer service) if there are updates to the manuals that may not have been included in the copy you bought (especially if it's been on the shelf for a year).

As silly as it may seem, there's a technique to replacing pages in a manual. Most information update sets consist of replacements for specific pages, new sections, and sub-pages. For example, you may be asked to replace page 17 with pages 17a through 17e. The first page of a documentation update packet should be an instruction sheet. It lists for every page, or every contiguous sequence of pages, the following generic commands, where n1, n2, m1, m2, etc. are page numbers:

Remove pages n1 to n2.
Remove pages n1 to n2 and replace with pages m1 to m2.
Insert pages n1 to n2 after page m1.
Insert section XX after section YY.
Delete section XXX.

Such instruction are intended to be followed in strict order, starting with the first, and taking no shortcuts. Errors in such instructions are rare. It's an area programmers are good at because it's the same procedure they use to update their own, internal, documentation.

I use a rigid protocol for doing updates. I'm right handed, so the following is a right-hand procedure:

1. Place the manual on your right. Put the update sheet package to its left. Put a wastebasket to your right.
2. Break the seal on the update package, remove the instruction sheets, and place them above the manual. Have a marker pen handy.
3. Assuming (the usual case) that it's a replacement sheet, open the notebook to the appropriate page number, and with your right hand, *rip out* the pages that are to be replaced and put them (neatly) in the wastebasket.
4. Open the rings and insert the replacement pages.
5. Mark the instruction for that sheet as done.
6. Close the rings and turn to the next page named on the instruction sheet.

Use a similar method for page insertions, section deletions, section insertions, and so on. Ripping out the pages to be replaced and doing it according to the above protocol assures that you'll never confuse a new sheet with an old sheet—not even if the wind blows through the window and disorders things, or if your cats decide to stage World War III on your desk while your back is turned. If a page is to be replaced one-for-one, and you can't immediately spot what's been changed, and if you're wondering if it's the correction of a mere typographical error or something substantive, then take the old and new sheets (the old one is torn, so you can't confuse them), align them, and hold them up to the light. Whatever differences there are now become obvious. If it's double-sided printing and it's too confusing, then make copies and compare the copies that way. Good manuals, however, save you the trouble and highlight the changes by a marginal notation. If you make a mistake, you can recover the old sheet from the wastebasket and use loose-leaf reenforcement rings to correct your errors. Most of my manuals updated this way have one or two such sheets.

I try to reserve an uninterruptible block of time to make the updates. I do it with as much concentration as I can muster and hold all calls as I do it. I don't delegate this task. Doing the documentation updates myself may be tedious, and it may seem like brainless work, but it it does allow me to review and spot all changes. So I'm really saving time by doing it this way.

HOW TO READ MANUALS

Don't take reading instruction manuals for granted. A good strategy may help. You don't read it like a book, starting at page one and going to the end: it's more like what Russians have learned about reading Pravda. They know that the first few pages will be filled with communist propaganda, blasts against the West, and junk like that. But information about yet another airplane crash in Siberia, or whether a shortage will get worse, is found in little one-liners at the back that look like classified ads. You learn, if you're unfortunate enough to live in the Soviet Union, to read Pravda backwards. It's similar for software information packages.

1. Install the update sheets before you start.
2. Read the overview section if there is one.
3. Read the command reference card. See how much of it makes sense. Note the commands you understand and those you don't.
4. Check the glossary for any terms whose meaning you don't know. Read the definitions of all new terms, and don't worry for now if you don't understand all the definitions.
5. Read the index(es) for terms that relate to your application, but don't look anything up.
6. Read the table of contents.
7. Flip through the reference manual one command at a time and read the first few lines or paragraphs of all commands that make sense to you. Look for the basic stuff first: see Chapter 3, Section 3.2. for a guide.
8. Read the "Before You Start" section and lay the manuals out in the order in which they are mentioned. For example: initial installation, tutorial program, advanced tutorial, advanced installation, reference.
9. Read anything they tell you to read if you haven't already done so. Start with initial tutorials and installation, and read the appropriate manuals before you do anything.

Reading the manuals this way takes me one day for most packages. Do it before you break the seal on the disk. Learn the joys of delayed gratification. Software no longer enthralls and mystifies. We're not pioneers going boldly where no man has gone before. It's not our task to seek out new life-forms, but to plod the well-rutted paths trod by untold legions before us. May your experiences with new software be dull, dull, dull.

Following the above reading program before you start is less romantic than a headlong plunge into a new package with only ignorance for a help-mate. It does take the zip out of it all. It converts what might have been a peak experience into something as mundane as learning how to use a new hammer. That's the idea.

THE BUG LIST

Every competent software builder, whether or not he admits it, maintains a list of reported bugs, confirmed bugs, deficiencies, complaints, items for a wish-list, and so on. Bugs are generally categorized by technical seriousness, which may not coincide with what's serious to you. Seriousness to software builders is a combination of the difficulty of repair, the number of complaints, the probability of occurence, and what the competitors might be doing. Really obvious bugs are fixed as soon as possible, and you should be able to get a new release for the asking. The remaining bugs and deficiencies can be classed into four groups:

1. Low probability, annoying, no serious data losses. More of a glitch than a bug: it will be fixed in a new release, along with several dozen of the same kind.
2. Nasty bug, no simple solution. The program is modified to avoid the bug by removing or reducing the feature: use it at your own risk.
3. Annoying bug, but there's a way of working around it.
4. A technical bug that affects many different things but with no obvious pattern: it will be fixed by the next release or version, but meanwhile, live with it.

It takes a while, using a new package, to spot bugs, to confirm that they're bugs rather than cockpit errors, and to decide how intolerable they are. At that point, I want to know what I'm dealing with. My future approach to using the package will depend on which of the above categories apply to which bugs. The above categories are also used by software designers, and as I've said, they have a list. But can you get that list? On those occasions where a software publisher had the self-confidence to publish the bug list, I have found it to be invaluable. The most important items on the list are those for which there's a reasonable workaround or precaution to take. Hewlett-Packard, for example, publishes bugs and workarounds in its user's group journal—but that's an exception.

Ideally, you should be able to contact customer service, ask for the current bug list, get it, and that's that. It never happens. The publishers, even good publishers, act like the CIA would if you were to ask them how many agents they have in Iran: "We have no bugs!" Then they admit that there might be bugs, as a theoretical hypothetical, mind you, but they deny that your symptoms have ever been seen before. They deny there's a workaround, and in fact, they'll make you feel like an idiot if they can, and that you have no constitutional rights to such information anyhow. Your chances of getting a bug-list from a publisher is about 1 in 20, and that's only if you're an expert in both computers and intimidation. The average user has about one chance in a thousand of getting the bug list, or even getting a confirmation that some kind of rotten behavior is the program's fault rather than his fault.

If it's that bleak a prospect, why bother? Bother because it's an exercise of collective pressure that will eventually result in better software from the publishers that survive. Ask for the bug list, just like you ask the auto dealer for the recall list to make sure that you know all the recalls that concern you. Ask for the workaround, precautions, and limitations lists. Report your symptoms in writing to the publisher's vice-president in charge of software quality assurance.*

---

*Most software development organizations don't have a VP in charge of software quality assurance: they don't even have a QA department. I send my letters to that fictitious VP in the hope of creating a self-fulfilling prophecy. Eventually, software publishers will learn that they should have such a department and that the function requires clout.

OTHER SOURCES

1. AFTER-MARKET BOOKS

Popular hardware or software, especially if it's bad and popular, generates a spate of after-market books. After-market books have titles like: "Getting the Most Out of BELCHWORD," "BELCHWORD Revealed," "Power BELCHWORDING," or "Advanced BELCHWORD Applications." Many after-market books means that there's something of value in the package despite its deficiencies. Furthermore, the greater the disparity between the package's value and the quality of its information package, the more activity there will be in after-market publications. That rates as a big plus. If software has a lousy information package but a terrific library of after-market books, then add the cost of the books to the package's cost. Be sure you explore the availability of after-market documentation before you condemn a package. The same applies to hardware.

2. COURSES AND SEMINARS

Just like after-market books, complicated but popular software will generate a demand for after-market training seminars. They're not cheap— $300 to $1000 for a one- to three-day seminar is the going price. Whether or not the software publisher sanctions these seminars doesn't matter. A publisher might decide that they're not good at the teaching business and encourage professional seminar vendors to do it for them. After-market tutorials and courses is another big plus for any package.

3. SUPPORT GROUPS

Support groups are the rage these days—from losing weight to dealing with terminal illness, being fired, hired, divorce, doing your taxes, marriage, children, and other catastrophies. Computer users have been creating and using support groups for more than thirty years—probably because computer use is as traumatic a human experience as there is. We call these support groups **"user groups."** For now, user groups are centered on hardware and almost every manufacturer has a users' group; but user groups for software are emerging, and eventually, they might become as important as hardware user groups.

User groups come in two flavors: **captive** and **free.** A **captive user group** is created and supported by the vendor (hardware or software). They usually publish a user-group journal and hold meetings. The journal's editorial staff isn't known for its stiff spine. They're employees, so don't expect too much in the way of revealing bugs, discussion of problems, and all rest. Articles tend to be upbeat, focus on new features, advance information, publicity, testimonials, tricks, applications, and other nonthreatening, bland stuff. Despite the fact that it's a censored publication, captive user groups and their journals are worth the price; which, because they're subsidized, is cheap.

Independent user groups come into being only after the user population is established and after enough of them are sufficiently disgruntled with the captive use group to go independent. When they work, they're like the English Parliament's "loyal opposition." They provide collective clout that vendors listen to. Independent user groups have had a major influence on technical developments at all mainframe computer manufacturers. Products have been dropped, modified, or created as a result of their lobbying. Strong groups like this have yet to emerge for personal computers; but they will.

User-group meetings are another matter. Captive or free, they're a great source of information—especially at the coffee klatch after the meeting. Many retailers dislike user groups because they can become an information center for discount purchase sources, or a clearing house for pirated software. Many hardware user groups are now creating **bulletin boards.** These are remotely accessible files which you can use to send messages, read what other people have to say, discuss problems, and all the rest. Typically, all you need is a modem and communications software. Bulletin boards run by user groups are replacing the coffee klatch as a primary source of information, and have the virtue of accessibility for individuals who can't attend meetings. Like all public bulletin boards, they have their share of utility, but also off-the-wall proposals and discourses, and graffiti.

4. PUBLICATIONS

Like user groups, there are captive and independent publications. Captive publications are cheap and you get what you pay for. Successful independent publications may go through an initial honeymoon period where they seek the vendor's support and are consequently unduly influenced by the vendor. But that's over quickly enough as the after-market vendors get into the act and take out ads that publicize their product to the hardware vendor's product's detriment. It's not likely that comparable journals will develop for software packages (e.g., for WORDSTAR, VISICALC, etc.) in the near future because, beyond tutorial programs, applications, and supplementary manuals, there aren't many after-market soft products to advertise. Independent journals are one of the best sources of information about anything. There are tutorials, technical articles, bitch letters, gripe columns, hints, kinks, and all the rest.

RESOURCES

BOOKS

Baber, Robert L. *Software Reflected—The Socially Responsible Programming of Our Computers*. North-Holland Publishing, New York, 1982. 192 pp.
    An off-the-wall book that software designers should read but won't. Read it, and maybe you can push from the other end. Learn why Western Civilization may collapse on New Year's day, 2000.

Beizer, Boris. *Micro-Analysis of Computer System Performance*. Van Nostrand Reinhold, New York, 1978. 404 pp.
    Technical introduction to the analysis of computer performance.

Beizer, Boris. *Software Testing Techniques*. Van Nostrand Reinhold, New York, 1983. 290 pp.
    Technical book on how to properly test software.

Beizer, Boris. *Software System Testing and Quality Assurance*. Van Nostrand Reinhold, New York, 1984. 358 pp.
    Technical/management book on software quality assurance.

Brand, Stewart (ed). *Whole Earth Software Catalog*. Quantum Press, Doubleday, New York, 1984. 208 pp. Paperback.
    Something of a "hacker" flavor, aimed more at people who are interested in "computer culture" than in using computers for something mundane like next year's cash flow projections; but lots of useful information and worth the modest price.

Curry, Jess W. Jr. and Bonner, David M. *How to Find and Buy Good Software— A Guide for Business and Professional People*. Prentice-Hall, Englewood Cliffs, 1983. 161 pp. Paperback.
    Useful checklists, forms, and procedures for evaluating and buying a package. Billing and accounting orientation. Cost trade-off analyses, worked examples.

Flores, Ivan. *Word Processing Handbook*. Van Nostrand Reinhold, New York, 1983. 552 pp.
    Ivan's big book on word-processing. Although this book has a dedicated word-processor flavor, almost all of it applies to word-processing as done in a personal computer. If you're a heavy word-processing user, or run a PC-based word-

processing group, you can't afford not to have this book as a primary reference. Every function is dissected and discussed—and if you've a mind to, there's probably enough information in the book to build your own word processing package.

Frankel, Philip and Gras, Ann. *The Software Sifter—An Intelligent Shopper's Guide to Buying Computer Software.* McMillan Publishing Company, New York, 1983. 254 pp. Paperback.
More of a massive checklist than a book in the ordinary sense. Look up most features and they're defined. You can then give them a weight corresponding to how important they are to you. I'd like to see this book as a software package. Lots of nice and ugly tales.

Gilb, Tom and Weinberg, Gerald M. *Humanized Input—Techniques for Reliable Keyed Input.* Winthrop Publishers, Cambridge, 1977. 283 pp.
Especially important for anyone who has to key in lots of data, or who supervises people who do. Important if you design your data-base application or select data-base packages. More lessons that designers didn't learn.

Glossbrenner, Alfred. *How to Buy Software.* St. Martin's Press, New York, 1984. 648 pp. Paperback.
Terrific source book. Lot's of good information on buying vertical packages. Telephone numbers of bulletin boards. Lots of technical material. Resources.

McWilliams, Peter A. *The Personal Computer Book.* Quantum Press, Doubleday, New York, 1984. 299 pp. Paperback.
Good introduction, kept up to date with constant revisions, but kind of cutesie. Worth reading.

McWilliams, Peter A. *The Personal Computer In Business Book.* Quantum Press, Doubleday, New York, 1984. 299 pp. Paperback.
As above, for business users.

McWilliams, Peter A. *The Word Processing Book.* Quantum Press, Doubleday, New York, 1984. 299 pp. Paperback.
As above, for word processing.

Weinberg, Gerald M. *Understanding the Professional Programmer.* Little, Brown and Company, 1982. 224 pp.
If you want to understand programmers and programming without becoming one, try this book.

PUBLICATIONS

BYTE—The Small Systems Journal. McGraw-Hill, New York.
Fat monthly covers almost everything in the personal and microcomputer field. Lots of ads. Good (but sometimes opinionated) reviews of almost everything. Letters to the editor with stuff ranging from silly to invaluable. Inside rumors. Articles at all levels from introductory to build-your-own computer. Worth buying even if you only read a few pages a month.

Data Sources. Ziff-Davis, New York.

Huge (several thousand pages) quarterly listing of hardware, software, vendors, and just about everything else. Names and addresses of everybody.

InfoWorld—The Personal Computing Weekly. InfoWorld, Menlo Park, Calif.

The *TIME* magazine of personal computing. Interviews with "personalities," rumors, roundups, reviews, sometimes outrageous editorials, and then there's Dvorak's column at the back which seems bent on getting a rise out of everybody in the industry (in rotation). Aimed at typical computer user, rather than hacker.

MICRO MARKETWORLD. CW Communications, Framingham, Mass.

Semi-monthly trade journal in newspaper format aimed at retailers, distributors and manufacturers. Controlled circulation, free to qualified subscribers. Good journal for keeping on top of things. Excellent surveys. Good for the multi-system buyer.

Mini-Micro Systems. Cahners Publishing, Boston.

Free to qualified subscribers (e.g., engineers). Consistently has the best technical reviews of hardware in the business. In a typical year they'll run through printers, hard discs, computers, plotters, modems, etc. For straight technical poop without BS and editorializing, this is the best.

New York Times. New York.

Regular column on personal computers and many stories in the business section.

Software Digest Rating Newsletter. Software Digest, Philadelphia.

Monthly ratings of the more important packages such as word-processing, spreadsheet, data-base, integrated software, accounting, graphics, and so on. Each issue covers a different kind of package. Rating criteria are copious and completely explained so that you can weigh the results to better suit your situation. Heavy emphasis on ease of learning, first-time users, and cockpit problems. Mostly IBM PC and compatibles.

The Wall Street Journal. New York.

An article or story on some aspect of personal computers worth reading, almost every day.

GLOSSARY/INDEX

After-market
    books, 40, 239
    hardware, 180, 183, **215**, 216
    journals, 240–241
    product, hardware or software purported to be compatible with a vendor's hardware or software but not sold by that vendor. The purpose of any after-market product is to enhance the product to which it applies. 127
    software, 46
ainu, a language spoken by 20,000 persons in Northern Japan; considered to be unrelated to any other known language. 12
air filter, 78–79
algorithm, any precisely defined procedure: especially one which is defined in mathematical terms. **196**–197
alpha particle, the nucleus of the helium atom, consisting of two neutrons and two protons. Alpha particles are ejected in quantity from the sun, nuclear reactors and old alarm clocks. They can cause *noise* in electronic circuits. If the alpha particle density on earth was half of that which is implied by the frequency with which programmers blame them for unexplained computer mishaps, then we would all glow in variegated shades of puce. 78
ALT key, 106, 128
anthropomorphism, 87, 92, 144, 145, 171–172
anti-static mat, an electrically conductive rubber or plastic mat put on the floor in front of a computer to syphon static electricity from the operator's body. Some mats must be connected to a proper electrical ground to work, otherwise their only effect is to impoverish carpet layers and enrich mat vendors. **78**
application
    compiler, 139
    language, a language intended to facilitate the design of a specific computer application such as accounting or retailing by use of specialized commands that make sense in that application as distinct from general purpose computer languages which are intended for programming any application. **15**
    software, software used to accomplish tasks in a specific application such as accounting or inventory control. Of late, however, this term has come to mean programs written in the specialized command languages of programmable

245

packages such as spreadsheet and data-base packages. For example, a stored sequence of operator commands used to create a customer file. **6, 8,** 218, **229**

arithmetic coprocessor, **184,** 188, 215

artificial intelligence, 172

ASCII code, *A*merican *S*tandard *C*ode for *I*nformation *I*nterchange. Most commonly used method of encoding the alphabetic and numerical characters into bits. 55

assembler, a program that translates assembly language into instructions that can be executed by the computer.

assembly language, a programming language in which each statement is usually translated into one computer instruction. **197**

assumption, design, 55

audio monitor, any device, such as a cheap transistor radio, or circuitry within a computer, which converts the computer's electronic impulses into an audible sound. **60, 78, 205–206**–207

auto-print mode. *See echo mode.*

Backaches, 149

backup, to copy data onto another disc or file, with the intent of protecting them from loss or corruption. Data loss or corruption can occur during the creation of the backup copy; short for *backup copy.* 67, 72–76

  copy, a copy of data or software made to protect against loss or garbling of the original. Good software can destroy good data for no good reasons while bad software does the same more often. Software designers attribute such destruction to the random workings of the universe and a perverse deity, but most data destruction is caused by software bugs. **2,** 32, 33, 70, 71, 73, 82

  key, 111

  method, 74–76, 193

  , object, **43,** 74–76

  , paper, 75

  , printer buffer, 75

  ritual, 76

  , wastebasket, 75

Basic, an early but still popular programming language available on almost every personal computer. Many personal computer programs are written in Basic. Basic is a dialect of *FORTRAN.* Basic was intended to be simpler to use than FORTRAN. The result was that FORTRAN development essentially stopped and that Basic is now as complicated as any other language. The only thing basic about it is the name. No two Basics are the same. **11,** 138

basque, a language spoken in Northeast Spain by about one million persons: considered to be unrelated to any other known language—not even *ainu.* 12

baud, a digital harlot; a unit of transmission rate that often corresponds to the transmission of one bit per second. "Three hundred baud" however, does not necessarily mean a transmission rate of 300 bits per second because the technical details of the method of transmission could result in a somewhat slower rates. For example, while a 2400 baud circuit could in some cases transmit 2400 bits per second, in most cases the effective transmission rate is only 1745 bits per second.

"before you start", xi, 169, 203, 219

benchmark, (1) a standard problem used to compare the performance of computers, operating systems, and software. (2) (rare) data stored for backup and recovery. (1) **201–202**

beta testing, testing of a software package conducted by an unbiased, uncorruptible, independent, tester under contract to the software's designers, operating under a meager budget and tight schedule. **19, 24**

Big Blue, IBM, from the blue color of their mainframe computers.

binary, a method of counting or representing numbers that uses only two symbols such as "0" and "1" or "finger up" and "finger down". Binary is used in computers because it is efficient. Humans using fingers and toes can only count to 99 using the decimal system but to 1,048,575 in binary. However, because six fingers and toes is congenital among the Basque, many of them can count to 16,777,215. **29, 44**

powers, 80

binding factor, **179**

bit, the smallest unit of misinformation. An acronym for *"Bi*nary digi*t"*. A bit represents either the numbers "1" or "0", or the logical quantities "true" or "false", but most often false.

block (of memory), any subdivision of a memory such as a main memory or a disc which is standard within a computer or for an operating system. Typically, block sizes are binary values with 128, 256, 512, and 1024 the most common. Block sizes usually, but need not, correspond to a disc sector size. **66**

boorish software, 154–157

bootstrap, the program or procedure used to get a program into a computer so that it can begin to malfunction. From the expression "hoist by one's own bootstraps". Bootstrap software is usually placed in a ROM. *See also: hot boot, cold boot.* 71, 207

branch, (v) the act of choosing one of several alternatives, as in a program or protocol; (n) the place in a program or procedure at which several alternatives are provided.

buffer, in politics, an artificially created country whose purpose is to mediate the abuse of two countries which it separates. In computers, an independent memory device whose purpose is to mediate the abuse of two adjoining devices, such as computer and printer—i.e. an electronic middleman. *See also spooler.* 191

bug, the essential ingredient of all programs: a glitch, error, goof, slip, fault, blunder, boner, howler, oversight, botch, delusion, elision, malfunction, hallucination, etc. **7,** 26–35, 151

categories, 31–33

, cost of, 30–35

list, 237–238

severity, 31, 33–34

symptoms, 30–31

bulletin board, a facility or file supported by (typically) a user group which contains messages, information, grafitti, notices, and all the rest which you would expect to find on an uncontrolled, physical bulletin board. Bulletin boards, in this context, reside in a computer and are reached by telecommunications methods. **240**

Bunch, The, as in "IBM and The Bunch". The five second-rank mainframe computer manufacturers: *B*urroughs, *U*nivac, *N*ational Cash Register, *C*ontrol Data Corporation, and *H*oneywell.

bundle(d), hardware and software are said to be *bundled* when they cannot be bought separately. In personal computers the operating system is often bundled with the hardware. *Cf. unbundled.* **8,** 14, 195

bus, **185**–186

   width, **184, 185**–186, 189

buyer

   responsibilities, 40

   rights, 40

byte, originally IBM jargon for "eight-bits", now universally adopted as standard terminology. Memory size is reckoned in bytes. A byte can be used to store one character in most alphabets. A popular trade journal devoted to personal computers.

C, a higher-order language useful for writing device control software, especially in communications and operating systems. 197

cable, 77, 187, 208–210

   compatibility, 209–210

   construction, 209

   , ribbon, 209

call, (v) to invoke the operation of a program or subroutine. Upon completion of its task, the program or subroutine *returns* to the calling (program or subroutine); (n) the instruction sequence used to activate the call. **7**

central processor, 182

Centronics interface, 208

character, a fundamental unit of data storage or transmission corresponding to eight bits. Also any printed, stored, or displayed natural language character. *See also byte.*

check software, **51,** 71, 207

chip, an integrated circuit. So-named because it is a small, thin, piece of material (5mm by 5mm, say) cut from a larger (10cm) wafer of silicon.

clock, **187**–188

   speed, **184, 187**–188

COBOL, an early programming language with a superficial but misleading resemblance to english. It is used mainly for business applications. It was intended to make life easy for "stupid" business programmers, but it's one of the harder languages to use.

cockpit error, an error made by a user or operator. Cockpit errors look like bugs to users and bugs reported by users are treated by programmers as "dumb cockpit errors". **33,** 39, 155, 162, 210, 215, 222, 237

code, (1) (n) *See statement.* (v) *See programming.* Often used interchangeably with "instruction" as in "machine code", with "language" as in "machine code", or with "programming", as in "coding error". (2) The specific bit pattern used to represent characters.

clobber, 65–66, 68

, key, **135**

, source, **139**

cold boot, a *cold restart* of the operating system, usually done by turning the power off and then on, or by means of a restart switch.

cold restart, the act of restarting a program in which the program is reloaded into main memory. *Cf. hot restart.* **62, 71**

command, (1) that which you type to get the computer to do something. (2) an almost obsolete synonym for computer instruction, as in "command set". (1) **2, 49,** 87–91

area, 94–95

buffering, **106**–107

capture, 137–138

, disc copy, 73, 76, 98

-driven, a package in which most operations are activated by typing letters or words, **54, 89**–91, 105, 114–132

editing, 131–132

file, 179

, file copy, 74

input, **87**

, keyed, 125–127

language, the set of possible commands typed or activated by the user to make a package do things. Usually, we speak of a *command language* only when the typed commands can be stored and then later used again with other data. **87–88**

logic, 115–116

, macro, 135–**137,** 179

menu, **220**–221

, mnemonic, **123**–124

, sequential, **116**–118

state, a state in which the computer interprets keystrokes as commands rather than as data. *Cf. data entry state.* **128**

, STOP, 65

storage, 132–141

structure, 115–116

, syntactic, **116**–118, 122

syntax, **49, 54, 120**–122

termination, 130–131

tree, 132

common subroutine, a subroutine which does a standard operation and which is used by different programs of a package. For example, a multiplication routine in computers which do not have multiplication hardware. Common subroutines are usually organized into a *common subroutine library.* **7, 24,** 133

communication, **14,** 38, 87, 161, 166, 167, 184, 191, 216, 240

, interpackages, 55

protocol, a protocol (i.e. procedure) used by computers, people, and other devices to communicate with one another. The mechanical equivalent of parliamentary procedures and often no less complicated. **221**

compiler, a program which translates instructions written in a programming language into a form the computer can misinterpret. **139, 197**

complain, how to, 154–157

computer, the twentieth century equivalent of thumb screws. 147

-bound, **179**

cost, 175

hardware. *See hardware.*

, home, **11,** 143, 173, 182, 183, 185

literacy, 11–13

, mainframe, **8, 10,** 147, 153, 180, 185, 193, 195, 201, 205, 240

, mini, **10,** 185, 193, 195

, personal, **1,** 30, 39, 144, 147, 153–154, 174, 180, 181, 182, 185, 193, 195, 199, 226, 240

phobia, 2–4, 12, 169

computor, a person who makes a livelihood by calculations, a professional arithmetician. The last computor is believed to have been a monk at the abbey of St. Eglise Demaldemer on the isle of Cormak, who in 1973 completed his compilation of tidal tables for Hudson bay between 1750 and 1800. The greatest computor was Hisao Kashimara (1860–1947) who mentally calculated the first ten-thousand digits of Feldstein's constant in less than an hour.

concurrent, when two or more programs operate quasi-simultaneously within the same computer. Control shifts back and forth between the two programs so rapidly that they appear to be working simultaneously. For example, printing one document while working on another. Actually, there is no real concurrency, because most computers can only execute one instruction at a time. 80, 191, 193

configuration, the combination of hardware and software you happen to be working with. 167, 210, 215–216

connector, 77, 187, 208–210

compatibility, 210

control

key, 106, 128, 163

loss, 32–33

software, that part of a package which controls and coordinates. *See also: executive, operating system.* **24**

conversion, the process or act of making the data produced on one computer or software package compatible with another computer or software package. Ease of conversion depends on time and place: conversions are always trivial and guaranteed by purveyors of replacement hardware or software, but almost impossible once the check has been signed. 64

copy

, backup, **2,** 32, 33, 70, 71, 73, 82

, master, 70, 227

different color, and so on. The cursor usually moves whenever a key is struck, but can also be moved by using the *cursor control keys* (if any). Other methods for moving the cursor include: *mice, joystick, touch-pads.* **99**

control keys, specialized keys used to move the cursor; the temporary function assigned to keys when used to move the cursor. The primary cursor control keys are UP, DOWN, LEFT, RIGHT, and HOME. These move the cursor one line up, one line down, one character left, one character right, and to the upper-left corner of the screen respectively. Modifiers to the cursor control keys may provide motion by words, paragraphs, screens, lines, etc. 99-100, 104, 126, 163

customer service, 32, 39, 144, 233, 237

cylinder, a subdivision of a hard disc. Hard discs with multiple recording surfaces are subdivided into cylinders. Each cylinder is subdivided into *tracks,* which are further subdivided into *sectors.*

Dangerous features, 55-56

data, the plural of *datum.* **2, 203**

backup. *See backup.* 74-76

base, any disorganized accumulation of data, such as an address book, a telephone directory, a recipe file, etc. after it has been installed in a computer. **9, 24,** 183, 243

manager, a program used to destroy, create, copy, expand, search, display, sort, print, insert, delete, etc. items and/or data into or of a data-base. Also a person responsible for the management and maintenance of a data base. **9**

software package, **9,** 32, 38, 43, 184, 190, 191, **203,** 218, 229

software package benchmark, 202

corruption, 31-32, 68

destruction, 32, 68

entry state, a state of the computer in which keyboard entries are interpreted as data rather than as commands. *Cf. command state.* **128**

, execution of, the grievous act of a faulty program when it interprets data as if they were instructions. Data execution has been declared unconstitutional under the VIIIth amendment by the high court because it is a cruel, but not unusual, punishment. However, it is one of those crimes which cannot be suppressed by mere legislation. **65**

input, **87,** 165-166

loss, **2,** 32

memory, 191

object, most often *object* alone. Any piece or collection of data when manipulated as an entity. An object can be a single bit, a field, a record, a file, a directory, a group of files, a path, etc. *See object.*

status lie, 161

structure, 81

datum, facts, information, statistics, etc. Computer professionals with higher degrees write "data are" and "datum is". In common speech, professionals and others singularize the plural "data" by saying "data is". Only pedantic fuddy-duddies *say* "data are".

deadly embrace, when two programs or program segments each requires the other to take the next step before it can continue. A software impasse. Deadly embraces most often occur between a program and the operating system, between two concurrent programs, or between parts of the operating system. **66–67**

debug, the act finding and correcting bugs. **14, 140**

default, that which the programmer assumes you want to do when you don't know or don't say what you want to do.

    hardware configuration, the hardware configuration assumed by a software designer. **214–215**

    values, **214, 219–221**

deleting objects, **44,** 81

delimiter, any character or fixed sequence of characters used to separate parts of a command or data entry. **120**

demo(nstration program), software legerdemain, flimflam, the primary tool of the software con-artist, the first refuge of incompetent programmers. Demonstration programs are the only software that can be theoretically guaranteed to be bug-free. 45–46, 199, **224–225**

design assumptions, 55

diagnostic program, a program used to determine what is wrong with a computer's hardware. Of course, if the disc is bad, or if the computer doesn't work, the diagnostic program will probably not run. If it does not run, or if it produces meaningless results, such as "the mayor's horse has diabetes", it has accomplished its primary purpose, which is to make you return the hardware to the shop for an extended vacation at an abominable cost. Diagnostic programs *are* useful, but they should be regarded with the same skepticism that one would regard the self-diagnosis of mental health or sickness as performed by a certifiably schizophrenic psychiatrist. **51,** 71, 207

dialogue, a conversation (or sorts) between computers and people, usually beginning with alternating interchanges and often ending with cryptic put-downs (by the computer) and obscene vulgarities (by the user) or vice-versa. 116–122

dip switches, from "DIP", an acronym for "*D*ual, *I*n-line *P*ackage". A set of tiny switches packaged in a container similar to that which is used for small chips. Often used to set hardware options and characteristics, but also used for some software functions. **215**

directory, a listing of files on a disc, often lost or garbled. Also called *index.* **68,** 161

    destruction, 68

    memory, 191

disc (also "disk"), used to mean several different related things. 1) a diskette or disc, which is a circular plastic sheet covered with magnetic material on which data can be stored, 2) a device used to store and retrieve data written on a diskette, and 3) an internal, high capacity storage device which is disc-shaped. *See also: floppy, hard-disc, winchester,* 7, 66, 77, **203,** 215

documentation, the totality of printed information by which a computer product (hardware or software) is defined and described. No project is complete until the weight of the documentation is at least ten-times greater than the weight of the product which it describes or the computer in which it runs. The amount of documentation given to users is usually inversely proportional to that which is produced.

dot-matrix printer, a printer in which letters are formed by printing microscopic dots which are part of an array or *matrix*. Usually, this term applies to printers in which the dots are formed by striking tiny wire-like hammers through an inked ribbon. However, burning heat-sensitive paper, spitting an ink droplet, or shining a laser beam on a sensitized surface, are also used. Dot-matrix printers are fast, relatively inexpensive, and can (usually) also serve the dual function of graphics printing.

draft-quality printer, any printer whose quality is so poor that it can't be seen in public. 227

dump, a printed representation of the contents of the computer's memory. Used mainly for diagnostic purposes during debugging or to impress and/or confuse and/or confute the unknowledgeable by huge lumps of printer paper. The typical dump which can be produced by even small computers weighs as much as the computer itself. It has been predicted that if the rate at which programmers produce dumps continues according to the present trend, the forests of equatorial Africa and most of Canada will be denuded by 2010. **140**

Echo mode, a mode of computer operation in which whatever is typed on the keyboard and/or displayed on the screen is also printed.

editor, (1) a form of quasi-life even lower than *hackers* or *pirates;* (2) a program used to edit other programs or itself. (2) **140**
entertainment software, 145, 204
EPROM, a memory device whose contents cannot be modified, but which can. Read *ROM* and *PROM* first for this one to make sense. An *E*lectrically *E*rasable *P*rogrammable *R*ead-*O*nly *M*emory.
ergonomics, concentration on the trivially rectifiable, putative, and unverified physical discomforts of using a computer (such as keyboard height and design or screen color) so as to divert attention from the psychic trauma induced by bad software in the false belief that if a misleading and/or abusive message is displayed in pleasant colors and at the right intensity, then it will no longer cause headaches. Formerly called *human engineering.* An appellation attached to any piece of furniture as an excuse to double its price. 144, **149**
error message, a message displayed by a program to indicate one or more of the following possibilities:
1. The program does not understand you.
2. You have asked the program for something impossible or illogical.
3. The programmer has asked you for something impossible or illogical.
4. The program has lost its way.
5. The programmer lost his way.
6. The hardware has malfunctioned.
Whatever the cause of an error message, its result is to infuse you with guilt as a substitute for programmers responsibility. 50–53
escape key, 105, 128–129
executive software, that part of a program or package which interfaces with the operator, controls peripheral devices, and schedules the operation of subsidiary programs. An operating system is the archtype executive software. *See operating system.* 24
extension, a part of a *filename,* usually consisting of a period followed by one to three characters, used to designate a property of the file, such as a program as in ".COM", or data, as in ".DOC", ".DAT", or ".INF". **56**
eyestrain, 149

Fear. *See also computerphobia.* 2–5
field, a subdivision of a record usually consisting of at least one byte, but not necessarily so. **25**
value tolerance, 165–166
file, an assembly of data typically organized into *records* that can be manipulated, by name, as a single entity. 14, **25,** 167
copy command, 74
name, the name given to a file. The first character is usually alphabetic. Typical filenames can be from three to eight characters long and may be followed by an *extension.* For example, < filename >.< filename extension >, as in "GLOSSARY.IND".
filter, (1) an electronic device which eliminates or reduces electrical noise: (2) in

some operating systems (e.g. MS-DOS, PC-DOS), a program or command that transforms data in some specified manner. (1) **211–213**

firmware, software not intended to be modified except by a programmer with expert knowledge of that package. **6,** 230

floppy (disc), (also *diskette*), a disposable, flexible, medium for temporary storage of data. Also the device which reads and writes onto the floppy disc. *See disc.* 167, **192, 203**

flowchart, a pictorial representation of the structure of a program or procedure. Flowcharts, although once popular, are now rarely used by programmers because they cannot accurately convey what a program does. Their use is almost completely confined to elementary texts, non-technical books about programming, and instruction booklets for taxpayers produced by the Internal Revenue Service. In this latter application, they achieve the same level of confusion that they once achieved for programs.

fluorescent lights, 77, 212

format, (n) a specification of the way data are to be organized; (v) the act of organizing data to a specified format, as in *"formatting a disc"*. **12,** 49, 64

    error tolerance, 164–165

FORTRAN, from *FOR*mula *TRAN*slator; one of the first, general-purpose programming languages; intended for technical and scientific work. 197

forward key, 111–112

frozen

  crash, 60

  keyboard, 62

  screen, 60, 62

function keys, any set of keyboard keys whose purpose is unspecified by the hardware and which can be given specific (temporary) meaning by software. **48, 94,** 102–103, **125,** 129, **218**

Garbage, faulty or meaningless data when entered into a computer; untested software. **29**

ghosts, 69–70

GIGO, *G*arbage *I*n equals *G*arbage *O*ut—the computer mavin's favorite cop-out; used to excuse almost any bug.

glossary, 49–50, 169, 235, 245–275

graphics, that which appears on the screen or which is printed and which does not consist of letters, numbers, and signs; e.g. pretty pictures; software used to draw pretty pictures. **9,** 101, 102, 182

  printer, any printer which can be used to print graphics as well as (actually, better than) text. 216

great lies of the Western world, there were only four great lies of the Western world prior to the introduction of computers:

  1. I gave at the office.

  2. The check is in the mail.

  3. Don't worry, I'm on the pill.

The fourth is too obscene to print. Computers have added the following to the list:

5. It's in beta-testing. 19
6. That bug will be fixed in the next release. 18, 231
7. It works fine on *my* system.
8. That (customer service) number is no longer in service.
9. Your copy of the disc must have been damaged in shipping.
10. Of course! You're not using a standard (printer, disc, paper, ribbon, electricity, etc.)
11. She's in conference.
12. Installing that release is a snap. 232

Hacker, (1) a derogatory term meaning an individual with skill in the abuse of computers for criminal or malicious purposes; (2) a skilled amateur; (3) a person skilled in the use of computers; (4) a computer aficionado as distinct from a computer user. The usage of this term has not yet stabilized. (1) 87, 146, 226

halt instruction, 66, 140

hard

disc, a memory device consisting of one or more inflexible discs, which are usually not removable. Hard discs can store a lot of data—typically, millions of characters. *Cf. floppy. See also disc.* **192**–193, 211, 213, 216, 227

software, like *firmware* only more so. Usually stored in an unmodifiable memory unit such as a read-only-memory (ROM). Considering the consistency of various computer-wares, hardware can be likened to a rock, software to sea foam, whilst firmware is like soft ice cream, and hard-software is comparable to twelve-day-old rice pudding. **6**

hardware, the physical components of a computer, such as printer, disc drives, and memory. *Cf. software.* **6,** 7–8, **203**

checkout program, a program which exercises and tests hardware components and reports which (if any) are malfunctioning and in what way. *See also diagnostic program.* **51,** 71, 207

compatibility, 216

default configuration, **215**

failure, 77–79, 210

installation, 214–215

manufacturer (or vendor), 8–9, 21, 152, 156, 180, 187, 196, 226, 230

options, 216

program, 6

speed, 181

status lie, 161

HARDWARE!, a programmer's cry of joy when she's deluded herself into believing that the hardware is at fault instead of her program. The counter-cry (actually a low mutter) by hardware designers and service technicians is "dumb programmer".

"hardwear", 6

headaches, 147, 150

heat, 78–79, 187

help, 43, 169

key, a key used to invoke a *help screen*. 43, 47,108, 113, 127, 129, 222

screen, information which appears on the computer's screen in response to the user's request for help. 43, 47–48, 121, 222

hexadecimal, also "hex", numbers represented in base-16 whose numerals are 1, 2, 3, 4, 5, 6, 7, 8, 9, A, B, C, D, E, F, 0. Often used because the value of any byte can be represented by a two digit hexadecimal number. The binary number 255 is represented in hexadecimal as "FF". *See also octal.* **134**

higher-order language, a programming language in which the programmer's instructions usually get translated into several machine instructions. Contrary to popular misconceptions, the "higher" the order of a language, the easier it is to use and the less the training required. The "highest" order languages are the commands inserted at the keyboard. **197**

HOL. *See higher-order language.*

home computer, a low cost, limited, version of a personal computer intended for education, games playing, and loading down the top shelf of the hall closet, but not for professional use. Typical price in 1986 dollars was under $500. *See also: personal computer, minicomputer, mainframe, supercomputer.* **11,** 143, 173, 182, 183, 185

hooks, **116**

horizontal package, generalized software intended to be used for many different purposes. Word processing, spreadsheet, and data base packages are the archtype horizontal packages. *Cf. vertical package.*

hot

boot, a restart of the system in which a fresh copy of the operating system is *not* read from disc. Most systems provide only *cold boots* while those that have hot boots, usually provide both. It's important to know which is which. Hot boots following a crash are acts of faith engaged in only by the hopelessly romantic.

restart, any restart of a program or operating system which does not involve reloading a fresh copy of the program.

human language, 87, 120

humidity, 78

hype, 223–225

Icon, (1) an object of religious significance or worship; (2) a pictorial representation of an object or concept; (3) in computers, the use of little ambiguous pictures on a screen instead of words to identify command or menu options—actually, for computer iconophiles, the first definition is most appropriate. (3) **90, 95**–98

iconic, the use of preliterate pictures to depict commands, events, and concepts, in the mistaken belief that adults entrusted with the daily use of equipment that costs thousands of dollars will be more comfortable with pictures which apes can understand, rather than with words, which distinguish man from beasts.

idiot proof, the first level of software quality. 166–168

, malicious, **166,** 167

illogical

condition, a condition presumed to be impossible by a programmer, but she built in protection against it just in case. 50-51, 81, 145, **159**

software, 170-171

impatience, human, 64

index, an arrangement of data (often alphabetical) used to provide rapid access to other data; such as the index of a book. Also the act of creating an index, as an "to index". *See also directory.* 53, 68, 245-275

memory, 191

information package, the collection of printed, stored, or programmed material which tells the user about a software package. *See also manual.* 39, **40-41**, 53

initialize, the act of bringing something to a known condition from which (generally) other operations start. For example, we initialize discs, computers, interfaces, etc.

input/output controller, 184

insertions, 81

install(ation), the act of adapting a copy of a program to a specific computer, set of peripherals, operating system, or user preference. 42, 71, 166, **214-222**

[of] hardware, 214-215

manual, 221

[of] operating system, 215-217

[of] package, 217-219

process, 219-222

recovery, 222

restrictions, 227

instruction, an elementary operation carried out by a computer—for example: add, subtract, test. *See also statement.*

manual, a random arrangement of possible facts and limitations whose understanding is essential to the proper use of a program but which cannot be understood unless you are an expert user of the program. *See also manual.* 2, 36-57, 134, 169, 224

integrated

circuit (also *chip*), an assemblage of microscopic electronic components on a single piece of silicon or similar material, packaged in a small container. Integrated circuits contain thousands to tens-of-thousands of components. They look like rectangular, black, centipedes. A typical personal computer has 200 integrated circuits.

software (package), (1) a group of software packages with a common appearance and file formats, and the ability to communicate with one another with the intention of executing a set of interdependent tasks. For example, the integration of a data-base, spreadsheet, word-processor, and graphics packages allows the use of a spreadsheet to do calculations based on data in the data base, to plot the results of the calculations and to then include the picture in a report. (2) Several unrelated software packages peddled by a publisher in one box. (1) **9, 11**, 162, 190, 195, 229

interface, the hardware, software, or procedural conventions whereby different pieces of hardware and/or software communicate with one-another; (v) to achieve bilateral communion between elements of a system. **13, 208**-209

interference, electrical, 77–78, 209, 212

interpreter, a program which operates by analyzing stored or entered commands one at a time and executing machine language subroutines which do the processing appropriate to that command. Distinguished from *compiled* programs which are translated into machine language by a *compiler*. Interpreters are flexible but slow. Most personal computer software operate as interpreters. 139, **197**

Jargon, 50, 169

joy stick, a gimballed stick in a box used to move the cursor to objects on a screen. An indispensible device for video games playing. Named after it's original use as an aircraft's control stick, with a probably obscene derivation, contrary to what most dictionaries imply. Most early joy sticks were adapted from preexisting devices that had long been used for radio-controlled model aircraft. *See also: light pen, mouse, touch pad, touch screen.* **100**

K, jargon for 1,024. Actually, 2 raised to the 10'th power. Because the successive powers of two are: 2, 4, 8, 16, 32, 64, 128, 256, 512, 1024, etc. we have a strange usage in which 128k is 128 multiplied by 1024, rather than 128 multiplied by 1000, yielding 131,072. The following table shows the interpretation of "k" for values commonly used in computer literature.

8k	8,192
16k	16,384
32k	32,768
64k	65,536
128k	131,072
256k	262,144
512k	524,288
1meg	1,048,576
2meg	2,097,152
4meg	4,194,304

The usage is inconsistent, and sometimes, "k" will have it's original meaning as an abbreviation for the greek *kilo* or 1,000, and sometimes not, and sometimes in the same document or even sentence. If you are buying, it pays to check if 256k is 256,000 or 262,144. Similarly, if a restriction is stated as 32k, it may be 32,000 or 32,768.

key, (1) the buttons on a keyboard; (2) the act of pressing such buttons; (3) a word or character group used to look things up in an index; (4) a word or field value by which records in a data base are accessed; (5) a bit pattern needed to decrypt an encrypted file; (4) **165**

, ALT, 106, 128

, BACKUP, 111

changes, 134–138

code, **135**

lockup, any condition of software in which programs or program segments have conflicting demands for resources, which the operating system cannot reconcile, resulting in a blockage of further work. *See also deadly embrace.* **66-67**

log mode. *See echo mode.*

loop, a continually repeating set of instructions executed by a program. A proper loop eventually terminates. Looping is a common mode of software failure, as in "it's looping" or "it's looped", which means repeating an instruction sequence without end. **66**

LSI, *L*arge *S*cale *I*ntegration.

luck, 79

lying, 145, 157–162

Machine language, the pattern of bits and data which can be directly interpreted by the computer. Erroneously used interchangeably with *assembly language.* Machine language is what results when assembly language is translated. Also called *object code.*

macro, a group of instructions or commands which can be manipulated or invoked as a group. 135–**137**, 179

mainframe

computer, a large computer system usually attended by a full-time, professional staff. Intended to satisfy a wide range of corporate processing. Typical price in 1986 dollars was between $400,000 and $4,000,000. *See also: home computer, personal computer, minicomputer, supercomputer.* **8, 10,** 180, 185, 193, 195, 201, 205, 240

software, 30, 147, 153

main memory, the internal, general-purpose memory used to hold data or programs.

malicious idiot proof, the second plane of software quality. **166**

manual, 2, 36–57, 134, 169, 224

, after-market, 40, 239

, hidden, 56–57

, how to read, 39, 235–236

index, 53, 235

, installation, 221

, reference, 48–49, 54–55, 235

, tutorial, 41–44

updates, 232–234

writers, 48

mass storage (device), a floppy disc, hard disc, or integrated circuit "disc", that can store more data than the computer's main memory. Mass storage devices are addressed by *blocks,* rather by *words* or *bytes.* Any data storage device which has twice the capacity of the largest storage device you now own. 66

master

copy, usually the copy of the software provided by the software publisher. The master copy should only be used to make *working copies.* 70, 227

user, 88, 107

mathematicians, 146

media, a suburb of Philadelphia; that on which data are stored—e.g., a floppy disc, magnetic tape, punched cards, paper, magnetic wire, punched paper tape, or a knotted string.

memory, any hardware in which data and/or software are stored. **4,** 189–192
management, 195
size, 159, 176, 189–190, 215, 217

menu, a set of choices presented to the user on the screen. Used to select commands, options, parameter values, etc. 91–98
, conversion to command mode, 108–109
display control, 107–108
-driven, a package in which most commands and options are selected by means of menus. *Cf. command driven.* **48,** 54, **89,** 90, 116–119
line, 94–95
nesting, **109**–110
, pop-up, **94**
selection, 98–105, 164
, abstract, **98,** 102–103,106
confirmation, 105–106
, default, 104–105
entry, 105–106
, hybrid, 104
, keyed, **102**–103
, keyword, 102–103
, mnemonic, **103**
, positional, **98**–102
tree, each menu has options which may elicit another menu which provides more details, additional options, or yet further menus. This leads to a tree-like conceptual structure of menus. **55, 109**–113

microcomputer, a small computer, such as a personal computer, built around a microprocessor chip. Typically, a microcomputer is built on a single printed circuit board and includes the main memory, I/O controller, and other devices.

microprocessor, usually a single integrated circuit chip which contains the major processing components of a computer; also (erroneously) used as a synonym for home or personal computers. 182–189

minicomputer, a small computer system intended for multiple, simultaneous users. Typical 1986 price was between $50,000 and $500,000. Lower end is often called "micro-mini" and upper end often called "super-mini". *See also: home computer, personal computer, mainframe, supercomputer.* 10, 185, 193, 195

Mister Spock, the ultra-logical Vulcan first officer of the Star Ship *Enterprise* (of Star Trek fame). 25, 28

mnemonic, (command), an abbreviated form of a command or a word with a similarity to the word that denotes the command's action; e.g., "ST" for "store", "FE" for "fetch". **123**–124

modem, abbreviation for *mod*ulator-*dem*odulator; a device which converts electrical pulses produced by the computer into sound tones (e.g., beeps and boops) and also converts sound tones into pulses. This is done because pulses cannot be transmitted accurately over the telephone network, which is designed to handle voices (i.e. human beeps and boops). **14**, 184, 193, 216, **221**, 240

monitor, (1) the TV-like device used by the computer to display data or graphics; (2) (obs.) *operating system.* (1) **2, 203**, 216

motor, 77, 212

mouse, a small rodent of the genus *mus musculus;* a pest; a small wheeled device with a cable (the mouse's tail) which is attached to the computer. Mice are used to overcome the hazards, exertion, and mental trauma, required to move the screen's cursor by use of cursor control keys; alternative to *joy sticks, light pens,* and *touch screens,* which serve the same purpose. 99, **100**, 215, 216

Network, any attempt to interconnect for a period of time, however brief, more than two computers. Network design often begins with a good acronym which is then released to marketing. Testing occurs only after sales are sufficiently high to warrant it, which is then followed by software design. **14**

nibble, a half a byte, naturally—four bits.

noise, unwanted electrical disturbance; a scapegoat for bugs; noise acting on data results in *garbage.* 77–78, 209, **212**

novice user, 41, 45, 75, 88, 107

Object. *See also data object.*
  backup, 43, 74–76
  creation, 43
  deletion, 44, 81
  fetching, 43
  language, for all intents and purposes, the same as *machine language.*
  naming, 43
  saving, 43
  status, 44

octal, number representation to the base 8, whose successive numerals are 1, 2, 3, 4, 5, 6, 7, 0; used in earlier computers whose word-length was divisible by 3 (e.g., 24 and 36). Octal is out of favor because the word lengths of most contemporary computers are divisible by 8. Octal marks the user as a hopeless romantic who sighs for the "old days". The octalarian's anachronisticism is exceeded only by die-hard macho users of binary. *Cf. hexadecimal.* **134**

operating system, a group of programs used to manage the operation of a computer including printers, discs, monitor screens, communications equipment, etc. Also includes utility software to copy discs and files, to format discs, to convert files, to call programs. Formerly called *monitor program.* **9, 26,** 66, 135, 179, **193–196, 204,** 205, 207, 215

  destruction, 69, 71

operator, any person forced to use a computer, as distinct from a *user,* who does so willingly.

option card (or **board**), any part of a computer not included in the base price without which the computer is useless. 215

orphanware, hardware or software produced by a now defunct vendor. **176,** 229

overlay, (1) a printed card or plastic device placed over or near keys to serve as a reminder of the key's current meaning; (2) one of several segments of a program when the entire program can't fit in memory; (3) to bring an overlay segment into memory; (4) to destroy (usually intentionally) the current memory content. (1) **127**

Pachinko code, a "clever" program whose control is achieved by dynamically modifying its own instructions so that the program bounces around like a Japanese pachinko machine: the worst kind of program there is—even worse than *spaghetti code.*

package, as in *software package,* a collection of one or more programs designed to accomplish a set of related processing task. *See also: program, software.* **1, 2,**

panic key, any key used to stop an ongoing action or to undo a prior command. For example: STOP, HELP, UNDO, ESCAPE, PAUSE. **62,** 65, 83, 127

parity, a way of coding characters or data so that it can be checked for errors.

parse, to make electronic sense out of statements in a programming language.

Pascal, a modern programming language with characteristics interesting to programming pedagogues; popular among personal computer programmers. 138, 197

password, a secret sequence of characters, conveniently written on the computer's keyboard, which permits only the password's owner to access sensitive information.

peek, a techie term meaning to examine the content of a memory location; the command used to "peek". *Cf. poke.* **140**-141

peripheral (device), a device connected to a computer, such as a printer, plotter, modem, light pen, mouse, or joy stick.

crash symptoms, 63

personal computer, a small, desk-top computer intended for serious professional use by one person at a time. Typical price in 1986 dollars was $3000. *See also: home computer, minicomputer, mainframe, supercomputer.* **1,** 30, 39, 144, 180, 181, 182, 185, 193, 195, 199, 226, 240

software, 147, 153–154

piracy, the felonious act of copying published works such as books or software in violation of copyright laws and/or contractual agreements with the publisher; illicit copying of hardware designs; especially when done for resale to a third party. **5–6,** 226, 240

pirate, an individual or group which engages in hardware and/or software piracy. 188, 226, 228, 231

plotter, a device used by a computer to draw pictures. 193

pointing methods, 98–102

poke, a techie term meaning to change the content of a memory location; the command used to "poke". *Cf. peek.* **140–141**

pop-up menu, a menu which "pops-up" on the screen when you hit the corresponding control key. **94**

power, 187, 211–213

 filter, **211–213**

 line, 211–212

 regulator, **212–213**

 supply, uninteruptible, **213**

 transient, 77

 user, any personal computer user who seems to know what she's doing. Often, a computer professional who happens to be using a personal computer. A user who has learned how to exploit most of the computer's capabilities. 88, 107

prerequisites, 42, 217–218

press, 157

printer, 167, **213,** 216

 bound, **179**

 buffer, **75,** 183–184

  backup, 75

  controller, 183

  memory, 191

 controller, 183

 crash symptoms, 63

 installation, 167, 215, 216

 interface, 208, 215

 interference, 78

 speed, 178, 184, 193

 staring, 178

printout, anything on paper produced by a computer printer. The veracity of a claim is significantly enhanced when presented as a printout. Printouts have usurped the prerogatives that in ancient times were reserved to priests and oracles. **2**

processing error, 32

processor bound, **179**

program, an organized arrangement of computer instructions designed to accomplish a set of specified processing tasks. **6, 12, 203**
, demonstration, 45–46, 199, **224**-225
, diagnostic, **51,** 71
memory, 191
status lie, 161–162
, tutorial, **2,** 45–48,

programmer, one who attempts to write programs. *See also software design.* 20–21, 58, 81, 144, 154, 164, 237
ego, 154
guilt, 159
immunity, 28–29
personality, 145, 146, 152, 153–154
training, 21–23, 160

programming, the act of attempting to write programs. 12, 13, 21, 26–28, 133, 138–140, 146, 154
language, a written language used by programmers which is then translated (by an assembler or compiler) into instruction which the computer can execute. Programs are written in a *programming language.* **10,** 11, 26, 120, 139, 162, 197
myths, 22

progress reports, 65, 176

PROM, *P*rogrammable *R*ead-*O*nly *M*emory, a memory whose content cannot be modified, but which can by use of special devices. *Cf. ROM.*

protocol, the verbal procedure used by diplomats to prevent dialogue between humans; about the same for computer protocols.
, communication, **221**

pseudo-crash, **63**-65

public domain software, software not protected by copyright or secrecy—generally of the caliber of things one expects to find in the public domain, such as graffiti in a public toilet. **5,** 197

publications, 240–241, 243–244

Quality, 4, 87
assurance (of software), a mythical state of being. 22, 24, 25, 29–30, 60, 79, 81, 152, 156, 166, 238

Radiation, 78

RAM, *R*andom *A*ccess *M*emory. This term originated when computers used a disc or drum for main memory—which devices could only be accessed in sequential order. Later, RAM also meant a disc—and you'll see it used that way in some older literature. It now means the computer's main, internal, semiconductor memory. **191**–192

ramdisc, a segment of a computer's main memory which is fooled into thinking that it's a very fast disc. 191, **197**

"read this first", xi, 219

record, (n) an organized arrangement of data; records are subdivided into *fields* and grouped into *files:* (v) the act of storing data, as in "to record"—rarely used—the proper jargon is "to write".

recovery, action taken with the intent of rectifying the effects of malfunctioning software. Also, the procedure or programs used to effectuate recovery. **58, 67,** 70–72, 73, 162

recursive, self-referential definition or process. Legitimatized omphaloskepsis. Recursive definitions are purely formal and devoid of semantics. They consist of examples and formation rules. If you understand a recursive definition or process, it's probably wrong. *This* definition of "recursive" being at the metalinguistic level, satisfies both the obscurity and self-referential requirement and is, therefore, recursive. 268

reference
    card, 48–49, 235
    package, 48–57, 235

release, to allow software to be sold or used; a number or designation which identifies that particular attempt at release; that which occurs after a corrected version of software has been widely distributed. A release is usually an interim package number interpolated between *versions.* Thus, between versions 2 and 3, we may have releases 2.21, 2.52, etc. **19, 34,** 35, 56, 230, 231, 232, 237

reset
    button, 67, 69, 71
    , false, **69**

resource depletion, 66

responsiveness. *See also performance.* 82

restart, to make a program start again, but without reloading a fresh copy. 62

retailer, 6, 38, 40, 156, 180, 219, 230, 233, 240

retry, 71

return, to leave a subsidiary program or subroutine and to resume operation in the program that had *called* the subroutine.

reviews, 157, 225, 231

rigidity, 145, 162–163

robust software, 81, 162–167

ROM, *R*ead *O*nly *M*emory. A memory device whose contents cannot be changed by software means. Often used for bootstrap programs or part of, or all of, the operating system. **191**–192, 230

routine. *See also subroutine.* 7

Saving objects, 43

screen, the monitor screen itself, but more often a specific visual presentation produced by a package. When a menu covers the entire monitor screen, it may be called a "screen"; a presentation produced by an application package for use by an unskilled data-entry operator. **24**

, corrupted, 60

, crazy, 60, 82

dump, (v) to cause that which is visible on the computer's screen to be printed; (n) a printed copy of that which appears on a computer's screen. **51**

, frozen, 60

searching, 196, 199

sector, an angular subdivision of the surface of a disc. A disc is subdivided into sectors and tracks. The smallest unit of data that can be read from most discs is the subdivision of tracks by sectors, corresponding (typically) to 256 or 512 characters.

seminars, 239

Seven Dwarfs, originally the runner-up computer companies to IBM, who was "Snow White": Burroughs, Control Data, General Electric, Honeywell, National Cash Register, RCA, and Univac.

shrieker crash, **63**

silicon, a gray-black shiny metal. The most common element in the earth's crust. Can be combined with oxygen to make sand and rocks. When purified to ridiculous tolerances, and then carefully corrupted by known impurities, it can be used to make semiconductors; the most common element used in semiconductor integrated circuits (or *chips*).

valley, an area south of San Francisco with a high concentration of computer companies and air-headed valley girls. Knowledgeable Valleyites are miffed over the fact that the electronic computer was invented in Philadelphia; but most valley dwellers believe that computers, software, and electronics originated there with the development of the first commercially successful personal computer; some even hold that the Garden of Eden had been there when the world was first created, but that point of view is held in derision by most Valley theologians.

software, generic term meaning individual programs, groups of programs, or segments of programs. *Cf. hardware.* 6–9, 79, **203**

, after-market, 135

, application, **6, 8,** 218, 229

, boorish, 154–157

, command-driven, **54, 89**–91, 114–132

complexity, 4–5

, control, **24**

cost, 6, 13–19, 30–35, 231–232

, long-term, 19

, mid-term, 18–19

, short-term, 16–18

criticism, 5, 157

, debugged, 14

design profession. *See also programming.* 22–24, 180, 190

development, 24–26, 39, 40
features, 4
"genius", 31, 147
, hard, **6**
, hybrid command/menu-driven, 90–91, 104
hypochondria, 84
, illogical, 170–171
incompatibility, 218–219
-induced stress, 33, 150–**151**–152
installation, 217–219
, insulting, 145, 170–171
layers, 6–7
limitations, 53–54, 80, 160–161, 224
manners, 157–172
, menu-driven. *See menu.*
, old, 34–35,
package, software which is sold; e.g., a program; a set of related programs, **1, 2,** 13, 26, 230
performance, 196–198
personality, 145–147
prerequisites, 42, 218
"programs", 6
, psychological screening of, 152–153
publisher (vendor), 6, 18, 24, 33, 34, 44, 55, 73, 74, 152, 153, 156, 166, 169, 180, 196, 212, 223, 226, 228, 229, 230, 231, 232, 233
quality, 2, 4–5,
    assurance, 22, 24, 25, 29–30, 60, 79, 81, 152, 156, 166, 238
release, **19, 34,** 35, 56, 230, 231, 232, 237
reproduction cost, 4
, testing of, 22, 24–25, 29–30, 166, 167
version, **15, 34,** 35, 55, 56, 218, 230, 231, 232
"softwear", 6
sorting, 64, 196, 199
source code, program as written by the programmer; that which is translated by an assembler or compiler into machine language. Software cannot be easily modified unless you have a copy of the source code. **139, 197**
spaghetti code, a program whose control structure is so entangled that a diagram of it resembles a bowl of spaghetti. Typical of bad, old software. The only thing worse is *pachinko code.*
special function keys. *See function keys.*
speed. *See performance.*
spell-checker, a program which checks and/or corrects spelling errors in a document. **11,** 32, 191, 196, 218
spooler. *See: buffer, printer buffer.*
spreadsheet package, a program which organizes errors and unverifiable assumptions into a rectangular array of cells, parts of which can be displayed on a

screen or printed. Cells can be related to one another by a variety of algebraic and logical disfunctions. The consequences of changing any initial fallacy can be immediately calculated, perpetuated to the ends of the array and of the world, and then displayed to 10 significant digits in any of many illegible forms. **9**, 32, 38, 72, 184, 190, 201, 202, **203**, 229

starting, 43, **71**

statement, a statement is to a programming language what a sentence is to a natural language.

static electricity, 78

status

    display, any display of a computer's or package's status, typically on a screen line reserved for that purpose.

    line, **95**

    monitor, also **SAM** (*S*tatus *A*ctivity *M*onitor); a device interposed in a cable connection which displays the signals which are passing on the wires; especially for cables between a computer and a modem. 14, **161**

step mode, a mode of operating a computer or package in which each processing step is initiated by use of a key, rather than having the program run automatically by itself. Step mode operation is used mainly for debugging. **140**

stereotypes, 2, 20–21, 143, 145

stinker crash, **63**

stop

    command, 65

    key, 62, 65, 82, 127, 129

stopping, 43

streaming tape, (alt. *streamer tape*) a tape recording device used to store a running record of everything written or modified on a hard disc, intended for backup purposes. 75

stress, 150

    , organizationally induced, 12, 150

    , software induced, 33, 150-**151**-152

subroutine, a self-contained, usually small, program segment that accomplishes a specified task. **7**, **24**, 133

    call, **7**

    , common, **24**

    tree, 7

suicide note, 60–62

supercomputer, very large computing complex in the multi-million dollar price range used for technical and scientific work or unusually large corporate data processing such as weather prediction, missile defense, and nuclear reactor studies. At any point in time, the hundred most expensive computers in the world are "supercomputers". Many of today's personal computers can outperform the "supercomputers" of twenty-five years ago. *See also: home computer, personal computer, minicomputer, mainframe.* 173, 185, 186

switch, any of several devices used to connect computers to peripherals. An "ABC" switch connects the C cable to either the A or B cables. An "ABCDE" switch

, broad, **195**

, sharp, **195**

Turing machine, **173**

tutorial

manual, 41–46

program, a program intended to train, by example and interaction, the operation of some other program. Many tutorial program need a tutorial program of their own. **2,** 41, 45–48,

, after-market, 46–47, 239

Unbundle, to allow the separate purchase of hardware and software that had formerly been purchasable only together; the means by which a hardware manufacturer with no taste or talent for software avoids the issue and the blame. *Cf. bundle.* **8**

underlay, **127**

UNDO key, 62, 83, 105, 111, 112, 129

update, (v) to make changes to documentation or software so that it corresponds to the latest available information or version; (n) the information or programs used to do the update; (n) the copy of the program or document which has been updated. The main difference between *update* and *upgrade,* is that updates are often free while upgrades are usually expensive. **6,** 230–234

cost, 231–232

procedure, 232

sheet, 235

upgrade, (v) to correct intolerable deficiencies of hardware and/or software by buying a later, more expensive, version of the same, with new bugs and limitations; (n) the copy of software, or the hardware which has been upgraded. **15,** 192

UPS. *See: power supply, uninteruptible.*

user, a masochist who willingly employs a personal computer. 181

"-friendly ", to condescend, demean, destroy, humiliate, induce guilt, infuriate, insult, and/or patronize, but with a smile. 36, 143–144, 153, 169

group, an organization of users of one vendor's products bonded by common misery. **5,** 231, 237, 239-**240**

, master, 88, 107

, novice, 41, 45, 75, 88, 107

utility, programs included in an operating system package intended to do a variety of utilitarian functions, but whose utilization is often beyond the ability of any but the utility's designer.

Value tolerance, 165–166

vaporware, software that's promised, announced, and/or advertised but never delivered; occasionally applied to hardware.

version, a fictional state of being intended to identify the how, what, when, where, and genesis of a software package. All problems will be fixed in the next version. Versions are usually numbered 1, 2, 3, etc. But may carry a two.

three or more digit subnumbers as in 3.14159. Such subnumbers are often called a *release number.* The "latest" version usually has the highest number and fewest bugs. **15, 34,** 35, 55, 56, 230, 231, 232

vertical package, a software package designed to satisfy the specific processing needs of an industry or occupation such as medical, retailing, or construction. 169, **195,** 218

vibration, 77

virtual button (or virtual key), a legend displayed on the screen which can be activated by either the use of function keys or by touching the screen (for *touch screen* computers). **102**

virus, a piece of destructive software which examines all the software in the system to see if such software contains a copy of itself. If the copy does not exist, the virus replicates itself into that software. As with real viruses, software viruses wait a while before beginning their destructive activities so that they can have ample time to spread to another host. Viruses could theoretically invade and replicate themselves into *every* personal computer in the world. The effect of a virus may range from a minor sniffle to the insertion of a time bomb which results in the complete destruction of all your software and data. It is not known if viruses have actually been introduced. Designers, however, can also build antibody software which kill software viruses. *See also: worm, time bomb, Trojan Horse.* 70

VLSI, *Very Large Scale Integration,* a type of integrated circuit or chip that contains 50,000 or more basic electronic devices; for example, microprocessor and memory chips. 181, 190

volapuk, an artificial language created by Johann Schleyer in 1880.

Waiting time, 178

warnings, 64

winchester disc, a type of hard-disc often used in personal computers; can store much data—5,000,000 to 20,000,000 characters is typical for personal computers.

window, the partition of a screen into two or more segments, each of which can misrepresent different data. 81, **108,** 195

word, a small unit of data used by a computer, typically corresponding to one, two, or four bytes. Early computers, however, had words of 12, 18, 24, 30, 36, 48, 54, 60, 66, 72, bits in length. Longer word lengths typically means higher speed.

length, **184-185,** 189

processing package, a program used for writing and editing text; the rationalization used by writers for buying expensive personal computers. **9,** 12, 72, 73, 147, 156, 166, 169, 184, 190, 191, 194, **203,** 206, 218, 229, 243

processing benchmark, 202

working copy, the copy of a program or package actually used to run the program, as distinct from the *master copy,* which is used only to make working copies. 218

work station, 182

worm, any deliberately or accidentally introduced piece of software which, once activated, goes about destroying other software or data. Worms can be introduced by *viruses. See also Trojan Horse.* **228**

write protect tab, a plastic tab about half the size of postage stamp used to cover a notch on 5″ diskettes and thereby prevent their being written on. For 8″ diskettes, the tab must be put on to allow writing and removed if writing is not wanted. Other storage media will surely evolve their own convention, leaving us all confused as to how to use the things. Because of this confusion, most users do not employ the tabs. Boxes of discs always have several sheets of write (read?) protect tabs which now serve the same purpose as a sprig of parsley on a steak. **32, 68**

Other Bestsellers From TAB

Other Bestsellers From TAB